Advance Praise for
Curation Nation

"Curation, not creation, is king, and Rosenbaum shows you why and what you can do with this knowledge. This is a great piece of research and analysis."

—*Guy Kawasaki,* cofounder, Alltop; author, Enchantment: the Art of Changing Hearts, Minds, and Actions

"From food to music to news to deals, a vivid picture of the necessity for curation. If you value your brand's future, read this book."

—*Lisa Gansky,* author, The Mesh: Why the Future of Business Is Sharing

"Big thoughts and real reporting—the essential guidebook for anyone paddling in the media flood."

—*Spencer Reiss,* WIRED

"Rosenbaum has assembled big ideas, bigger egos, and more than enough information to catch you up, in a hurry."

—*Seth Godin,* author, Linchpin

"The primer for how information is going to be processed in the future and how information businesses are going to prosper."

—*Michael Wolff,* author, The Man Who Owns the News *and* Burn Rate

"Curation is one of the most important trends in media and business today—*Curation Nation* makes sense of it for you."

—*Jeff Jarvis,* author, What Would Google Do?

"Hits the bull's-eye in exploring what matters in our digital world."

—*Jon Miller,* chief digital officer, News Corp

"Rosenbaum has the answer to information glut."

—*Douglas Rushkoff,* author, Program or Be Programmed

"A map that leads brands to relevance in the next Web."

"Steve Rosenbaum has LIVED curation as a business value for several years. You need this information in your consideration set for the new marketing world."

"Teaches you three key things: Be authentic, be passionate, and be trustworthy. Rosenbaum's secrets can help you get your curation game up and stay two steps ahead of the competition."

"Explains how our friends and colleagues are emerging as our most trusted editors."

"Steve Rosenbaum is a genuine visionary."

"In a world filled with user-generated content, users are becoming editors. It's called curation, and Steve Rosenbaum explains why this is such an important trend."

"Steve Rosenbaum has seen the future and bottled it for all future curators."

"Steve Rosenbaum has become a Web video pioneer. So when Steve talks about curation, people should listen—I do."

"Steve Rosenbaum understood the power of online communities well ahead of the pack. Now he is talking about the impact of collaboration, and we'd all be well advised to listen."

—*Jon Klein,* former president, programming, CNN

"A practical guide for how the digital world will evolve in the next decade."

—*Howard Morgan,* partner, IdeaLabs and First Round Capital

"Rosenbaum explains the role curation is playing in our Twitter and Facebook world."

—*Robert Scoble,* blogger, Scobleizer.com

"Contains the prescription for turning this new open, accessible world of information into a more profitable business."

—*Stephanie Agresta,* EVP, social media, Weber Shandwick;
author, Perspectives on Social Media Marketing

"Offers an easy-to-read and coherent vision of twentieth-century media."

—*Jack Myers,* author, Reconnecting

"The future of digital living is curation. Read and enjoy."

—*Shelly Palmer,* author, Television Disrupted;
host, NBC Universal's Live Digital with Shelly Palmer

"A savvy look at the full-on revolution in communications, buying and selling."

—*J. Max Robins,* vice president and executive
director, the Paley Center for Media

"Steve Rosenbaum has a gift: he sees things before anyone else. Now in *Curation Nation,* he's sharing that gift with the rest of us. Don't miss out. Read this book!"

—*Alan M. Webber,* cofounder, Fast Company

"The instruction manual for organizing the data of our post-digital world."

"Bursting with fresh insights, relevant case studies, expert interviews, and revealing anecdotes—all in the service of a compelling thesis from one of the true pioneers in media and technology."

"To make sense of our information flood, we need to combine human and machine intelligence. *Curation Nation* helps us understand why machines can't do it alone, and why they need our help."

"Required reading for modern retailers."

"Offers a compelling case for the art, craft, and enduring value of human judgment."

"A must-read if you care about media, marketing, or the emerging voice of consumer amplified by the Web!"

"Of all the power shifts that are redefining the competitive environment, none matters more than the rise of readers, users, and customers as the true power players in business and media. Steven Rosenbaum understands how to do great things in this new environment, and in *Curation Nation* he explains his ideas and makes them come to life. There's nothing more exciting than learning from someone who is inventing the future. That's what Steve is doing—and this important book shows all of us how to do it too."

CURATION
NATION

CURATION
NATION

WHY THE
FUTURE OF
CONTENT IS
CONTEXT

HOW TO WIN IN A WORLD WHERE
CONSUMERS
ARE CREATORS

STEVEN ROSENBAUM

NEW YORK   CHICAGO   SAN FRANCISCO
LISBON   LONDON   MADRID   MEXICO CITY   MILAN
NEW DELHI   SAN JUAN   SEOUL   SINGAPORE
SYDNEY   TORONTO

1 2 3 4 5 6 7 8 9 0 DOC/DOC 1 6 5 4 3 2 1

ISBN 978-0-07-176039-3
MHID   0-07-176039-3

Interior design by Mauna Eichner and Lee Fukui

This publication is designed to provide accurate and authoritative information in regard to the subject matter covered. It is sold with the understanding that neither the author nor the publisher is engaged in rendering legal, accounting, securities trading, or other professional services. If legal advice or other expert assistance is required, the services of a competent professional person should be sought.

—*From a Declaration of Principles Jointly Adopted by a Committee of the American Bar Association and a Committee of Publishers and Associations*

Library of Congress Cataloging-in-Publication Data

Rosenbaum, Steven C.
  Curation nation : how to win in a world where consumers are creators / Steven Rosenbaum. — 1
    p. cm.
  ISBN 978-0-07-176039-3 (hardback)
  1. Online social networks. 2. Market segmentation. 3. Management. I. Title.
  HM742.R67 2011
  658.8'02—dc22

                              2010047465

To my family, Pam, Max, and Murray, who are able to shine light in interesting places, ask puzzling questions, and genuinely enjoy the process of discovery that is the underlying journey of both a book and a life. And to my mother, Eileen Landay, who raised me to appreciate the rhythmic clickity clack of an IBM Selectric typewriter— long before a computer keyboard or mouse ever existed.

CONTENTS

PREFACE

As I did a final read of this book before handing it off to the publisher, I had a revelation.

This book is curated.

It is the result of an editorial process unlike anything I've ever experienced before. As I reached out to many of the smartest and most thoughtful people I've either met or read, I found that each of them had been thinking about and shaping their vision of their work around the concept of curation.

Jeff Pulver, a serial entrepreneur who's seen the future since he was nine years old, sees the conferences he puts on as an act of curation. He chooses the dates, the venue, the speakers, and even who he wants to see in the audience. He mixes voices he knows and trusts with new people who are doing important and exciting things in what he calls the *now* Web, the real-time data that is optimized by Twitter. Jeff is one of the kings of curation whose ideas you'll find throughout this volume.

Esther Dyson is both a creator and a curator. Her work in health, technology, privacy, international relations, and innovation makes her one of the most prolific connectors today. Esther's decision to aggregate and share knowledge is prodigious. As the founder of the groundbreaking PC Forum conference, she was able to fill a room with the world's most extraordinary intellects long before the thing we now know as the Web was a public utility. But her content sharing includes her love of a daily morning swim. Wherever she is in the world, the morning pool is photographed and shared on Flickr, an act of content creation, she says (http://bit.ly/curate10).

Elizabeth Schlatter is one of the few people in this book who's actually got the word *curator* on her business card. An academic and museum professional, she's both energized by and challenged by the massive changes that are taking place around her once rarified profession. As she found the word *curation* being adopted by a wide variety of people without Ph.D.s, she decided to dig in and find out exactly what was going on. Like any good academic, she did research, talking to her peers and a wide variety of people who are adopting the word *curation*. Is the newfound popularity of curation good for her colleagues? Or, as some told her, a "dilution" of the craft and its importance? A good question worth exploration.

Robert Scoble is an omnipresent tech blogger and video maker. Scoble is best known for his blog, Scobleizer.com, which he began while he was a technical evangelist at Microsoft. Scoble has declared curation is the next "billion dollar" opportunity and wonders aloud as to whether he should "create or curate" as tech news breaks in Silicon Valley. Scoble says a curator is "an information chemist. He or she mixes atoms together in a way to build an info-molecule. Then adds value to that molecule."

Alexa Scordato is the smartest young person I know. She's smart because she has a remarkable understanding of how lucky she is to be born in the postdigital world. She describes herself as being born on Live Journal, growing up on Facebook, having a professional life on LinkedIn, and an ongoing dialog with friends and clients on Twitter. She is "always on" and thinks a good deal about the need to "reverse mentor" folks who are trying to translate their worldview into the newly connected digital, curated-content world.

Andrew Blau is a media analyst, thinker, and scenario planner. Andrew is copresident of Global Business Network. GBN works with companies and not-for-profits to adapt and grow in the face of mounting uncertainty, whether it's uncertainty about their future, the future of their industry, or the future of the world at large. Certainly the massive change in data production and the flood of content from new and often untrusted sources creates massive instability. His scenario on the future of independent media in 2004 projected unfathomable change, and if you read it today (http://bit.ly/curationnation2), it turns out to have been a roadmap for the next six years. What does Blau see as the next chapter? Curation clearly plays a central role.

Those are just 6 of the more than 70 people I interviewed for this book. From corporate leaders like News Corp's Jonathan Miller to Edelman's Steve Rubel. From BlogHer's Lisa Stone to Modem Media's Jean-Philippe Maheu. There's a whole new world of content strategists, with Brain Traffic's Kristina Halvorson leading the charge. And there's a groundbreaking group of brand marketers and e-tailers like Zappos' Tony Hsieh and Pepsi's Bonin Bough. Privacy is emerging as a critical issue in this era of both purposeful and accidental sharing, so Jules Polonetsky from the Future of Privacy Forum and Stanford University's Lauren Gellman are critically important voices. And then there are the content makers both old and new—some embracing, some struggling with this new era of consumer curation. The team at AOL is thinking hard about content and folks like Michael Silberman at New York Magazine and Renee Jordon at Readers Digest's *Taste of Home* are exploring new and exciting ways to mix created, contributed, and curated content.

Of course curation isn't without its critics. Mark Cuban is perhaps the most colorful, calling all curators "vampires," and enjoying all the media attention that Count Dracula commands.

And Andrew Keen, whose rant against amateurs has given him a permanent spot on the dais, sides with Cuban, and suggests that curation is just another attempt of the liberal elite to control the conversation under cover of democracy. But there's no shortage of those who argue to point passionately: Seth Godin is happy to poke holes in Cuban's thesis. And Bob Garfield, who's dark-but-prescient book *Chaos Theory*, published first in 2006, says that the road ahead for brands and advertising is paved with complexity and danger.

That we live in a digital world is certain. That you can report and gather and edit a book immersed in this digital world was by no means a certainty. But here I must give credit to both the partners and technologies that made it possible to write a book about such a fast-moving topic and do it without the historic lead time and resources that such an undertaking would require.

ACKNOWLEDGMENTS

First, my appreciation goes to my publishing partners at Huffington Post, Business Insider, Mashable, and FastCompany: many of the early themes of this book began as posts on their pages, and only as the links and comments grew louder did it become clear to me that the topic of curation was ripe for a lengthy and detailed exploration. And while my virtual explorations were eye-opening, the real-world ones were certainly equally important: from my days at the Monaco Media Forum to the mind-expanding week at TED 2009, and finally—but significantly—to my South By Southwest talk titled "Curationism vs. Creationism: The Great Debate." It was in Austin that it became clear that the issues and opportunities around curation were going to drive not just the emerging future of my company, Magnify.net, but of the next iteration of the real-time Web.

Second, thanks to the editorial team that embraced this idea from its nascent form and helped shape it into a coherent text. My gratitude goes to John Wright, a writer's agent, who is both supportive and demanding at the same time. He never let me cut corners or leave questions unanswered. And thanks to Leila Porteous, my editor at McGraw-Hill, who was able to shepherd the work and this author through what was at times a daunting process and a looming deadline.

And finally, my thanks go to the folks who've made the work possible: my amazing team at Magnify.net, who've become the best curation toolmakers on the Web today. By listening to our partners and customers, and sometimes by taking leaps of imagination, we've been able to build both a business and a vision for content on the Web. They provide daily inspiration and keep me grounded in the real-world realities of making business sense of all this. Particular thanks to Filip Szymanski, who was my partner in crime for many of the interviews throughout the book and acted as videographer, Turk wrangler, and transcriber as the volume of content grew on an almost daily basis.

And most important, my content partner, proofreader, editor, and sometimes-pointed critic. Since 1982 we've formed and launched four companies together, and now this is our first book. She wouldn't want to admit that hers is often the only voice to say "this doesn't make sense," but in this world of always-on content and instant blog publishing, having an editorial conscience who is willing to roll up her sleeves and read rough drafts that are sometimes spot on and other times . . . well, let's just say that on occasion I'll shoot high and miss the mark. Pamela Yoder is a curator's curator—and we all need one of those in our lives.

1

CURATION: WHAT IS IT?

When I was 13 years old, I was a magician. I don't mean card tricks and parlor tricks. I was into the big stuff. Harry Houdini, The Great Thurston, illusionists, escape artists, and mind readers. And back then, there was no shortage of gizmos and books and apparatuses that a young boy could buy. There were catalogs and magazines that featured page after page of gleaming boxes, swords, silk scarves, and grandly adorned illusions. If you had an allowance, there was always some great new magic trick ready to help you amaze your audience. In magic tricks, there was an endless abundance. What was a boy to do?

Well, there was a solution: a special place where magicians in the know went to see the latest gear up close, watch demonstrations by great prestidigitators behind the counter, and end up spending their hard-earned allowance money on the *right* new gizmo. It was called Tannen's Magic Store, on 44th Street in Times Square. And although it was a four story walk-up, anyone who found the place could be assured of a few hours of deft salesmanship and some insider knowledge as to which magical flourishes were popular, which of the latest shiny illusions didn't work, and which patter would keep your audience mesmerized. Tannen's was nirvana for a young magician. Sure, the store had a catalog, but that was for suckers. The smart money knew that if you trekked to the store, you'd get a better deal and buy the right stuff. I didn't know it then, but the folks at Tannen's exposed me to my first truly curated experience. They separated the good gear from the cheap knockoffs, they added a special aura of knowledge and experience—and they turned a deck of cards with a mimeographed set of instructions into a treasure. They added context, meaning, and knowledge. I loved that place, and I still do. Even as magic has fallen out of favor for this generation of boys and girls, Tannen's remains a curated experience that has kept it solvent, and special, since its founding in 1925. Buying a magic set at Toys "R" Us just can't compete. The difference between a curated retail experience and a generic one isn't limited to magic shops. As we'll soon discover, brands and retailers who are standing out in this noisy world are increasingly replacing abundance with smaller selections of carefully chosen offerings.

CURATION COMES IN MANY SHAPES AND SIZES

There are some words that arrive in our world meaning one thing and over time morph into a new idea.

Tweeting was a thing birds did, before Twitter. Now the word has new meaning. It used to be that you could learn about people you were interested in by researching them in print or by asking their friends. Now you Google them. The remarkable pace of change is having an impact on more than our lives and our interactions, it's changing the very words we use to describe what we do.

Today, the word that describes much of what's changing is *curation*. It's both a new word and an old one.

In the past we lived in a world of disciplines. The senior editorial leadership at magazines were known as editors. The folks who chose which TV shows played on a TV network were programmers. The people who picked which things would be on the shelves of your local stores were retailers. Each of these professions involved choosing the right items, putting them in the proper order, and creating a collection that was appealing to an audience or consumer. Oh, and there was that rarified individual who selected objects of art to present in a museum or gallery: they were called curators.

Today, curation is the coin of the realm. Film Festivals curate their program. Web sites curate their editorial. The team at the shopping site Gilt Group curates the items it offer for sale. *Curation* was once a word that seemed to mean highbrow, expensive, out of reach of mere mortals. But today museum curators must compete with media curation at Newser, collections of handmade crafts at Etsy, or the curated collection of the best roll-on luggage at Squidoo. Certainly curation means quality, but now quality is in the eye of the beholder.

Curation, as we'll come to explore it in the pages that follow, comes in many shapes and sizes. It is critically important to understand two things. First, curation is about adding value from humans who add their qualitative judgment to whatever is being gathered and organized. And second, there is both amateur and professional curation, and the emergence of amateur or pro-sumer curators isn't in any way a threat to professionals.

Curation is very much the core shift in commerce, editorial, and communities that require highly qualified humans. Humans aren't extra, or special, or enhancements; humans *are* curators. They do what no computer can possibly achieve. There's far too much nuance in human tribes and the taste of groups and individuals. Curation is about selection, organization, presentation, and evolution. While computers can aggregate content, information, or any shape or size of data, aggregation without curation is just a big pile of stuff that seems related but lacks a qualitative organization.

There are places where we're going to see curation happen first, mostly editorial enterprises such as Web sites, magazines, and other media. And although it may seem like curation, as a trend, is declaring war on old institutions we've known and trusted, the simple fact is that curation is going to save these organizations, not destroy them. Not long down the road, curation is going to change the way we buy and sell things, the way we recommend and review things, and the way we're able to mobilize groups of like-minded individuals to share, gather, and purchase as groups. Curated experiences are by their very nature better than one-off decisions about what to buy or whom to trust.

But the real power of the trend toward a Curation Nation is that, for the first time, we can see a future in which individuals can galvanize and publish their passions and knowledge in a way that will create value from personal passions and niche expertise. Imagine a time when your love of travel, fine wines, and collectable lunch boxes each provides a revenue stream. Okay, maybe not a full-blown stream, but a revenue trickle; when these microcareers are knit together, your curated knowledge can evolve from a hobby to an avocation to one of the many gigs that pay the rent, keep your kitty in cat food, or help you save for a college tuition. Which is to say, curation is about something different than disintermediation. In fact, it's about re-mediation. It's about adding quality *back* into the equation and putting a human filter between you and the overwhelming world of content abundance that is swirling around us every day. Curation replaces noise with clarity. And it's the clarity of your choosing; it's the things that people you trust help you find.

Curation is an exhilarating, fast-moving, evolving idea that addresses two parallel trends: the explosive growth in data, and our need to be able to find information in coherent, reasonably contextual groupings. No one doubts that we're shifting, as author Clay Shirky says, from an era of content scarcity to one of content abundance. And while that seems on one hand bountiful, it's also quite impossible. Imagine trying to find a needle in a haystack. Now try to find that same needle in a thousand haystacks. Now, try to find three related needles in a billion haystacks. Yikes! If you think of those needles as words or ideas, forming a coherent sentence is flat out impossible. It's in just such situations that curation comes to the rescue.

CURATION TO THE RESCUE!

As we fumble around for a clear picture of the future, curation comes up in some places we might not expect. Looking for E.T. the Extra-Terrestrial or a bit of a flying saucer? NASA's Office of Curation (Yep, they actually have one of these—check it out at http://curator.jsc.nasa.gov) describes its mission as "tasked to curate NASA's current and future collections of extraterritorial samples. Curation includes documentation, preservation, preparation, and distribution of samples for research, educational, and public outreach.

Looking for some silky and sultry undergarments? The Canadian company Panty By Post offers luxury women's panties curated by subscription. The combination of a curated collection and re-curring delivery isn't limited to panties. There's a similar offering from ShoeDazzle, a monthly subscription to a handpicked series of stylish shoes.

What if you find yourself hungry on a Saturday afternoon at the Brooklyn Flea swap meet? Founder Eric Demby tells *New York Magazine* he personally curates the food stands so you can count on a good tamale or great grilled cheese sandwich. Most people prefer having an array of interesting food options curated for them rather than settling for the always-risky sidewalk mystery meat from New York's ubiquitous street vendors.

Curation has always been the process of discerning quality. But in an era of abundance, the definition of quality needs to evolve suit its intended audience. Do you want to know the best place to en-joy a Nascar race? Well, then don't ask me, because I can't tell one driver from another. But ask a Nascar super-fan, a highly engaged and deeply passionate enthusiast, and he'll have lots of advice and pointers and links to help you get your bearings before you set out to the track. Are you a Nascar curator? Could you be? Someone's going to grab that gig, so maybe it should be you?

There are some places where curation simply works better than undifferentiated large collections.

Certainly curated retail should provide a better experience than large undifferentiated box stores. As Alex Williams explains in the *New York Times*, "among designers, disc jockeys, club promoters, bloggers and thrift-store owners, curate is code for 'I have a dis-cerning eye and great taste.'"

But to be fair, the curation of art or shoes or even women's lingerie may not be anything new. This trend, from the hallowed halls of museums to banal retail shopping, is still very much about gathering groups of real things in the real world. The place where curation is a new idea is within the bits and bytes of the World

Wide Web. Because the Web is essentially still new, and the speed of its growth and ubiquity is unparalleled in human history, there's a demand—even desperation—for new systems and behaviors to manage the tsunami of content that envelops us every day. From Facebook to Twitter to blogs, newsreaders, LinkedIn, text messages, e-mails, updates from Foursquare, voice mail, and now the iPhone's FaceTime video voice conversations . . . the sheer volume of digital data available or assaulting us is both dazzling and exhausting.

Über-blogger Robert Scoble describes the flood of data that overwhelms him most waking hours: "I have TweetDeck running with the real-time streams and can see it flowing down the screen—and I'm only following 20,000 people out of two hundred million people on Twitter, so I'm just seeing a little water in the gutter compared to the Mississippi River that could be going through my screen. And we're all trying to deal with this, we're all trying to find interesting stuff and share it with our friends. People need ways to deal with this constant stream of information."

The solution isn't to bail out, to get "off the grid," as some weary netizens proclaim. Fred Wilson, a New York venture capitalist and one of the folks who's got his pulse on the Web start-up community, routinely declares "e-mail bankruptcy" and empties his inbox. Overwhelmed with input, he waves the white flag of digital defeat and tells his potential correspondents they'll simply need to write again. Their previous e-mail was dispatched into the digital ether. That doesn't work, of course. And Wilson knows it. But lacking tools to filter the flood, he's got little choice. That's all changing, though.

Boston science writer Joanne McNeil, writing on tomorrow museum.com, describes the emerging role of curator by suggesting we begin with the root of the word. "Start by thinking about the etymological roots of 'curate'—to take care of. Information surplus creates different challenges in preservation and archival record keeping. There are 'digital ethnographers,' slightly fewer 'cyber anthropologists,' but media is most in need of digital historians like Jason Scott providing historical context. Someone who can determine the 'and this' from the 'don't forget' in fickle Internet memes. Implied by the word *curator* is an intuitive sense of pattern recognition . . . More visual than a mere editor, the Internet curator requires a sense of the relationships between words, images, space, and shapes."

But I still haven't answered the question I set out to resolve for you in this chapter: what is curation, exactly?

THE ORIGIN OF CURATION

Let's start with where the need for a new word came from.

It's 1977, and as a young magician I was looking for some deep dark secrets. I'd found my way to a closed, private collection of magicians' memorabilia and personal papers that was held at the Lincoln Center Library for the Performing Arts. Buried inside the white marble halls, beyond the public stacks and out of view—the mysteries of the great prestidigitators were carefully recorded in formidable bound volumes. Only the intrepid students, hungry for information, could find their way to these secret stacks, and only then could they gain access. I arrived at the front desk and confronted a librarian who had no plans to let me into the Lincoln Center collection. To her surprise, I took a membership card to the Society of American Magicians out of my pocket. With the proper documents and a signature on a new Lincoln Center library card, I was able to gain access to the secret shelves. Long, dusty, quiet columns of rare books. Dog-eared card catalogs produced with manual typewriters. Each dark oak drawer organized by ritualized numbers. DDC: 793.8 LCC "Death and the magician"; DDC: 793.80922 "100 years of magic posters," Card magic was 793.5. Those numbers were like a decoder ring; if you knew "793," you had a map to where the secrets of magic were kept. I knew the code. I was in.

In the past, organization was simple. Small groups of things where organized by a group of daunting and often stern people known as librarians. In 1876 Melvil Dewey copyrighted a proprietary system of library classification: the Dewey Decimal System. The method organizes books in repeatable order for library shelves. The idea was that you could find the book in the same place in any library in the world. And, for a period of time, Dewey was the Google of its time. But the nature of the Web's openness swamps Dewey. Since librarians no longer stand between content creators and library shelves, a rigid and inflexible taxonomy simply doesn't work. On the Web anyone can publish and anyone can access published pages, so the role of the human archivist needed a digital counterpart.

In 1998 two graduate students at Stanford University began to commercialize a search engine known as Google. The company's mission was "to organize the world's information and make it universally accessible and useful." The sheer size and openness of the Web made human categorization impossible. Today Google runs over one million servers in data centers around the world and processes over one billion search requests and 20 petabytes of user-generated data every day.

Dewey was a human system, with a rigid digital classification. Google replaced human classification with digital discovery and a "black box" formula that ranked pages based on a complex and changing algorithm that let Google determine a page of data's relative value for a particular search term. The concept of page rank was powerful, and it resulted in a taxonomy that created an entire industry of consultants and advisors who helped Web-content makers increase search engine optimization (SEO).

That Larry Page, one of the Google cofounders, understood that the unit of measure for Web content was pages rather than domains, URLs, articles, authors, sources, or any other dimension helped to shape the Web for almost 10 years. That the concept of *page* and Larry's last name were the same will go down as one of those great coincidences of history. While Sergey Brin, Google's other cofounder, is no less brilliant, there's no useful way to create a measure of quality called a Brin—though arguably Dewey did that very thing back in 1876.

We're moving along a continuum, first from human categorization (Dewey) to automated organization (Google), and now the sheer volume of data—and the nuance and complexity of it—overwhelms search technology. We're at a moment when what is emerging is something totally new.

We are on the verge of a data tsunami. Really. "Between the dawn of civilization through 2003, there was just five exabytes of information created," Google CEO Eric Schmidt told the audience at the 2010 Techonomy Conference, in Lake Tahoe. "That much information is now created every two days, and the pace is increasing. People aren't ready for the technology revolution that's going to happen to them."

Of course Schmidt is right. He knows the data better than anyone, as a very large portion of it is moving through the massive data centers that Google has built around the world. But it isn't simply the volume of data; it's the speed. The Web is now moving in real time: what happens *now* is delivered *now*. Jeff Pulver is a serial entrepreneur who was an early investor in Vonage, the Voice On the Net company that hit it big. Now Pulver only talks about one thing, what he calls The State of Now.

Says Pulver, "Living and experiencing information in The Now is just different when compared to the way we are used to experiencing things. Since the launch of the commercial Internet in 1993 we may have been on-line in real-time, but we experienced access to information that was slightly old to ancient. Today access to information has changed so much in the past year that today we are now living in 'The State of Now.'"

Now means data comes at you fast, and it's harder to determine relevance, accuracy, or even sourcing.

It is inevitable that we end up talking about needles and haystacks again.

"We are going to have more and more stacks of haystack and we are going to need people to find the needles in the haystacks," Scoble says. "You can see that Twitter is moving. Where is the new human pattern in that Twitter stream that we need to collect and save and talk about and argue about stuff like that? And that first process starts with curators who see a pattern in the world that needs to be discussed."

Andrew Blau is a researcher who has presciently foretold changes in media distribution and content creation. Now he's watching a new, historic emergence of first-person publishing.

Says Blau, "It used to be it was expensive to create and expensive to distribute—to amplify speech—was held in very few hands, held to high standards by people, by governments or by societies. That meant that very few people had that opportunity to amplify speech. Now that cluster, that nexus, has been irretrievably broken."

Today publishing tools have been set free, Blau says. Cost, ownership, and barriers to entry are all gone, almost overnight: "The ability to amplify one's voice, to amplify that beyond the reach of what we have had, reflects a change of course in human history. A lot of the discomfort people have about the kind of current riot of voices is that it's irresponsible, it's dumbing us down. What happens when anyone can actually speak to a very large audience? Now the whole dynamic of how stuff gets made and moved and managed has been changed so fundamentally that the gatekeeping function that we've come to expect is gone."

Of course, all big changes have unintended consequences. Blau says that the old problem—limited access to the tools to amplify speech—has been fixed by the Internet. It used to be that making and moving information was so expensive that the question of who was going to get permission to speak was a central social and political issue. But now speech is more democratic.

That development, not surprisingly, creates a new problem. "The problem is who gets heard," Blau says. "The real issue that remains is access to an audience. Because that's hard. Access to technology has become trivially easy for most people in the industrialized world, and increasingly easy for people in the emerging economies around the world."

In trying to humanize the problem of too much democratization of speech, Blau channels the wordplay of Yogi Berra: "There'd be some wonderful thing that he would say—'The problem when you can talk to *anybody* is that you can't talk to *anybody*.'"

There's no doubt Blau is right. Speech is easy; being heard is hard and getting harder, because computers can't distinguish between data and ideas. Or between human intellect and aggregated text and links. This lack of esthetic intelligence in a tsunami of data changes the game.

THE HUMAN ELEMENT

No longer is the algorithm in charge. Human curators have become essential software. What emerges is new human and computer collaboration. It's what former *New York Times* technology writer and AOL editorial director Saul Hansell calls bionic journalism—a cyborg creature that is part man, part machine. A massive gathering engine that finds, sorts, organizes, and then hands aggregated information to a human for a final review and editorial approval.

Before you get scary images in your mind of Arnold Schwarzenegger as the Terminator or the out-of-control WOPR (pronounced "whopper"), the fictional military computer featured in the movie *WarGames*, take a deep breath. The important news of the emergence of a Curation Nation is that humans are very much back in charge. If for a moment it seemed like some algorithm along the lines of Google News would automatically assemble "The Daily Me," today it's clear that our individual interests are more than a series of tags. The esthetic judgment that makes us choose a book or a bottle of wine or a favorite restaurant are a complex concoction of data and human taste.

In an era of data abundance, the thing that is scarce is taste. In the old world, a handful of media outlets and large corporations could set the agenda for political discourse, pop culture, and emerging trends. Mass media, as it was known, was not created by human demand for the same brand of jeans or the same tube of toothpaste; it was created by technology. Television allowed a single point on a network to broadcast a signal in real time into the living rooms of a geographically diverse and culturally different population. The result was that for a time we had a shared story that was the drumbeat of our culture. TV shows, national news, consumer products were all marketed to a mass culture and created mass demand. But technology giveth, and technology taketh away. And now, thanks to the magic elixir of bandwidth and hardware, we've all got a television broadcast studio in our pocket, a printing press on our desktop, and a radio station in our iPod. Mass media just went *kaboom*.

And while technology fueled the creation of mass media, mass content creation and aggregation tools are now driving the creation of micromedia and the job of Web curator.

Writing on SocialMediaToday.com, Rohit Bhargava defines the job of the future in the following curation manifesto.

MANIFESTO/JOB DESCRIPTION: CONTENT CURATOR

In the near future, experts predict that content on the web will double every 72 hours. The detached analysis of an algorithm will no longer be enough to find what we are looking for. To satisfy the people's hunger for great content on any topic imaginable, there will need to be a new category of individual working online.

Someone whose job it is not to create more content, but to make sense of all the content that others are creating.

To find the best and most relevant content and bring it forward.

The people who choose to take on this role will be known as Content Curators. The future of the social web will be driven by these Content Curators, who take it upon themselves to collect and share the best content online for others to consume and take on the role of citizen editors, publishing highly valuable compilations of content created by others. In time, these curators will bring more utility and order to the social web. In doing so, they will help to add a voice and point of view to organizations and companies that can connect them with customers—creating an entirely new dialogue based on valued content rather than just brand created marketing messages.

It's worth remembering that content isn't the same thing it used to be. In fact, you may be surprised to know the folks at Zappos, the Web e-commerce site that is legendarily known for its customer service, consider every item they sell on their site content. There's a team photo on the wall of their Las Vegas headquarters with a caption that reads: "The Content Team, formerly known as Product Information." Information about shoes, headlines in the *New York Times*, data about New York City subway arrival times—it's all content. And it's all hungry for curation.

WHO ELSE IS A CURATOR?

Are rappers, DJs, and bloggers considered curators? The American Association of Museums thinks the answer may be a somewhat shocking yes. Writing on the AAM blog, Elizabeth Schlatter broke the news to her fellow museum professionals: "Over the past few years, the words 'curate' and 'curator' have become increasingly prevalent in describing activities outside the museum arena. In addition to the word's use as a synonym for 'select' and 'present,' . . . 'curate' is also being used in job titles and in related products and functions."

What prompted this pop culture reflection of the normally staid museum world? It may have been this headline from the equally staid *New York Times*: "Ludacris as Curator of His Own Hip-Hop Museum." Schlatter explains, "The concert review described how the musician Ludacris featured guest rappers and DJs famous in the '80s and '90s in his own new recordings and live performances. Praising the inclusion of songs and appearances by other artists in the concert, the reviewer wrote, 'A cavalcade of guests emerged to take the stage for a few moments each, a showcase of New York hip-hop history with a devoted fan as curator. It turned this show on its ear.'"

Wow, that has to be a tricky thing for folks with Ph.D.s from the nation's most respected universities to read. Here's an up-from-the-streets rapper who's taken on the mantle of curator and the *New York Times* seems more than willing to give him the title. Ludacris isn't alone. Chris Anderson, the frighteningly bright and occasionally acerbic organizer of the famous TED conferences introduces himself as TED's chief curator.

And, indeed, I consider myself a curator too. During my work in the film business, I've spent a piece of my career gathering and organizing footage around one of the most dramatic and pivotal events of my lifetime. In the days after 9/11 in New York, I worked with both amateur and professional filmmakers to gather stories and documentary footage of the attacks on the World Trade Center. The result of that effort was a film I directed titled *7 Days in September*. The resulting archive, more than 500 hours of video of the attacks, and the week's aftermath became known as the Camera-Planet 9/11 Archive. And what did I determine—back in 2001—was the appropriate title for my role as caretaker of the archive? Well, it was, of course, curator. Don't get me wrong: in many ways what I did with the 9/11 material is classic curation. But I did it without the credentials or training that the museum community requires to confer that title.

This trend, Schlatter reports, has the curatorial community struggling to understand their new role in pop culture. "The growing use of the term 'curator' in other fields, while misleading to many, fools no one who is actually in the industry and knows about the scope of activities that a curator undertakes," says independent curator Michelle Kasprzak. "The use and abuse of the term outside the field indicates how opaque the contemporary art world and its processes may be to the rest of society, but perhaps we should welcome this as a teaching moment, where what curators do can be discussed and illuminated in a broader context."

I'm not sure that the guy curating grilled cheese at the Brooklyn swap meet considers this a teachable moment. But for all of Kasprzak's snark and superiority, the new class of curators that

Robert Scoble represents aren't losing sleep over the concerns of the old guard. What does he say to the Ph.D. crowd? "Get over it. I love people who have investment in a word because they spent 20 years doing something. How they get a little uppity about, 'Oh, that's my word and you can't use it.'"

In fact, Scoble doesn't buy that the word has changed or been diluted. He thinks he's a curator in the very essence of the word. "I talked with museum curators, and they do the same thing I do," he says. "Only they're trained to look at art and see a pattern and explain that to other people. 'Van Gogh did this, and this, and this. I see a pattern, I was trained to recognize this pattern, and now I'm going to explain that to you in the museum.' They write cards or do audio tours, etc., to explain what this pattern means to us. That's exactly what I do with Twitter. So, if they say, I'm diluting their value to the world, I don't think so. I'm not a trained museum curator, I can't explain to you what a painting that Van Gogh did means. I don't have that expertise. I can tell you what a tweet from Tim O'Reilly means. That's my training. So, if you think that takes away some value you had to the world, I think you're wrong."

In the face of this democratization of the word *curation*, some in the museum world are a bit more welcoming. Schlatter quotes Kristen Hileman, curator of the Baltimore Museum of Art, as saying, "it is intriguing to think there is something so evocative in the vocabulary describing my job that others want to use it to articulate their own abilities or services."

It's clear that the museum world isn't going to allow its professional credential to be drawn into broad public use without putting up a fight. Here again, Schlatter is able to quickly synopsize both the trend and the implicit objection: "The word 'curate' could be attractive because of its implied prestige, suggesting that objects, experiences or people are being chosen and presented by an expert best equipped with the necessary knowledge and experience."

And Baltimore Museum's Hileman explains, "In short, I can see the appeal of a knowledgeable specialist making selections or recommendations in an information and image-saturated culture."

Troy M. Livingston, vice president for innovation and learning at the Museum of Life and Science, in Durham, North Carolina, targets the crux of the issue: "I think the threat to curators is that if we allow anyone to participate, will that lessen the value of what curators contribute? There's a sense of resistance and fear perhaps in the curatorial profession because of this. I mean, some curators probably hate Wikipedia because there's no oversight. But we're living in a Wikipedia world."

Which brings me to the painful, ugly, but inevitable truth of the pages ahead. Most readers of this book will be reading it through the fog of their nondigital selves. We are not digital natives. How do I know this? Okay, well, first of all, you're reading a book. Sorry, but that's so . . . um . . . long form. And some of you were born after 1982.

To keep me honest in this journey to the heart of curation, I enlisted the advice of my friend Alexa Scordato. She is a digital native. She's 24, she wrote her first blog post when she was 11, she was the first generation of Facebook kids, and she's already had six jobs. At least.

"I wake up every morning with my iPhone next to me, and before I even get to work I probably have responded to 15 to 20 different e-mails, Twitter direct messages, and maybe five text messages," Alexa tells me.

"You take someone like me who was a tween on LiveJournal and MySpace, a college student on Facebook, a professional on LinkedIn, a Web professional on my blog, and then the world needs to be more forgiving for people who are in their twenties today—because who we were at the age of 13 is still the same person that we are today. However, we live in a world where that entire identity that we've been exploring for the last decade is indexed by people."

Alexa's generation has been named by some marketing people as the Content Generation. Generation C. The Web site Trend watching.com published a post in 2004 exploring the emergence in consumer brand advertising aimed at Alexa and her peers, which invited them to make content around their brands. But Jim Richardson, founder of the British consulting firm Sumo, has suggested that the C in Generation C should stand for not only content, creativity, and connectivity but also curation—designating the millions of young people who create, organize, interpret, and share pictures, music, video, and opinions on these Web sites. Richardson reasons, "They curate 'stuff,' which says something about them, or, probably more realistically, says something about how they would like to be seen. I don't think the term 'curator' means a great deal to these young people, but I think the act of curating does mean something. It helps them to say to the world who they are."

And Alexa, in describing herself as a "digital guinea pig," agrees: "I think that's sort of the beauty of the digital media, that we have these tools at our disposal to basically not only curate the world around us but also kind of curate our personal selves and who we want to present to the world."

Richardson adds that while Web 2.0 culture allows everyone to curate content, it complements rather than replaces the role of the professional curator: "I think this is a fresh and exciting way for people to interact with museum content, and in doing this they are also exposing more people—their friends, peers—to that content. At present, there is a trend toward looking to the public to impact the content of exhibitions, but realistically the amount of work that it takes to develop an exhibition really requires professional involvement."

Schlatter asks the rhetorical question: can a DJ be a curator? But digging in, it's hard to think of a DJ as anything other than a curator. After all, curators explicitly aren't creators. They don't make content or art or sneakers. Curators don't make anything from scratch. But as Colby Hall, the editor in chief of the Web site Mediaite.com, explains, "Being a DJ is exactly what a curator does. They are able to take songs that are written by other people, performed by other people, mixed and distributed by other people, and create an experience that is entirely new." Sometimes, even better. If you've ever been to a party with a great DJ, you know how great that can be. Now remember a party with a terrible DJ? Often he played the same songs, sometimes even in the same order, but a bad DJ just doesn't get the pace, the rhythm, the vibe of the room right. Well, curation is kind of like that. If you don't get the choices right, and the timing right, and the pacing right—then each song that is knit together into musical montage that makes the whole more than the sum of its parts. Which is to say, musicians need DJs and DJs need musicians—the business model question notwithstanding. We've got a whole book of pages ahead to help sort out how makers, publishers, and curators all get paid in the new curation economy. But *new* is the operational word here—and new rules mean new rulers. No longer is the owner of the distribution system the king of the castle. Today, curation is king.

CONTENT STRATEGISTS

While the emerging curation ecosystem may leave the highbrow and pedigreed museum curation crowd with a furrowed brow, there's another group who are equally troubled by the rise of human-powered finding and filtering—and that's the code-centric solutions crowd that has been searching for the holy grail of machine-powered (or crowd-sourced) finding and filtering. This is the aggregation camp. And they too are anxious to see the emerging but noisy curation community replaced by elegant code.

Blogger Clinton Forry has the most cogent distinction I've read so far:

- Aggregation is automated

- Aggregation collects content based on criteria in the form of metadata or keywords

- Criteria can be adjusted, but remain static otherwise

- Follows a preset frequency of publishing [as available, weekly, etc.]

It isn't that Forry thinks aggregation isn't important, it's that he thinks it doesn't do the whole job. It gets you only partway there. He explains ". . . aggregation excludes the important, active, and ongoing editorial approval from the process of gathering content. Aggregation has its place. It is easy to set and forget. It requires considerably less staff resources. With carefully selected criteria and sources, it may actually serve the purpose you seek."

Forry is one of the new and growing number of consultants and advisors who call themselves content strategists. These are folks who are hired to make sure that Web sites are built to encourage vibrant content, rather than stale "publish and forget it" content. He defines curation this way:

- Curation is, in part, a manual task

- Starts with sources to parse

- Evaluates content individually based on established editorial criteria

- Weighs content based on context, current events, branding, sentiment, etc.

- Publishes approved content on appropriate schedule

So, if you buy the notion that we're moving from a world of content scarcity to content abundance, and that you—like all of us— are facing content overload that verges on an endless fire hose of data coming at you from the moment you wake until the last time you check your e-mail, texts, voice mail, blog posts, and direct Twitter messages—then curation isn't just something that may happen, it's something that *has* to happen. The alternative is a harrowing experience straight out of *Max Headroom*. You may remember the short, mind-exploding advertisements that fictional investigative reporter Edison Carter exposed when his networks decided to broadcast them even though they killed people. Well, it turns out we're living in a universe of blipverts, and while they may not be killing us, they certainly are making day-to-day life in the world of the data avalanche hard to cope with. Without a coherent human filter to create contextual and digestible information, the noise is rapidly approaching a place where it drowns out the signal. Unchecked, the data will make our collective heads explode. *Kaboom!*

2

THE HISTORY OF CURATION

As the face of work in America changes, folks who've had full-time jobs increasingly find those jobs are turning into gigs, or short-term assignments. *Entrepreneur* magazine reports that 90 percent of U.S. companies use outsourced labor, a figure that has grown from 6 percent to more than 27 percent since 1990. The freelance nation even has people with full-time jobs looking for ways to turn their passions, knowledge, or skills into a revenue stream.

The result is the emergence of the pro-sumer, a consumer turned part-time professional.

What makes this model so powerful is that it allows a new class of curators to emerge who are in many ways more deeply committed to their narrow fields of interest. While mainstream media will shift their senior correspondents at the White House to cover the Justice Department or education or health care, a passionate enthusiast with a fervent love of collectable lunch boxes is far more likely to build a fan base and a reputation as the best source of curated information about them. The king of collectable lunch boxes isn't shifting to Beanie Babies or Matchbox cars anytime soon. Is the idea of an amateur with a passion becoming a curator a new idea? Hardly. Early curators stuck to a core concept of adding value by finding, sorting, and publishing digests or collections. Eventually some of them grew large enterprises based on the concept of finding and filtering.

Take for example DeWitt Wallace who, while recovering from shrapnel wounds received in World War I, began the hobby of gathering and condensing articles from monthly magazines. Sometimes he would rewrite them. The magazine was, of course, *Reader's Digest*. The original business plan, such as it was, had estimated an annual $5,000 of net income. But Wallace was wrong.

THE STORY OF *READER'S DIGEST*

DeWitt Wallace was born in 1889 in St. Paul, Minnesota. His father was the son of a Presbyterian minister and the president of Macalester College. As a young boy Wallace raised chickens and vegetables, and ran an electrical repair service. Piety and knowledge were part of his upbringing.

Wallace attended Macalester from 1907 to 1909, then transferred to UC Berkeley. He dropped out in 1912 to return to St. Paul, taking a job at Webb Publishing Company, which published agricultural textbooks. In 1916, Wallace realized that few farmers were aware of the vast number of informational pamphlets available for free from state and federal government offices. He gathered up a list and sold more than 100,000 copies throughout the Northwest.

Wallace enlisted in the army during World War I and was wounded, landing him in a hospital in France for four months. He passed the time reading American magazines. It was during his convalescence, far from home, that Wallace began to think about other magazine readers and just how much material there was to absorb. Surely for readers who didn't have so much free time, the volume of magazine content would be overwhelming. An American overseas—he had the germ of an idea for a business.

Wallace was shy, introverted, and by some accounts even antisocial. He was uncomfortable with strangers, soft-voiced, and spoke in fits and starts. But inside the world of magazines, he had an uncanny sense of what people would read and how to get to essence of an article.

Wallace returned home and spent nearly every day of the next half year in the Minneapolis Public Library reading magazines. He read, cataloged, and condensed articles. His plan was to create a compendium of a wide variety of subjects, abridging articles so they could be read quickly. His prototype of the *Reader's Digest* had 31 articles from magazines including *Atlantic Monthly*, the *Saturday Evening Post*, *National Geographic*, and *Ladies' Home Journal*.

Wallace showed a sample of his magazine of magazines to the sister of a college friend, Lila Bell Acheson. Acheson loved the idea; in 1921 he proposed and they were married. Their husband-and-wife partnership would turn out to be one of the most productive and successful in publishing. After 12 publishers turned them down, they decided to produce the magazine on their own. The Wallaces mailed out several hundred circulars advertising a magazine with "each article of enduring value and interest, in condensed and permanent form." When Wallace and his wife returned from their honeymoon, they found 1,300 subscribers had paid $3 a year for the magazine. *Reader's Digest* was born. The couple went to work out of their basement apartment in New York's Greenwich Village, copying articles for the first issue, which appeared in 1922.

By 1929, the magazine had 290,000 subscribers and had a gross income of almost a million dollars a year. Forty years later, there were 40 international editions with a worldwide circulation of 23 million. The magazine launched in the People's Republic of China in 2008 and changed its tagline to "Lives well shared." Gathering and sharing in print for more than 70 years was a very good business indeed. With more than 100 million readers around the world, *Reader's Digest* is the most popular magazine of all time.

The couple was an unlikely duo; Wallace was a tall, somewhat stooped man with a tweedy demeanor of a college professor, while his wife, Lila, was outgoing and confident, with a sweeping optimism. Yet together, his innate sense and her marketing savvy made a remarkable team. Later, one of his editors would remark, "If Wally likes it, automatically 12 million other people will like it."

That the *Reader's Digest* became a phenomenon can be attributed to a number of things. No doubt Wallace had an uncanny knack for choosing and packaging Americana. But the mix of stories was unique in both its breadth and brevity. These were hallmarks of the *Reader's Digest* brand and style. The variety of subjects covered, included science, social service, education, government, politics, industry, sports, travel, nature, and biography, among other topics. Popular columns such as "It Pays to Increase Your Word Power," "Humor in Uniform," "Life in These United States," and "The Most Unforgettable Character I've Met" gave the publication a spine. The magazine was unfailingly optimistic, a kind of pocket-size Andrew Carnegie of the era. Wallace was able to take the essence of the upbeat American idea and turn it into a publication. As the *New York Times* explains, "In Wallace's magazine, one hears an incredibly American voice saying, in short simple sentences, that one can improve one's life, improve one's health, and, in fact, improve the world, if only one has adequate information. It always implies that there is no problem without a human solution."

Keep in mind that when *Reader's Digest* was born, those were the days before television and there was no mass media. But the *Reader's Digest* was able to gather, synthesize, and package a view of America that was culled from a wide variety of sources. And much as Wallace discovered in that hospital bed during his postwar recovery, readers around the world were looking for a bite-size American magazine that encapsulated the American Story.

Reader's Digest was a powerful American export. As *Time* magazine explained, "In the long run, Wallace's greatest contribution to the nation may be found in the cumulative effect of his overseas editions The Digest articles—depicting the innate decency, kindness, and simple virtues of ordinary Americans, the triumphs of a George Carver or a Helen Keller—have probably done more than all the Government propagandists combined to allay the fears, prejudices and misconceptions of the United States in other lands."

THE STORY OF *TIME* MAGAZINE

While Wallace was in a hospital bed considering the overwhelming volume of magazine content and the need for a filter and an abridged package, that same idea was taking shape across the ocean.

The year was 1916, and while Wallace was graduating from a public high school in Minneapolis, the young Henry Luce was graduating from the elite prep Hotchkiss School, in Connecticut.

He was the son of American Protestant missionaries in China and arrived in the United States at age 14. As biographer Alan

Brinkley reports, "He had overweening ambitions even then, along with a highly developed sense of his own importance. He had none of the advantages that his classmates' money could buy, and knew so little about American popular culture that prep school slang was alien to him. By graduation he had become editor of a campus publication and boastfully labeled it "First in the Prep School World.""

Luce was just 24 when he and a classmate conceived of the world's first "weekly news-magazine": *Time*. They even invented the word *news-magazine*. But *Time* wasn't to be known back in 1923 as a magazine of writers; it was instead a collection of news of the world—a concise summary that was published weekly and marketed around the United States. *Time* was able to make the ideas and articles of the world available to U.S. readers, serving as a single source of information for middle-class people with a need to be well-read but without the time to pore over the world's periodicals.

That both Luce and Wallace were sons of preachers seems worth noting here. At a time when America's horizons were opening—both men took the passion of their politics and fused them with an evangelical zeal and missionary sense of purpose to spread the word of American ideas—as filtered and contextualized with content from the world's publications. These were hardly unbiased digests; in both the case of *Time* and *Reader's Digest*, the choices, the tone, and the delivery were all means to an end. These were aggregated and curated content vehicles to be sure, but they where hardly automated—in fact they were chosen and summarized with purpose. Rather than objective, these were both subjective publishing empires.

In 1923, as Luce was readying *Time*'s debut issue, he had a clear vision for what the newsmagazine was going to be: cogent, compartmentalized, and clear. The language woven throughout was rooted in the founder's classical education and employed vivid turns of phrase such as *wine-dark sea*. Also, under the steadfast guidance of *Time*'s first editor, H. L. Mencken, the wit on display in *Time* was fashionably irreverent. Michael Kinsley, writing in the *Atlantic* about Alan Brinkley's biography of Henry Luce, acknowledged Brinkley's observation that Luce was looking to filter information with the form that became known as the "news-magazine": "Brinkley, the first biographer to have access to all of Luce's letters and other documents, confirms that *Time* was intended from the start to be what we now call 'aggregation' or (if we're being hoity-toity) 'curation.' Although it later succumbed to bureaucratic bloat—an insane system of researchers feeding material to reporters that fed it to writers—at the beginning it was just a lot of smart-ass Yalies rewriting the *New York Times*. Brinkley describes sliced-up copies of the *Times* and piles of foreign magazines everywhere around the offices. Luce's idea, and that of his business partner, Briton Hadden, was to condense all the news busy people needed to know into one weekly read. The magazine, Luce wrote, would 'serve the illiterate upper classes, the busy business man, the tired debutant, to prepare them at least once a week for a table conversation.' There was not a lot of brooding about other people's intellectual property rights."

CABLE TV IS BORN

If Luce and Wallace were the first aggregators of text, John Walson may well have been the first video aggregator: way back in 1945, fewer than 10,000 televisions operated in the United States. Walson and his wife, Margaret, had a small shop set up to sell and install GE appliances in Mahanoy, Pennsylvania. In 1947 they began to sell TV sets. Mahanoy, however, was a town in a valley, with Pennsylvanian coal-country mountains on all sides. The result was poor signals for Mahanoy residents. While John Walson had perched an antenna on a utility pole on nearby New Boston Mountain to demonstrate the TVs, it didn't help the local townsfolk once they'd brought a new set home and turned it on. The three Philadelphia over-the-air broadcast signals just weren't going to make it to the living rooms of Mahanoy. In June 1948 Walson connected his mountain antenna to both his store and a number of his customers' homes that were on the path from the mountain to his shop; the result was the first of what was then called community antenna television (CATV). That day, the televisions in his store window displayed the nation's first cable TV. He charged customers $100 for installation and a monthly fee of $2.

Much as Luce and Wallace had the same revelation that the world needed concise new digests back in 1922, Walson had the same insight. Walson was one of a number of entrepreneurs in the hills and valleys of central Pennsylvania who trudged up mountains in search of over-the-air signals that they could capture and bring down into their towns on amplified cable strung down from the mountains. By 1952, 14,000 subscribers were getting their signals through 70 start-up cable companies. As cable was wired from home to home, from town to town, cable systems began to realize that they could deliver more than signals from nearby broadcasters, and aggregation of signals from other broadcasters—like Ted Turner's superstation WTBS, in Atlanta—helped fuel the transition from a solution that improved local signals to a vast network that could become a delivery system for programming that didn't originate from a broadcast tower. Cable TV evolved, from aggregation and curation to creation.

What's important for the emerging new class of content aggregators and curators today is that there's a proud tradition in start-ups building businesses that help organize emerging new content sources. *Reader's Digest, Time,* and the companies that became Comcast and Cablevision all began when they determined a customer need. In the case of the magazine aggregators, there was no debate about copyright or revenue sharing—or frankly even about business models. Luce and Wallace both knew that if they provided value to readers, content creators would need to partici- pate, and if they didn't gather readers—there would be no need to concern themselves with sources—they'd be out of business. No doubt there were plenty of other folks who tried content gather- ing who failed; those names are lost in history. And 30 years later, when broadcast television left living rooms in Pennsylvania with- out broadcast TV, it was again the early entrepreneurial curators who stepped in and found the signal, strung the wire, and won the hugely valuable prize of having the cable in the home that, with time, prevailed over broadcast signals.

AN ABUNDANCE OF CONTENT

Now let's get in our time machine and flash forward 50 years or so. If you were Luce or Wallace or Walson today, what problem would you want to solve? Back then, content was precious, and distribu- tion and organization were the key factors. But today, distribution is ubiquitous. The Web touches most people and places, and WiFi certainly keeps people and devices connected whenever and wher- ever they choose.

Today the problem is about abundance—about content, or, more accurately, about data, overwhelming us and the systems we have in place to organize it. So if Luce was transplanted to the cur- rent day, he might well be curating not a single magazine called *Time* but a series of Web sites with aggregated and curated brands about politics, science, business, travel, world affairs, and a host of other aggregated verticals. Today the innovators are the content entrepreneurs, passionate individuals who are using the powerful leverage of the Web and the coming era of overwhelming abundance to explore a new kind of editorial business. Their passion can't be faked.

THE STREAMING GOURMET

One example of passion and curation creating a new and exciting content mix is San Francisco's Amy Wilson. She is a former high school physics teacher and administrator who has always liked to make things with raw materials. Her story begins with her mom, a dedicated cook in her own right, and a childhood spent in the technology hotbed of Silicon Valley. "My love of food and cooking was instilled in me by my mother, who still makes everything from scratch," she says. "Living here in the Bay Area and working at a school in Sonoma County helped feed my obsession with all things culinary. After having my second child, I decided it was time to work from home, and I wanted to do something related to Web 2.0 technology and quickly realized it would need to have a connection to food."

She began looking for a Web project and found that her preoccupation with "all things culinary" led her to create her own blog and curation project. As Wilson explains it, "I decided a year ago that I wanted to create a video-sharing site for people passionate about food and drink, and I wanted it to be easier to use than the other culinary video sites on the Web—easier to find the videos you're after and easier to share videos you like."

The result was StreamingGourmet.com, a social-networking video-hosting site devoted to food and drink. Wilson handpicked over 2,000 high-quality videos from around the Web and sorted them into easy-to-navigate categories. Members can upload their own videos, which are often featured and promoted on the site and on other social networks such as Facebook and Twitter, where

StreamingGourmet has a strong following. Wilson says the aim is to be a compendium of video recipes as well as a source for other fun food- and wine-related videos—one-stop shopping, if you will.

Although the site is still just getting started, Wilson has embraced curation with the zeal of an inventor, evangelist, and explorer. She's found her calling. Not in making food. Not even in making food videos. But in finding, sorting, and sharing food videos.

StreamingGourmet hasn't become profitable, but that may not be the point. Wilson is enjoying a good deal of attention and garnering paying clients as one of the pioneers in the culinary Web space. "People are reaching out to me," she says. "I am currently in discussions with a celebrity interested in creating a cookbook and Web site with video. None of these opportunities would have come my way without the credibility that resulted from curating the site."

The question then becomes whether Amy Wilson is leading a trend or just enjoying a hobby of collecting videos for fellow foodies. Well, as it turns out, even global media phenomenons are rapidly being embraced, some would say overtaken, by talented, passionate content curators.

While Wilson harnessed her passion for food, other would-be curators are able to see a trend on the horizon and crown themselves the king or queen of a certain emerging domain. Take, for example, the story of Paul Wood.

SUSAN BOYLE'S FIRST BIG FAN

Paul Wood is a construction worker in London who's got the bug for building video networks in his spare time.

So on a Saturday night in London back in 2009, Wood decided on a lark that the career of an unknown singer named Susan Boyle might take off when *Britain's Got Talent* broadcast her performance.

He'd seen her in the auditions and decided to take a risk. He bought the URL Susan-Boyle.com and Sunday night—moments after the broadcast—he had a fan site for her up online.

What Wood didn't know and couldn't know was that somehow Susan Boyle connected with a wide variety of people in a deep and powerful way. Why is that? First, you need to see the clip to understand. We can spend a sec and try to psychoanalyze the public: for some, the music is what it's all about; for others, it's the ugly duckling that spreads her wings. But then again, it may just be that given the economy, with people feeling so beaten up, watching an underdog triumph was just too much to resist.

It hardly matters. She totally owned the gig, and now she's a rocket. And the best part? This isn't some contrived media event from the pop-culture factory. This is a real woman with real talent.

Susan-Boyle.com has created an "instant" destination where people can connect, share stories, record videos, and watch Susan Boyle's performance. It is a feel-good site, with most viewer comments gushing with enthusiasm and support. There is something that feels good about watching a community grow organically around such a positive media moment and personality. We just don't have enough of this stuff these days.

After four days of going live, Wood's Web site was getting close to a million page views a day, and, as of today, it has over 42,000 registered members.

The *Wall Street Journal* reports that the site's soaring traffic makes it the number one site for Susan Boyle fans worldwide, providing a unique mix of tearful user-submitted video testimonials, network clips from the Web, and a live Twitter stream of Susan Boyle fans that updates around the clock from a fast-growing global fan base.

It is also worth pointing out that only in the technologically connected world we live in could such an event be possible. Millions of people flocking to a virtual destination and forming a flash-mob-style community, never meeting one another but finding a real outlet to come together and share in the moment. Who says technology is making us numb to personal interaction? It was Wood's curation efforts that made the site possible, since he in fact never made a video. He simply created a home for fans looking for a place to share, link, and view one another's videos. And what about the business side? One year after the launch, after some reasonable advertising revenue, Wood told me he sold the site to a group of fans and "did well." A curation project with a happy ending.

EVERYTHING OLD IS NEW AGAIN

Amy Wilson at StreamingGourmet has a plan to keep growing her curation franchise. Says Wilson, "I'd really like to be able to harness the food blogging community more, and to do that, it has to be easy for content on my site to be linked back to content on their sites. Food bloggers want to do more with video, but then they realize how difficult and time-consuming it is to make a video, so if I can help them learn so that they can publish good content quickly, then that could really drive growth at my site."

So is curation now only the realm of start-ups and entrepreneurs? Media consultant and Columbia University professor Ava Seave says that she's seeing big media brands embracing the curation equation as well. And you'll hardly be surprised who's leading the trend.

"A client I worked with called *Taste of Home* is a great example," Seave says. "*Taste of Home* is a division of Reader's Digest. And what's really interesting about *Taste of Home* is that it was the original user-generated material company that started as a magazine before the Internet age. Where the readers would contribute recipes. So it's all about food and recipes."

The Reader's Digest Association was already deeply committed to aggregation and curation. User-generated content was an obvious next step. So when RDA acquired *Taste of Home*, it found itself squarely in the user-generated content business. At first it was a highly successful magazine of user-submitted recipes, and the next step was to take that model to the Web.

"*Taste of Home* has taken that idea and basically run with it in terms of its electronic presence on the Web. It has a very active set of users of its Web site, as well as content from all sorts of places," Seave says.

Video plays a key part to its curation solution. "They have their own videos and they have videos from across the Web that are appropriate, and they manage to use them well; their readers and users participate in whether these are good videos or bad videos," Seave explains. "Advertisers really like it. So they have a sort of combined hybrid situation where they have print publication, they have user and reader engagement, they have really a flow between print and electronic and they have a curation aspect of it across the board, and so that's a really successful business."

So if someone ever tells you that you can't make any money gathering and curating content, just mention DeWitt Wallace and his Reader's Digest Association. Chances are that person has never heard of him, but, trust me, he did just fine.

3

BIG-TIME CURATORS ON THE RISE

he funny thing about innovation is that the old guard always cries foul, and the new folks storming the castle always claim that they can break all the rules in the name of progress: "Get out of the way—here comes the *future*," they declare. They're right, pretty much, but that doesn't make the transition any less painful or the folks who are forced out of a job any less pissed off. If you were the best darn buggy-whip maker around when the horse-drawn carriage was replaced by the automobile, chances are you weren't terribly excited about Henry Ford and his newfangled Model T.

For me, the moment that everything changed happened in a pretty unlikely place, and with a very unusual cast of characters.

The location was the principality of Monaco, a tiny bit of remarkably privileged earth on the north-central coast of the Mediterranean Sea, bounded on three sides by France. It's the kind of place you expect to run into James Bond driving an Aston Martin with a martini in hand. Instead, I found myself talking with Arianna Huffington.

HUFFINGTON POST AND THE EMERGENCE OF THE LINKED ECONOMY

Arianna Huffington has reinvented herself more times than Larry King's been married. Huffington has been a conservative pundit, the wife of a wealthy conservative businessman, a published author, and a Democratic candidate for governor of California. But all those incarnations seem relatively unimportant when you watch just how clearly she has seen the future of publishing.

But before we get to my moment in Monaco, let's go back to 2008. The first time I saw Huffington speak, she was standing in front of a room of media types at the New York Yacht Club preaching the gospel of the linked economy. Huffington's view of publishing was simple: writers need links; publishers need links. No matter who you are, a homegrown blogger or the *New York Times*, the site that sends you traffic is going to be a key partner. She was sure that the Huffington Post could be a good partner to content creators without having to pay them. I'm pretty sure no one knew what she was talking about. But she was forceful, unwavering, and determined, speaking in her now-famous accent that seems like it should come straight out of the mouth of Eva Gabor on *Green Acres*.

Across the room of gainfully employed media execs, her message was taken with polite bemusement. She was charming and well-meaning, but wrong, of course. This breakfast was when she was gearing up to be a big force in democratic media as the presidential election approached. Even as her traffic grew, media veterans seemed comfortably confident that once the elections were over, the era of Huffington Post would fade into the background, and the trend toward aggregation and curating content would soon be over. Then a funny thing happened. The election came and went, and the Huffington Post continued to grow. It morphed from a left-wing democratic site to a collection of topics, such as media, technology, sports, comedy, food, and the environment. From June 2009 to June 2010, the *New York Times* Web site nytimes.com gained just 2 million unique visitors while the Huffington Post's uniques nearly doubled. And from September 2010 to June 2010, the gap between the *Times* and the Huffington Post has narrowed from more than 12 million to just 6 million. If both news sites continued to grow at the same rate, the Huffington Post would overtake the *Times* in unique visitors by mid 2011.

How did she do it? There are a few secrets that have been shared in closed circles that I can reveal here.

First, the Huffington Post isn't one set of content; it's actually three very different kinds of content presented in a slickly blended presentation. There is a core team of paid HuffPost reporters and editors. They cover beats such as politics, media, and technology. They report and blog editorial that is effectively about 60 percent of the site's content; 40 percent has been published elsewhere. Historically, reporting has been fact-based and objective, while blogging is crafted for the Web, allows for more opinion and often includes facts that are modified or updated after the blog's original publication.

Huffington is able to say that she is both linking to and being linked from the wider Web. This curation mix gives the Huffington Post some exclusive content, the ability to break headlines, and protection from critics who say all it does is steal content. *Steal* is not my word, but it is one often tossed around by some of the older, more established media executives in reference to HuffPost. Huffington has her fans, of course, but like anyone breaking new ground, she's got more than her share of enemies as well.

The second set of sources is Huffington Post bloggers, a large group of well-regarded leaders in the worlds of tech, politics, media, and the arts. These well-known writers, and celebs and other notables who contribute one-off pieces, create a sexy mix. Huffington exerts a bunch of effort, making it easy for folks like Henry Kissinger to fax in op-ed pieces. For the less tech-savvy, HuffPost will actually take the fax and type it into a blog post—a modern-day scribe for the digitally unsophisticated. For others, a user name and password allows self-publishing and posting. This creates a large volume of unedited posts from vetted sources. Simply put, this is DIY publishing, with HuffPost acting as the host and brand presenter. And while the HuffPost staff curates the bloggers when they join the network, they aggressively do not review, copyedit, or fact check what these unpaid volunteer bloggers provide to the site.

Then last, HuffPost editors scour the Web and their sources for content that is topical, breaking, edgy, compelling, or just a bit salacious; those images and brief excerpts are placed on the page in big splashy layouts. All this is fed into a technology platform that is built on WordPress, which is a Web-based blogging platform, but is actually more like WordPress on steroids. Behind the curtain, HuffPost editors watch every link, every page, every post, and make changes in headlines, layouts, and images—testing just what results in readers clicking on links. This happens in real time, creating a publishing marvel that morphs as readers express their interest with their mouse clicks. It is as if the *New York Times* could know in real time just which articles are engaging readers and then make editorial changes to keep the pages fresh and the readers reading. That's the positive view.

Critics, however, say that using technology to create headlines that incite clicks is pandering, not publishing; that a headline about an actress's "Most Sexy Movie Scenes" is going to always perform better than images and reporting from Rwanda. But the numbers don't lie, and readers like what they see at HuffPost.

And it's important to point out that Huffington didn't invent a politically oriented Web site of aggregated links. That honor belongs to Matt Drudge, whose Drudge Report back during the 2000 election was able to garner massive page views with little more than a page of links and a single big splashy headline. Today Drudge's format hasn't changed, and he's still bringing in huge audiences every day. His site is certainly smaller than Huffington's, but he does the job with a much smaller staff. Huffington's staff is comparatively vast, and with so much venture capital invested, HuffPost is under pressure to make a profit soon, before investors get restless.

As the leading proponent of aggregation and curation, Huffington spends a disproportionate amount of time proselytizing and defending the emerging practice. But two years is a very long time in Web evolution. Just 24 months after getting polite applause at the yacht club, Huffington was on the world stage as a media darling at the invite-only Monaco Media Forum—where the likes of News Corp's Jonathan Miller rub shoulders with the likes of Tony Orsten, CEO of Abu Dhabi Media. Huffington was pitted against Germany's media giant Axel Springer's CEO, Mathias Döpfner, the hard-charging defender of premium content and pay walls, who smiled and waved his hand at Arianna's "money losing experiment." But Huffington, who'd learned how to arm wrestle media barons by that time, said with a sly laugh, "You continue to be paid, I'll continue to be free, and let's meet back here next year and see whose business is growing." The audience seemed ready to bet on the newly minted media baron: a Web-publishing juggernaut that had just crossed 8.4 million unique visitors a month. Newspapers, the core of the Axel Springer enterprise, seem like an idea whose day is clearly passing.

Huffington, who *Time* magazine called the Web's new oracle in 2009, is clear about the fact that what she's doing is changing things, and some of that change will have a negative impact on so-called old media. She explains, "We are certainly at a turning point leading to the tipping point—an exciting prospect in my view. There needs to be a distinction between saving journalism and saving newspapers. The idea that you can go back to a pre-Internet world where you can create walled gardens around content, and charge for admission, is simply futile. Those who try that are going to fail." She's speaking about Mathias Döpfner, CEO of Axel Springer, of course. She goes on, "Today we live in the linked economy, not a walled-off content economy. The challenge is to find different ways to monetize links among media through advertising or micropayment or whatever, not subscription for exclusive content. In this environment, good journalism will survive, and even flourish, though most newspapers—except for a handful of the very best papers and magazines in every national market—probably will not. There will be more bottom-up, citizen journalism, which is great."

For Huffington and a whole host of other aggregator and curators, it comes down to where the law says they can link and share content without crossing the line into stealing. Attorney and Web publisher Dan Abrams of Mediaite.com explains, "When we link, we follow the 'fair use' ground rules, quoting no more than two paragraphs from another medium and then linking to the original story on the original site. That generates an amazing amount of traffic to the original site. It is not a one-way street."

And Huffingon concurs: "Half of our traffic at HuffPost comes from links and searches. The question for newspapers is how they monetize those links."

Döpfner said that given the choice between free beer or paid beer, the thirsty would drink the free beer if they're both good quality. He's brewing better beer and wants to charge, but Huffington is giving away his brew. But he misses one key point: Huffington Post's distribution system doesn't need his content; there are plenty of other beer-makers happy to stock her shelves. Döpfner believes his content is unique, while Huffington sees it as little more than commoditized data.

Huffington isn't shy about the tsunami of change that's coming to media as result of her linked economy. After all, putting your head in the sand won't do anything other than leave you with an ear that is full of sand. According to Huffington, "The answer of the mainstream media can't be to huff and puff to try to blow down news aggregators. If they got what they wished for, it would be a one-way ticket to oblivion because they would lose huge chunks of traffic driven to their sites."

For creators—people who've spent their careers making content and trying to sort out an economic model—curation can seem like an end-run around hard work. And so the conflict ultimately comes down to this: Is curation about saving money? Or about adding value? The answer, it appears, is yes to both.

THE PUBLISHERS' CONUNDRUM

"A lot of it is economic, doing more with less, and it has crossed every media industry," explains Allen Weiner, research VP of the Gartner Group. "If you think about the tools you want to give an editor to make him or her more complete, you want to give them curation tools." It could be "something they add to their own content. As more old media companies attempt to do more with less, publishing tools that allow this efficiency without demeaning the product quality . . . [are] going to be very important."

Weiner's comments are made all the more prophetic when you know that the Gartner Group's founder and namesake—now many years out of the firm—has taken to preaching the power and importance of curation.

When I went to visit Gideon Gartner in his stunning penthouse apartment looking over both New York's Central Park and Columbus Circle, one thing was immediately clear: Gartner's research provided advice on future trends and helped to shape wisdom for corporate buyers of Gartner Group data. Both Gartner and his clients have profited from his keen insight. Back in 1979 when he began, the stock and trade of his analysis was in observing trends and data, and making detailed reports and projections about the future. Today, with the Gartner Group sold and his fortune safely in the bank, his antennae are no less keenly attuned and his hunger for new trends and market-moving theories no less driven. Just a few minutes into the conversation, Gartner is struck by the frustration of trying to get the right information from the Web in a timely manner. "It's impossible," he says, imploring his visitor to see the future with him. "Impossible to imagine data and information in the future *without* curation." He waves his hand toward file cabinets full of clippings that are his self-made curation solution. But, he says with frustration, it doesn't work. Too much data. Too fast. Too unfiltered. At 75 years old, Gartner doesn't need to be worked up about anything other than the majestic view out his window. But curation is what has him fired up.

AN OLD MEDIA STAR BUILDS A CURATION EMPIRE

If Gartner and Huffington are an unlikely pair of allies, consider Dan Abrams, a mainstream media anchor turned aggregation entrepreneur. Dan is the son of the nation's preeminent first amendment attorney Floyd Abrams. He grew up with the free-speech rights of journalists as nightly dinner-table conversation.

Abrams graduated from Columbia University School of Law in 1992 and quickly found himself the chief legal correspondent for NBC. He covered landmark trials such as *Bush v. Gore*, and as NBC grew its news presence with the cable channel MSNBC, Abrams became a staple of the channel. By 2001 he had his own hour-long show on MSNBC, *The Abrams Report*, and made regular appearances on *NBC Nightly News* and the *Today* show. Abrams was, by any measure, a network TV star.

So, as Huffington Post was expanding beyond politics, Abrams decided that there was a niche for a Web site wholly devoted to coverage of the media. Rather than raise money from private investors or venture capitalists, Abrams reached into his pocket, founded Mediaite.com, and set out to gather, editorialize, and curate content around the world of media. One of Mediaite's early observers, Slate, remarked, "The site name sounds vaguely medicinal, like something you'd give to a toddler suffering diarrhea." But Abrams wasn't discouraged. He brought on Colby Hall, another mainstream media content creator with the mission to create an edgy aggregation site.

"In our wildest fantasy we hoped that in one year we would have a million customers a month," Abrams says. "Judging by other Web sites, we thought that the media news niche was realistically maybe 500,000. And one year later we're on pace to have 1.4 million unique visitors."

That growth has had given Mediaite the ability to attract the interest of Madison Avenue, and advertising on the site is taking off.

"I don't believe curation and aggregation are going to go away," Hall says. "The forms by which people curate and aggregate are certain to evolve, whether it be video, text, audio, or any other interactive entertainment experience. But what will never change is the role of developing the sharp, focused, and unique point of view. And as long as that exists, the curation aggregation will always be second to telling an interesting, unique story that that people will want to read and discuss."

Having a boss who is both a media aggregation mogul and an attorney isn't always easy, as Hall explained to me while sitting in a room full of 20-something Web editors who were crawling and linking, and writing snarky headlines. It often comes down to how much is too much for links and in particular video excerpts.

"Dan will come in and say, 'I think that that's too much.' Then we'll have an earnest and frank and very pleasant debate, which typically circles around context," Hall reports. "He'll say something like, 'Well that part doesn't really make sense unless we have the setup before.' The setup may not necessarily be newsworthy, but it provides the necessary context."

According to Hall, the day-to-day decision making about editorial is squarely in his corner. But there's no doubt that Abrams's keen understanding of the law—and of journalism—has helped Abrams and Hall lead the way in the news-curation space and protect Mediaite as a business.

For Hall, there's little doubt as to what will happen next. "I think when the apparatus is in place, the eyeballs and the advertising revenue is there," he says. "What we will be providing through our point of view is incremental eyeballs. In a perfect world I would love people to recognize that our value is our taste, sensibility, and talent in curating."

But Hall acknowledges that the rules and standards around curation are evolving and hardly settled. "We have constant conversations with CNN, MSNBC, FOX News," he says. "And we do our level best—it's in our best interest to have an amiable relationship and to work hand in hand because we understand that the world is shifting dramatically right now. We're building an audience, but it's in our best interest to avoid an unamiable relationship with the creators of this content."

NEWSER: THE PUGNACIOUS PROVOCATEUR

Hall and Abrams work hard to wear a white hat in the world of curation. But not all the players care about being seen as playing nice. Author and blogger Michael Wolff has made a career out of biting the hand that feeds him. As an early new-media mogul, Wolff's early CD-ROM company Wolff New Media was a victim of the early dot-bomb bust. But rather than dust himself off and try again, Wolff instead penned a book that became a manual on what not to do when starting an Internet company. The book, *Burn Rate*, bought Wolff street cred as an outsider. So he went on to pen a column for *New York Magazine* that routinely savaged folks from the New York media scene, which made him an honored but feared guest at most of the trendy industry parties. When *New York Magazine* went up for sale, Wolff tried to buy it with a few partners; when that didn't work, he was quickly out of a job. His acerbic wit landed him a position at *Vanity Fair*, but as Wolff once confided to me, he wasn't sure anybody read him or the magazine itself. "It's a pretty magazine, good to have on your coffee table," he said. Translation: his cutting, take-down articles in *VF* just didn't get people mad enough to count. He was risking being out of the cool kids' club. A tell-all book about Rupert Murdoch briefly bounced him back in the headlines, even if it did earn him the internal "enemy for life" moniker at Murdock-owned *New York Post*.

So while Huffington and Abrams looked to make aggregation respectable, Wolff launched his Web site with the same gusto for angry e-mails that he'd honed at *New York Magazine*. Dubbed Newser, the HuffPost knockoff sported the bold tagline "Read Less, Know More." He would make reading mainstream media obsolete by creating an über-aggregator, critics be damned.

Says Wolff of the original work he does in synopsizing and reporting from, for example, the *New York Times*: "The articles are too long, and our editor Carline Miller and her team take a 1,200-word *New York Times* article and reduce it to 65 to 110 words, without losing one piece of information. So that's the imperative online. You have to take in much more information than we're accustomed to taking in offline in the same amount of time. I think it's not just the *New York Times*. All the city newspapers are imperiled. Many are in bankruptcy. Many are or will be in bankruptcy in short order. It is really hard to imagine a successful model except cutting and cutting. Even then, I think that gives you another year of breathing room, and then it will eventually catch up with you."

It's worth keeping in mind here that Wolff's career has been built on writing tough, often combative, pieces on large characters within the media landscape. Knowing that, his attacks on the *New York Times* seem particularly savage.

"We're just at a point where it's very clear that a new technology has come along, and it's better," Wolff says. "The *Times* has tried to have a foot in both worlds. I would say at this point, they're doing neither successfully. I think you would be hard-pressed to find reasons for being optimistic about the future growth and development of that business."

Wolff's willingness to gnaw on the hand that feeds him goes so far as to taunt content sites that he links to, causing what may well be the first public battle over curation. Wolff, linking to the site The Wrap, edited by Sharon Waxman, finds himself faced with a request to not link to her work. His answer: "Go pound salt." While folks like Huffington see curation as reciprocal and say that they'll take down links if requested, Wolff sees his work at Newser as adding value and believes that he's well within his rights to excerpt, copy, and refer to posts on sites like The Wrap. Waxman cries foul.

"What we do is really curation, which I consider a much more careful selection of relevant content," Waxman explains. And she is sure there should be rules around curation that everyone lives by: "I certainly feel that all aggregation should involve proper credit and a link. That just seems good manners. And most people on the Internet do that."

Keep in mind here that Waxman isn't suggesting folks ask permission before they link or abstract—the Web is far too diffuse and nichified for that to work. She just wants to be able to say "Take it down."

"Newser has never approached us about using our material," Waxman says. "We have asked that they stop using our material or sign a syndication agreement. At the very least, they should follow their own stated policies. They're not even doing that consistently. They're telling us they'll use our material in any way they like."

In fact, Wolff's reaction to Waxman may be a sign of things to come. He's been cavalier to the point of daring any organization to sue Newser if it thinks he's doing anything wrong. Let the games begin!

So far Wolff seems to be right: there's been no lawsuit filed. Aggregation and curation live in the murky world of fair use, which has wide and broad safety for journalists. Here it seems, curation has a lot of latitude.

As Huffington sees it, the standards and practices of the media world are coming to her. "What's happening now is a convergence," she says. "When we launched the Huffington Post, we were worlds apart. There was the legacy media that were very, very skeptical about blogging or the future of online media. And there were the start-ups like the Huffington Post. Now the *New York*

Times is doing a lot online. And we are hiring more and more reporters. So I think we're moving toward a hybrid model."

Today HuffPost has 6,000 bloggers with passwords who can post at will. Much as the *New York Times* or the *Washington Post* has room for op-ed writers who are published but not paid, HuffPost provides infrastructure in that editors choose which posts to feature. Clearly, Huffington sees the glass half full: media companies that engage and evolve will survive. Wolff, on the other hand, sees the old guard dying off, unable to adjust to the new mindsets, cost structures, and editorial skill sets required to thrive. HuffPost's growth in readers, contributors, and revenue suggests that Huffington's link economy is winning the day, as more mainstream publishers move to the hybrid model that she innovated.

USER-CONTRIBUTED CONTENT

The other secret sauce of HuffPost is user contributions, in the form of comments. The site invested early and significantly in moderated comments, far from the wild west of many early blogs. It has a full-time staff of 20 just to review comments—with the power to approve them and to remove objectionable ones—and the human curation of these contributions makes for frothy and mostly civil dialogue. In June 2010 alone, the site received a staggering 3.1 million comments. "Self-expression is the new entertainment," Huffington explains. "People don't want to just consume information, they want to participate. Recognizing that impulse is the future of journalism."

Huffington is in many ways the poster girl for curation. She curates her bloggers, choosing voices that are distinctive and unique. She curates her reporters, putting a small number of journalists to work, but making a lot of impact with them. She curates the linked stories, choosing provocative pictures and testing headlines that work and drive traffic. And she curates comments, editing for civility and discourse. Overall, the efforts that Huffington Post extend to source, mix, and manage multisource content into a coherent collection of well-edited verticals is appreciated. Clearly it's something readers like.

From news to community to e-commerce and even to brands, curation is a new meme being touted by top media makers, entrepreneurs, and thinkers. Former content *makers* are becoming content *curators* to grow their businesses extremely quickly and to build fortresses of content that will make them leaders in the new digital world order.

In the end, the future of content is a battle of computers versus humans. Huffington's vote is for humans, they are what's worth paying attention to. "There's no way you can supersede human editing," she says. "We have a clear attitude. The whole thing is about editors following their passions."

Huffington, Wolff, Abrams: these are smart, serious folks. And while they've all got their own take on how news will evolve, they all agree on one thing: curation will be key to the future of journalism. Writers, editors, publishers, and readers all ignore it at their own peril.

4

CONSUMER CONVERSATIONS AND CURATION

t's easy to look at curation as a powerful change agent for editorial enterprises such as magazines and newspapers, and that is certainly the case. But it's far more powerful than that. Brands, which for so long were able to tell their story with the massive voice of one-way advertising, now find that consumer conversations about their products are happening in big, public, uncontrolled ways. They need to embrace curated content and at the same time remain careful that they don't unleash the wrath of customers who may end up both empowered and unhappy.

In a world where brands no longer control their own story, a single unhappy customer can create a firestorm that galvanizes consumers into an army of complaints. This kind of negative engagement is a new thing for marketers, a kind of mass media turned upside down.

But there's power in passion, and passion doesn't have to be a positive thing. There's the phenomenon of consumers who are mad as hell and willing to blog about it. There are lessons in those stories too.

DELL HELL

Jeff Jarvis is a journalist who's found that he is no longer able to use his former power as a columnist for *Time* magazine to get CEOs to return phone calls. But way back in 2005, in the days when the Web was still emerging as a consumer power platform, Jarvis was sold what he describes as a lemon computer from Dell. What Jarvis knew was that you could put any corporate name into Google and add the word *sucks* and you'd quickly get a listing of all the complaints or issues that faced a brand or corporation. So Jarvis penned a blog post titled "Dell lies. Dell sucks." Serious stuff. The result should be required reading for any brand marketer trying to understand the power of the aggregated and curated consumer.

Here's Jarvis's post in its entirety.

June 21, 2005

Dell lies. Dell sucks

I just got a new Dell laptop and paid a fortune for the four-year, in-home service.

The machine is a lemon and the service is a lie.

I'm having all kinds of trouble with the hardware: over-heats, network doesn't work, maxes out on CPU usage. It's a lemon.

But what really irks me is that they say if they sent some-one to my home—which I paid for—he wouldn't have the parts, so I might as well just send the machine in and lose it for 7–10 days—plus the time going through this crap. So I have this new machine and paid for them to FUCKING FIX IT IN MY HOUSE and they don't and I lose it for two weeks.

DELL SUCKS. DELL LIES. Put that in your Google and smoke it, Dell.

What's interesting, of course, is that this isn't journalism or lit-erature or even a well-constructed argument. It's a rant. Short and sweet. Anyone could have written it. But his blog, BuzzMachine, had some traffic and some power, and so the post had impact.

What it did was get noticed by other unhappy Dell customers. It got picked up by reporters who wanted to know what Dell was doing about the problem. And it tested Dell's ability to understand the changing power and voice of consumers on the Web.

Between June 2005 and August 2005 Jarvis posted a number of follow-ups.

Dell hell: Seller beware

July 1, 2005

The age of caveat emptor is over.

Now the time has come when it's the seller who must be-ware. Caveat venditor.

A company can no longer get away with consistently of-fering shoddy products or service or ignoring customers' concerns and needs.

I tested Dell and they failed. Their customer service mech-anism did not recognize a machine and service pattern and customer that were a mess. They didn't try to fix it.

I could have stayed on the phone for hours and gone up a tier at a time playing the customer having a psycho fit (ask anyone who has heard me go after customer service people who don't serve: I play the role well).

Instead, I chose to write about the saga here. I chose to elicit the sympathy and conspiracy of fellow pissed-off Dell customers. I chose to see whether Dell is listening.

They are not.

Their media people were not reading the media that mat-ters—media written by their very own customers. This page is already No. 5 in Google under Dell sucks. I gave them time. They failed.

So then I emailed their media department and told them to read this blog. I gave them a cheat sheet. They didn't. They failed.

Jarvis goes on at length about his attempts to fix his computer and teach Dell the power—and the danger—of the emerging con-sumer as public Web publishers. Eventually he even suggests that Dell literally hire him to come in and teach the company about blogs and the customer voice. What is important about the Dell Hell moment is that it was early, and unlike really angry customers who want to destroy a brand, Jarvis was truly looking to present what academics (and Oprah Winfrey) call a teachable moment. His warning shot that negative consumer sentiment can be gathered and amplified was ignored, it appears. Jarvis bought an Apple computer. And brand marketers continued to ignore consumers at their peril.

In less than two years, Jarvis's handful of personal blog posts had been taken as a rallying cry and grown from a single consumer rant into a full-fledged platform of consumer unhappiness and anger. Connected consumers had demands. This was a shocking revelation, to say the least.

COMCAST MUST DIE

On Thursday, October 4, 2007, the next shot in the growing shift from passive consumers to engaged consumers was fired. Bob Garfield, a well-known media reporter on NPR and a magazine columnist registered the blog name ComcastMustDie.com. The first post read:

> Actually, I have no deathwish for Comcast or any other gigantic, blundering, greedy, arrogant corporate monstrosity, What I do have is the earnest desire for such companies to change their ways. This site offers an opportunity—for you to vent your grievances (civilly, please) and for Comcast to pay close attention . . .
>
> Congratulations. You are no longer just an angry, mistreated customer. Nor, I hope, are you just part of an e-mob. But you are a revolutionary, wresting control from the oligarchs, and claiming it for the consumer. Your power is enormous. Use it wisely.

In a separate post, he explained why consumers are rising up and what he felt Comcast had wrought.

> Partly because you [Comcast] have behaved so arrogantly till now, and partly because the world has changed around you, you now must answer to a Greater Power.
>
> Us.

Garfield had three main demands of Comcast:

1. You will recruit a standing panel of customers to consult, brainstorm, complain and advise every step of the way . . .

2. You will host a website soliciting customer feedback of every kind . . .

3. Most importantly of all, you must recognize that none of this should be a PR move you have made through gritted teeth in extremis . . .

Garfield's rant exploded as unhappy Comcast customers found the site. It seems that while *sucks* is great search engine bait, *Comcast must die* was also very effective. You can search YouTube and easily come across the promotional video that helped build the buzz for ComcastMustDie.

Garfield estimates that 10,000 visitors and 1,000 comments were registered in the first two months of the site's operation. Garfield explained the change this way: "The world has changed, in that its customers are no longer passive victims of the corporate agenda. We are stakeholders. We not only wish to have a say in how things are done, we not only demand a say in how things are done, we have the power to get our way."

On September 7, 2009, Garfield declared victory, posting on the ComcastMustDie site, "ComcastMustDie.com has now evolved. This is partly because we have declared victory against Comcast, a vast, greedy, blundering, tone-deaf corporate colossus which, in less than two short years, has finally seen the light. But tone deaf no more. To quote the abolitionist Wendell Phillips, 'Eternal vigilance is the price of liberty.' Thank you, and congratulations."

Comcast had first ignored, then attacked, and finally engaged in listening to its customers—even unhappy ones. It put a social media team in place and began monitoring the Web and Twitter for service issues.

LISTENOMICS

The irony of the Comcast tale is that Garfield had spent a large part of his career as the columnist for *Ad Age* who reviewed advertising. He was an advertising *expert*. When I sat down with him in 2009 at the social media epicenter of the world—the South By Southwest Interactive conference (SXSW), in Austin, Texas—Bob hadn't lost his faith in the power of the emerging consumer revolution. Far from it.

"There's stained underwear right up and down Madison Avenue," he told me with a rueful grin. He went on to explain just what's wrong with conventional advertising: "Brands have hitherto been able to dictate their entire stories. They've been able to craft it from beginning to end and put it on your television machine. What they're scared about is that they don't have control of their own stories. And they have no control over what is being said about them." Example: Comcast.

No longer can advertisers control, which leaves them little they can do except aggregate and organize. "They want more than curation. But curation's the best they can hope for," Garfield said.

But fear not, he's got a prescription: listenomics.

According to Garfield, listenomics is what happens when marketers, media, and all institutions that hitherto had dictated from the top down—from the U.S. government to Proctor and Gamble—learn the art and science of shutting up and paying attention to what is being said among their various constituencies. After all, those people on the receiving end are the real stakeholders, and now with their online voice, they're collaborators, participants, and members of a community.

Garfield's listenomics appears to have made more sense to Comcast than Jarvis's Dell Hell did to Dell: while Jarvis reports little change in how Dell engages unhappy consumers, Comcast quickly recognized Garfield's aggregation of anger as a powerful and potentially disruptive force. Comcast made changes based on the consumer organizing of Garfield and his MustDie site. Comcast now has employed a real-time customer service Twitter team under the handle @ComcastCares, which was launched by Comcast customer service manager Frank Eliason.

ONE-TO-ONE CUSTOMER SERVICE

Frank Eliason joined the customer care team at Comcast just a month before the ComcastMustDie site went live. I reached out to Frank, trying to understand how much of Comcast's reaction was a result of the Garfield corporate death threat. Was his job simply crisis management? Eliason says no. As he describes it, he was hired to manage customer service when a powerful blogger (Michael Arrington from TechCrunch) tweeted about a tech issues. ComcastMustDie was just another source of unhappy customers for him and his team to engage proactively.

Eliason explained that one of the most successful things he did at Comcast was to create an in-house newsletter to highlight customer issues for management. The voices of unhappy customers seemed to resonate more with management than Excel spreadsheets did. Eliason is a Comcast loyalist, even though he has since left the company. But he's the first to admit companies ignored customer service for far too long. He told me, "Customer service leaders for all companies have been weak for a long time. Over the past 20 years the service industry has been focused on shortening call times, becoming more efficient, et cetera. They never shared the impact upward. Now it is the customers' turn."

But what about the lurking concern that one-on-one customer service doesn't scale? That Twitter can't be made efficient? While it's fair to point out that bloggers like Michael Arrington may catch the eye of a corporation, you get the sense that Comcast really *does* start to learn about its customers by listening.

Eliason explains, "Using that argument, phones would never scale and neither would e-mail or chat. Social media scales in a much easier fashion than any of these other communications channels. First of all you have a means to broadcast messages out which can reach millions very quickly. Beyond that, you can easily queue up a tweet, assign it to somebody, and have them respond. Most companies do not have to get that sophisticated today, but the tools exist now."

Eliason's core message is "Keep it personal."

PEPSI FINDS SOCIAL MEDIA REFRESHING

In the few years between Jarvis's and Garfield's first salvos and now, a handful of brand marketers have figured out that consumers are going to have their impressions and product issues aggregated and curated, for better or for worse. While lots of brands have jumped on the Twitter bandwagon, tweeting about various brand activities, Pepsi has been perhaps the most active leader in inviting customers to participate in the brand and help shape both the products and the marketing.

Pepsi has taken seriously the change that Garfield is shouting from the rooftops. Bonin Bough, the director of digital and social media at PepsiCo explains, "If you listen to what people have to say and give voice to their perspectives, you can inspire people and empower their ideas." This may not seem like the words of a soda and snack food company, but Pepsi is putting its brand and its money where its mouth is by pledging more than 20 million dollars to a crowd-sourced grant program, with public voting determining who gets the grants. Each month, Pepsi will award up to $1.3 million to the winning ideas across six categories: Health, Arts and Culture, Food and Shelter, The Planet, Neighborhoods, and Education. It's a listening campaign that is meant to send a message to a new generation of connected consumers. Frank Cooper, Pepsi's chief consumer engagement officer, explains the company's social media initiatives this way: "We want to become a catalyst in the culture rather than act like a big brand announcing something." Cooper does admit that this "goes against all the systems put in place that were designed for mass marketing." Pepsi's Mountain Dew brand is reaching out to its core customers, inviting them to participate in planning the brand, and even the events for the DEWmocracy, as they call it .

DEWmocracy is engaging fans by having them campaign and vote to determine which of three new Dew flavors would be rolled out by PepsiCo; the destinations, activities, and venues for the DEWmocracy: The Flavor Campaign tour were also largely determined by fans. They were told that they would be calling the shots on which cities were visited and on the specifics of the activities that would take place in their areas, including helping to choose venues. Fans also were invited to rally friends to participate in creating content, including posting photos and video content online, and to vote for their favorite flavor. You can't dispute the math: Pepsi distributed 60,000 samples of flavors, met 100,000 consumers, and generated more than 1.5 million total impressions.

Cooper explains that the DEWmocracy campaign "started with a simple question" that asks "What if we gave the power to our consumers to lead product innovation?" Pepsi did just that. The result was the creation of Mountain Dew Voltage. Cooper calls Voltage "one of the most successful product launches in PepsiCo beverage history."

But Pepsi didn't just focus on consumer content. The Pepsi Refresh Project "looked to add value to a community or a real-life social network," Cooper says. "We knew that our consumers wanted to play a central role in developing and promoting ideas that they believed would move the world forward."

Cooper sees a massive change in media and the potential of a brand. "The Pepsi Refresh Project has expanded our consumers' perception of what the Pepsi brand can be: Pepsi remains a fun brand that leads culture," he says. "However, it also has social responsibility, a sense of purpose, built into its behavior."

Bough explains, "We collaborated with organizations that are dedicated to making a positive difference in the world to design and implement the Pepsi Refresh Project. Each month we accept 1,000 submissions, and all the ideas that comply with our official guidelines are then posted online for public vote. We're doing our part to bring transparency to the process by featuring a monthly leader-board showing which ideas are getting the most votes."

Pepsi is working to make the process open, with both an advisory board of nonprofit leaders and a team of ambassadors ranging from start-up founders to activists to neighborhood advocates.

Bough says it's about aligning the brand with positive social change: "Our theory of social change is that new ideas are born from optimism, a curious mind, and a creative spirit. We can make a difference by equipping people with the means to bring their ideas to life. And we believe social media and digital engagement can fuel, extend, and inform these efforts."

And it appears that some of the companies that first were exposed to the power of consumer voice online and didn't pay attention are drinking the Kool-Aid. Jarvis says Dell got the message, and years later Dell CEO Michael Dell told Jarvis, "No company can exist anymore on the idea that it's just three people." The era of the all-powerful CEO, CMO, and COO has been replaced by a crowd-sourced aggregation of suggestions, feedback, and complaints.

TAKING CONTROL OF THE BRAND

So what are the action items that this change from mass media to consumer-controlled conversations can offer? Well, there is a shift in how the buyers engage companies: no longer do they need to accept the "take it or leave it" attitude of many companies they do business with. Instead, they can say, "No, I think I'll change it and take control of the brand." The tools to amplify consumer concerns are only growing stronger, and there's a business opportunity in becoming a consumer evangelist for an aggregated community of customers who haven't had a voice before. So imagine you harness the power of formerly powerless consumers and pick a topic, brand, or endeavor to aggregate and curate.

Take cruise ships, for example. Which tours are great? Which ones are a rip-off? Is there one unhappy customer on board or a ship full of disappointed travelers? Only human curation can filter the noise and alert travelers. That's a site that can be quickly authentic and have a positive impact on travelers looking for curated data.

Now, imagine curated human data brought down to your neighborhood. Unvarnished human experience about local repair companies, lawn services, plumbers, and chimney sweeps. Who's gathering and curating the raves and rants in your hometown? Someone surely is doing so. The important thing to know here is that curating brands or public figures doesn't require you to get permission. In fact, a truly authentic site or community may not want to be authorized by the brand so that it can be both a passionate fan community and a transparent truth teller if the brand or the public figure does something that doesn't sit well with the users.

While crowd-sourced data most certainly gives people power and shifts the ability for consumers to speak with what Andrew Blau calls "a massive megaphone," crowd content without curation tends to drive the thoughtful voices to the edges and amplifies the loudest and most outrageous voices. It doesn't encourage civility, accuracy, or thoughtful dialogue. But when you add a human editorial layer, a curatorial perspective that organizes gathered content and community participation, you get real results. Bob Garfield wanted Comcast to hear unhappy customers, and he curated a community with such passion and visibility that Comcast had to listen.

As curated consumer conversations take hold, there will not be a brand, a service, or a company that won't have an independently curated ad-hoc watchdog group that will emerge to give feedback and filter customer reaction to goods and services. There's no doubt that there will be plenty of the XYZ Company Sucks sites, but that's not likely to be where the majority of customers will end up. Instead, reasonable and balanced communities curated to be about honest feedback and customer solutions will emerge as a new and powerful force in consumer-and-brand interaction.

Curation is the future of consumer conversations.

5

CONTENT ENTREPRENEURS: THE NEW CURATION CLASS

have a confession to make. I'm a content crook. A newspaper thief.

I'm pretty sure that Rupert Murdoch would say I stole intellectual property.

I started at a very young age. I was nine years old, and as a young man, I always seemed to want to be an entrepreneur. I remember clear as day the first time I noticed all that valuable content just sitting there. Waiting to be repurposed. It was pure gold, and no one seemed to see it but me.

Up and down my suburban street, piles and piles of almost brand new newspapers set out by the curb to be picked up by the town's recycling truck.

I knew they were valuable, because my mom and dad read them eagerly each day. On Sundays they were part of a family tradition that included bagels and lox. Newspapers were valuable; after all, people paid for them. And these slightly used copies were simply stacked in neat, crisp piles, there for the taking.

Now, I understood that they weren't worth the full price. They were a day old. But they couldn't be worth nothing. Surely someone would be willing to buy day-old newspapers at a discount!

And so, I set off, with a red wagon and a dream to be the neighborhood's best-known proprietor of day-old newspapers. "Extra, extra, read all about it. Get your day-old news here!" I chirped as I went from door to door. I figured not everyone had the paper delivered; maybe they'd rather get a bargain on day-old news.

Selling newspapers isn't easy. And selling newspapers that are slightly used turned out to be a bit of a challenge. But sure enough, I sold a few. And found that there was some value left between those pages. My work as a used-newspaper sales boy didn't last for long, as I found more lucrative employment selling polished stones (Hot Rocks) and then performing as a magician at local birthday parties and Elks clubs.

But I was reminded of my used-news experiment the other day. The debate over free versus paid news distribution continues to create a dividing line between conventional printed news distribution and today's digital Web delivery.

A few questions I found myself pondering: Was I stealing news when I resold the newspapers left by the sidewalk? Did the owner of that newspaper have the right to give me the right to resell it?

Back then, the paper was Long Island's *Newsday*. Today, it's owned by the cable giant Cablevision.

But if *Newsday* had known that I was selling day-old news, would it have cared? Certainly it would have said that I was profiting from the paper's hard work, and it's true. I think I made almost five dollars a week. Back then, a newspaper was a product. A physical thing. But today the news is digital. It moves at lightning speed and is delivered to my desktop computer almost instantly.

What if I were, as a nine-year-old boy, to embark on my used-news project on the Web today? It would, I suspect, look a lot like the Huffington Post: news, gathered and organized and resold. Did I add value back when I was dragging my red wagon around? Hard to say. I did bring my used news to my neighbor's door, so that was helpful. But if I were doing that today, likely I'd do more. I'd select news from various sources, and I'd filter, sort, and curate my take on the links of the day. And in the end, sure, I'd charge something for my repurposed news service.

Mr. Murdoch would call that theft. Mark Cuban, another outspoken critic of aggregation, would call me a vampire. And I think I'd argue today, as I did back on Ward Street, that gathering up things that are set out on the sidewalk for all to see and delivering them to a new customer is me participating in the democracy that is free speech, news gathering, and redistribution.

I know nine-year-olds see the world in a pretty simplistic way, but the more I think about my used-news endeavor, the more I think both my neighbors and I got it right. I was trying to add value by providing a slightly dated, lower-cost news service. And my neighbors, other than a few generous souls, determined that the cost of fresh news wasn't cost prohibitive. If they wanted the paper, they'd get the delivery boy to toss it on their lawn the day it was printed.

If anything, my business was way ahead of its time.

CURATING CONTENT: THE EARLY SEARCH FOR NEW MODELS

Today, we need more context and organization around information. So if that means more nine-year-olds are cutting and pasting the *New York Post* or the *Wall Street Journal*, well, to me that's something that can only lead to good things for readers and media barons alike.

So, it might seem odd to you that I went looking for a bit of a history lesson on the roots of content curation at News Corporation, the media empire built and run by newspaper baron Rupert Murdoch. But, entering 1211 Avenue of the Americas and walking through the newsroom of the *Wall Street Journal*, I couldn't help but feel as if I was in exactly the right place.

There, in the corner office, was one of my favorite media executives, Jon Miller. He is the CEO of Digital Media at News Corp., overseeing the digital properties including the once-mighty MySpace. But I wasn't there to talk about the current squabbles between Murdoch and Google, or the free versus paid questions that have been brought to the fore as Murdoch has erected pay walls and called into question the whole concept of free content on the Web. Miller's trajectory in media parallels the growth of the curation ecosystem, so I wanted to get his point of view on where all this was going. But first, how did he end up as the guy to try and fix both AOL and then MySpace?

Miller graduated from Harvard in 1980 and took a job as a researcher with the FCC on the anticipated impact of cable TV. As he surveyed people regarding whether they'd pay for cable if it came to their town, it became clear that cable was going to spread fast. Miller explains, "I thought, 'If it comes to this city, people are going to go for it if there's more programming. I should go figure out how to make some programming.'"

It's worth noting that the early days of cable programming were, in Miller's words, aggregated broadcast signals. There was no such thing as *original* cable programming. Miller saw the future and jumped on it.

Miller found a job in production, at first making commercials. Then he shifted to programming, with a gig at WGBH in Boston. And then in 1987, using his God-given talents as a really tall guy— six-foot-four to be exact—Miller worked his way into a great gig at the NBA as vice president of programming at NBA Entertainment. Back then few games were on TV, and many weren't even recorded. Miller changed that—and the league mandated that all games had to be recorded. It was a very rudimentary setup, just three cameras recording to three-quarter-inch U-matic videocassettes.

This would be the foundation of what is now the highly valuable NBA archives. But back then it was all they could manage to get even basic metadata captured as the raw footage was screened. "The tapes would come in and literally we had kids out of college who got paid next to nothing to label every play, descriptors like pass left or right," Miller recalls. "This became the archives of the league and when you wanted to put out a TV show or supply your network operators or whatever, you just go back and find stuff for commercials. But before that, it wasn't even recorded."

No longer did the NBA have just live games, now it had media assets. Early footage of Michael Jordan, Larry Bird, Hakeem Olajuwon, Magic Johnson, Isiah Thomas, Charles Barkley, Patrick Ewing, and Dennis Rodman were being recorded as cable sports channels were arriving on the scene.

Says Miller, "It became a basis on which you can think of yourselves as a media company. Now you have a library and now you have archives. It is like a film library but in this case it is footage of games and players. And the most important question was, what was more valuable: aggregated content, as in games, or disaggregated content, as in plays. Plays became highlight reels and stories. Games were their own self-contained things. If you think in media terms, it is like the trailers and highlights versus the film. Which was the most valuable part and how could they work together?"

The answer turned out to be both. The powerful thing about monetizing a film library is that you can use the same material in multiple markets and they don't cannibalize each other. The annual value of the NBA's television rights was pegged at $400 million a year through 2008, and that doesn't include the future clip royalties.

Then, after a stint at Viacom and Barry Diller's Studios USA, Miller took on the unenviable task of fixing AOL. It was 2005, and the problems were written large on the front door.

AOL was an ISP (a dial-up Internet service provider) in a world that was going broadband. You didn't have to wake up in the morning and have cognitive dissonance around that. AOL knew it couldn't sell its dial-up business and that it was going to go to zero—and fast. And, since parent company TimeWarner owned cable, the broadband business was already taken. Miller needed to imagine a new AOL with a new focus: "There aren't a huge number of options, but I thought, 'How do you figure out how to make a lot of content that people want to consume, since you're essentially an aggregator of lots of other peoples' content and services?'"

Searching for a content creation model that was Web-driven, low cost, and could create a large volume of material, Miller turned to AOL executive Jim Bankoff, who introduced him to entrepreneur Jason Calacanis. Weblogs Inc., Calacanis's company, was creating a network of low-cost blogs, what Miller called "magazines on the Web."

The first one to catch his eye was the tech blog Engadget. Says Miller, "Engadget was a Web magazine on an incredibly distributed low-cost model. Peter Rojas was the creative force; Brian Alvey, technologist; and Jason Calacanis created the model and the ability to stamp these things out with a lead curator. Then we could plug that in to what I call 'the machine,' our sales operation." With Weblogs, Miller was able to find a model, both technical and editorial, to curate low-cost content. Back in 2004 the deal wasn't seen as a slam dunk with the execs at TimeWarner HQ. Miller now reveals that he had a hard time selling it to his bosses.

Miller says his bosses challenged his basic assumptions, asking him why content was going to matter. But harkening back to his early precable TV days, he saw the same phenomenon affecting the Web. More bandwidth, in this case broadband, meant that users would consume more content if it was offered. "It was almost that simple," Miller says. "Without broadband it was a lousy experience so it was limited in what the Web could do. With broadband it wasn't as limited. It's not much deeper than that."

Miller decided the solution was to have AOL buy Weblogs Inc., the editorial properties that Calacanis had spun up, and the technology that his partner Brian Alvey had developed. Check in hand, Miller went shopping.

"I met him [Calacanis] at Four Seasons hotel in L.A., I said I should come by your office. You know, it was part of my process. I bought a lot of Internet companies and had seen a lot of companies. Generally, you go in and you kick the tires, you get vibe, you see what's going in the office, you meet the people."

But that was his first surprise: Calacanis explained there was no office.

Miller says, "I go, 'Wait a minute—no office?' "'Yeah,' and he explained to me, he pulled up on his computer, he could see all the bloggers and what they were doing that day, that hour, that minute, who was posting, how many responses they got, and it was all there on the screen. And that was like the lightbulb going off. I was like oh my God! It was from all over the country."

If Jon Miller was able to look out across the country and see that the emergence of cable TV was going to create a huge demand for content, what does the coming deluge of content create a need for? Miller sees a massive content creation explosion in the next five years, as phones, tablets, and social networks all encourage and even automate the creation of data, feeds, choices, Diggs, and Facebook "Likes." Content creation explodes, and the need for filters goes from being helpful to being essential.

"MTV fine-cut the network business in a sense, cable took what was a network, i.e., NBC, which would have kid's programming, women's programming, adult programming, late-night comedy all during the course of a 24 hours—news, et cetera, all in a 24-hour day— and it basically took each of those and made networks out of each of those. And they were big, broad ideas: CNN equals news, MTV equals youth and music, Nickelodeon equals kids. They were still big swatches. And what that told you is what was coming, which is as more bandwidth appeared both on television and something called the Internet, the cuts got finer. So now news is not just one idea, it's a zillion ideas. And you could see the process was just going to keep going into finer and finer cuts."

ALL ABOUT ABOUT.COM

Elsewhere, another media executive with a similar entrepreneurial bent had been seeing the same trends as well. Let me save you the suspense and tell you that Scott Kurnit ended up inventing the forefather of curated Web content, now called About.com. But how he discovered and developed About is worth a bit of background.

You know that show on cable TV called *Mad Men* about the drinking, smoking, snappy dressers of Madison Avenue in the 1960s? Well, Kurnit grew up in a family with a "Mad Man" as a head of the household. His father was an advertising executive during the golden age of Madison Avenue. Kurnit was born in 1954 and experienced firsthand the transformative power of TV. "Wow, this changes everything," he remembers thinking. But while most folks thought of TV as a one-way medium, the young Kurnit quickly moved from local TV programming to being the head of programming at a Columbus, Ohio, experiment called Qube. This was the first test of interactive TV from a company known then as Warner Cable, long before Time and Warner merged, and longer still before TimeWarner merged with AOL. Which is to say a *very* long time ago.

We'll just have to wonder what the world would have been like if Qube had been given more than the relatively tiny $40 million in R&D money that it was given. It might well have been what we now think of as the Internet, but on two-way TV. But, as Kurnit tells it, Warner owned a game company called Atari. Atari made a billion dollars one year and lost a billion in the next. The year that there was a billion-dollar loss, Warner Cable pulled the plug on the interactive experiment known as Qube.

But the young Kurnit didn't forget what he'd learned at Qube: People wanted choice, but they wanted curated choice. They wanted a clear set of options and both data and information in a digestible but interactive form. Kurnit was hooked on narrowcast interactive media. Only there was really no such thing in 1983. Kurnit left in search of the holy grail: interactive TV. After a seven-year stint at the pay cable network Showtime, Kurnit arrived somewhat skeptically at Prodigy, an early Internet service provider. "Prodigy, I think, recruited me, but it is a terrible, terrible, terrible service. I'm fascinated by interactivity because of my early Qube roots. I never unpacked my boxes."

In 1994, instead of staying with Prodigy, Kurnit, at age 38, saw the future and understood that the Web was going to be a game changer; he decided to dive in headfirst.

The experience he had at Prodigy told him that the Internet was going to be transformative. To him, the analogy was the impact that individual cobblers and metalworkers had in the 1600s and 1700s—that same spirit was being exhibited by young entrepreneurs working out of their garages to build software companies and Web sites.

Kurnit took the metaphor of pickaxes and shovels to heart, and formed the Mining Company, a human-curated Web service that was dramatically different than companies like Yahoo that were building huge Web catalogues by hand. For Kurnit, even back then, it was all about curation.

The Prodigy model was expensive centralized curation. Kurnit wanted to adopt a decentralized workforce so he could take advantage of people working out of their own homes. His plan was to get better talent at a lower price and cover a wide range of topics. While he launched the Mining Company, his main competitor, Look Smart, had 100 employees.

"I didn't like their model—it was inefficient. I liked our model for any number of reasons," Kurnit says. "If we had a hundred people and they cover all the topics, then I wouldn't get that, so I wouldn't get the passion, I wouldn't get the knowledge, the expertise, the quality of the service wouldn't be good, the way you talked about it to consumers wouldn't be as powerful.

"The plan from the beginning was to harness the passion of the guides; we'd call them curators today. The original plan was to cover everything. We set out to dig up the gems, polish them, and present them. That was the metaphor of the Mining Company. Our original taxonomy was 4,000 guides. So we had a guide for white wine, red wine, Spanish wine." But as the company started to hire, even with low-cost remote guides, Kurnit knew he had to focus the vision. "I remember the meeting when it became clear the economic model isn't going to work; we have too many people, for too little revenue, to motivate the people to both stand out and be stars and to make enough money," he says. "We need to have wine. So we went from 4,000 to 750 guides. Had we stayed at 4,000, we would have probably broken the business."

As the Web was taking shape and the early leaders were forming, Kurnit invented what would become About.com.

The model was pure from the beginning: the idea was that with a distributed workforce, an individual could handle only so much work. But Kurnit didn't want personal politics or friction. So core to the model was one passionate guide per topic.

For example, the person at the helm of a site about anesthesiology was—you guessed it—an anesthesiologist. As a result, About .com guides had both passion and sector expertise. Kurnit and his team curated the guide selection—curating the curators, if you will—but then he let them manage their own content verticals. If you think it sounds like blogging before the advent of blog tools, you'd be half right.

"The beauty of guides is that they were passionate about their areas, so we went and found them, we recruited them, we trained them . . . These people were and are independent contractors, which is a very careful line you can't cross," Kurnit says. This relationship works well for both parties, according to Kurnit. His company doesn't need to have the guides on the payroll as full-time employees, and the guides feel ownership over the content they create and are compensated very well. "The market was built to ebb and flow with the Internet," Kurnit says thankfully, so when the dotcom industry went bust in 2000 and 2001, he reduced his staff from 600 to 100 and let about 300 of his 750 guides go. "People made less, but they could afford it because we weren't, for most of them, everything—like I'm still an anesthesiologist, so I can do this," Kurnit says. "So we were able to ride through the Internet winter of 2001 and then grow back to where we have about 800 guides."

Kurnit describes a small but critical shift in the company's focus that happened when it changed from the Mining Company to About.com. "On day one we didn't have any articles because we just started, so the job was if the U.S. government had weights and measures data, we'd use it," he says. "Then you'd see your traffic increase, and then you think we should probably produce our own weights and measures page and then we would get the traffic on our pages." In other words, the company realized that people valued information on things that were already relevant to them, rather than a general survey of the Internet, and adjusted its content to reflect that fact.

One ironclad rule Kurnit implemented was that each and every About.com page has the same look, feel, and color scheme. Kurnit says, "So it's only if you're the CEO and you're a product guy that you can say *no no no no no*. Red, three shades of gray, no purple, no blue, no green. Red and three shades of gray, cuz when these get found in search engines you need to know what it's about, even if it's subconscious. Number two: consistent tools across the sites, so that when we roll out something new, we can roll it out across the system. So there's consistent user experience—so when a guy comes home and he's used the composite material site, he can show his wife the pregnancy site and he instantly knows how to use it."

THE FUTURE OF CONTENT

For guys like Miller and Kurnit, who started their careers in the television business but were already looking past it to what would come next, curation isn't a buzzword or a trend; it's the future of content and nothing less.

Says Miller, "I believe that there has to be curation, which by the way can run the gamut from traditional media like magazines and newspapers to bloggers like Michael Arrington. The social systems will do it with friends and your social graph. And the volume of content will continue to explode, which will create more content than advertising can support. So advertisers will need curation. In the end specialists win, the greater the specialization, the greater the win."

And Kurnit's take is clearly in the same spirit: "There's no question the crowd is more efficient than directed individuals. So it's interesting that About.com holds core to its 750 guides one guide per topic area, and I think for About, it continues to do very well, that's a very good idea. If someone were starting About.com today, you wouldn't do that model. The temptation to let everyone do it and let the best guy bubble to the top would just be so overwhelming that you'd have to do it. Interestingly, it wouldn't be as good, and we've seen that."

"Specialists win," Miller says. "They understand their user base. They understand how to connect with them. Typically they're starting smaller; they have a different cost structure. And they tend to nail it, and that's the key to success."

So Jon Miller—who turned basketball games into media assets, who shifted AOL from dial-up to a platform for nichified digital content verticals, and who's now handing content gathering and organizing tools to MySpace users—says the future is all about gathering and sorting content with new tools, and consumer engagement. As he says, "Aggregation allows people to go after categories. The costs of starting them [targeted sites] come way down. Before, they had to do more than that because you would have to go through the kind of venture pathing—you know, of multiple rounds of financing that could amount to $20 or $30 million of capital or more—before you could be successful. Now, you shouldn't need anywhere near that. So that you can have lifestyle businesses that, you know, for hundreds of thousands of dollars that, you know, could do very well for you."

For observers who aren't running the day-to-day meat grinders of big media companies like News Corp., trends that began back at the early days of Qube and the NBA are now very much the future of a curated experience. Says Jeff Jarvis, a well-respected thinker on Web content and author of *What Would Google Do*: "My über-view here is that the future is entrepreneurial more than institutional and that we're going to see a whole bunch of entrepreneurial efforts. And those are going to reach critical mass, and those are going to be brought together in networks."

Rohit Bhargava, the author of *Manifesto for the Content Curator*, is able to document a job that Miller had remarkably foretold. Bhargava says that in the near future—content on the Web will double every 72 hours. This staggering data explosion will overwhelm the current search algorithms and the search methodologies that have heretofore made the Web discoverable. No longer will people be satisfied with text links and obliquely recommended results. Hungry content consumers will want valid, contextual content on topics we can hardly imagine. This will create demand for the new role of content curator. This will be an act of love at first, but as curators provide value, they will attract attention, and attention is worth money. Already we see the building blocks of this trend as Facebook traffic exceeds the traffic on Google. Facebook users are community curators already, finding links, images, and media that they share with their friends and family. In time, these citizen-editors will become central to helping clarify and validate content on the Web. This change is significant, because it will both help create the new human-filtered Web and open the door to a whole new class of curators and curatorial efforts that will be full-fledged paying jobs.

6

TOOLS AND TECHNIQUES

So, you're ready to dive in and be a curator. Not just as a hobby but as part of building a brand, a business, and even—*gasp*—earning a living.

Well, to do that you'll need to think about your business in three parts: publishing, advertising, and syndication. It's those three legs of the stool that will get you going, bring you revenue, and over time build a business. While the individual tools may change over time, the basic thesis is tried and true. How can you create a content site that is engaging and easily updated and current? Then, how can you find revenue once visitors start to come to the site? And finally, how can you reach out and tell the story of your site so that more folks will show up at your front door and tell their friends? Sounds simple? The good news is almost everything you need to build a curation-centric business is free. So you can get started right now.

But let's first walk through the three building blocks and give you some guideposts so you can explore the tools without too much pain.

PUBLISHING

There are a number of great ways to get your site launched right now. To some extent, you need to think about what you want your site to feel like. Spend time looking at sites you like and think about their business models. Think about what it costs their creators to make the sites and how they earn a living from them. For example, the *New York Times* has a large number of paid reporters, editors, and photographers. Their model is based on being part of a large institution with its own revenue stream. So unless you have very deep pockets, that may not be the way to go.

Oh, and since this is a book about curation, think more about sites that gather and organize links and excerpts. Take a look at Techmeme or Business Insider or Gawker. These are sites that use a mix of gathered and curated links, a bit of original reporting, and a lot of effort to package and promote their brand so Web readers will come to expect that they've got the right curated collection.

Here are three examples of different kinds of sites:

1. *Big media: USA Today*

2. *Curated/created mix: New York Magazine*'s pop culture Web site, Vulture

3. *Pure curation:* Media reDEFined, Techmeme

For the purposes of our journey into the world of tools, I'm going to assume that you've decided to be a curated/created mixer. You've decided that you want to be the go-to source for all folks looking to be serious fans of barbecue. I don't mean a weekend grill jockey or the Fourth of July burgers-and-hotdogs hero—I mean a serious barbeque aficionado. Competitive cooking. Serious eats. Okay, so put on your apron and fire up the grill. It's time to get cooking—and curating.

Step 1: Pick a Platform

The good news is that you've got plenty of choices; the bad news is that you've got plenty of choices. If you're going to be a blogger, then there are some great, solid solutions in WordPress, Movable Type, and Blogger.com. Each has its own fans and critics. Of the three, Blogger probably has the least flexibility. Both WordPress and Movable Type have big communities of free plug-ins and templates, and freelance designers who can help you grow and enhance your site as your editorial needs and skills grow. TypePad.com is the hosted version of Movable Type, so you don't need to pay to set up your own server. This isn't a technical book, so I'm not going to get into the ins and outs of each platform; a quick Google search like "Word-Press versus Movable Type" will get you into the conversation.

Another popular option is one of the growing microblog platforms like Tumblr. Tumblr.com is less for long-form writers and more for folks who want to have lots of quick hits: links, photos, posts, and so on. It's called microblogging. It's super easy to get started, but as with all things, the simpler it is, the less likely you'll be able to enhance it to be a full-fledged Web site down the road. So pick with care if you want to use one of these software platforms.

Here's a tip. If you really like the look, feel, and functionality of a site, you can always use the "view source" menu item in your

Web browser and then search for a few platforms like "WordPress" within the HTML code; you should be able to tell which platform the site is built on. Oftentimes, that's the best way to find the platform that mirrors your needs.

Step 2: Find Your Sources

Here's the big *aha* moment for content curators. Okay, to begin with, for the purposes of this chapter we're going to be building a championship barbecue site. The first stop is Wikipedia. Sure, I know the obvious keywords, such as *barbecue*, but I want to get a quick overview of the other words that could help attract appropriate content. The goal is to find the places on the Web that can be sources for content to populate the site.

Quickly we learn that there are a number of keywords that need to be part of your aggregation search times. Both *barbecue* and *barbeque* are proper spellings. In Canada it's called broiling. Keywords matter—a lot—because part of the service you're going to provide to your visitors is sorting out the difference between broiling and grilling. Visitors are folks that have forgone the hunt and peck of search, and are looking for contextual, curated content.

Keyword Search Terms

Next, let's build a collection of search terms that can help you find both content and later advertisements for your site. These terms will be your keywords—the text that is linked to content on the Web—and that will be linked to or excerpted on your site.

Here are some tools for keyword searches:

- *SEMRush* is a research tool for both search engine optimization (SEO) and pay per click (PPC) keyword data. It has a free version, and a paid version with more results.

- *Compete.com* is a research tool for keywords and sites. If you want to know which other sites are in the barbecue space, Compete can tell you for free. And not only can you find sites, but you can see which keywords they're using and how they've measured up over time.

- *Rank Tracker* is a tool you can use to see where your keywords rank (http://www.link-assistant.com/rank-tracker/).

- *Wordtracker.com* may be the best-known of the tools in this space. Wordtracker claims that more than three million people use it to manage their keyword research and link building campaigns. That's a big number, but it's probably right.

But for simplicity's sake, let's just start with the Google keyword tool (https://adwords.google.com/select/KeywordToolExternal). When you search any topic (such as barbecue) with it, Google quickly responds with 100 top keywords, ranked by search demand. This is powerful, free data that you can use. If you're thinking about what kind of curation site you want to build and you're deciding between barbecue and fried chicken, this search tool will tell you that barbecue is a more popular search. More Web visitors are going to be looking for your site if you build a barbecue editorial site.

Here's just a sample of what Google returned for barbecue:

barbecue recipe, gas barbecue, barbecue restaurants, barbecue restaurant, barbecue rib ,barbecue catering, barbecue cooking, barbecue grilling, barbecue marinade, barbecue beef, barbecue grills, charcoal barbecue, barbecue menu, Weber barbecue, outdoor barbecue, barbecue tools, barbecue tips, barbecue accessories, barbecue smokers, barbecue ribs, barbecue rub, grilling, stainless steel barbecue, grill, pork barbecue, gas barbecue grill, barbecue set, buy barbecue, barbecue review, barbecue tool, barbecue reviews, barbecue smoker, barbecue chicken recipe, barbecue caterers, barbecue pork, barbecue take out, barbecue grille, bar b que, barbecue steak, barbecue rotisserie, barbecue meat, barbecue marinades, barbeque recipes, bbq recipe, grilled barbecue, barbecue pork tenderloin, cheap barbecue, barbecue salmon, barbecue corn, barbecue dining

Yes, there's a lot of data, but don't freak out. It turns out that barbecue has lots of niches and keywords and categories. This is very good news; it's why the Web needs *you*. There's so much complexity in all the content categories that someone is going to sort through those keywords and find a way to turn that data into coherent content. The key to that collection of search terms is that you can see in that cloud of data both the topics that you'll want to include in your site and the potential ads that you'll be able to attract. Now, not every search term is an editorial category. For example, Weber is the name of a brand of barbecue grills. You may not want to have an editorial category called "Weber," but you sure might want to have that company's ads on your site or reach out to Weber's ad agency to see whether it wants to sponsor it. Poking around in the tag cloud, a collection of related words ranked by popularity, the phrase *barbecue kings* jumps out, so let's name your site that.

And using just the keywords *BBQ, barbecue,* and *barbeque,* here's what an automatic aggregation solution delivers: a collection of video content, organized by keywords, by topic, and by search terms—but most important, with videos chosen and featured by *you*. So the computer does the heavy lifting, but you get to share your favorite barbecue videos.

Link: http://barbecuekings.magnify.net/

RSS Feeds

Next, let's go in search of some RSS feeds. RSS stands for really simple syndication. It's a way for you to find content within a category and have it pushed *to* you rather than having to search for it. You can get RSS feeds by putting keywords into an RSS reader. There are a number of choices, but for this exercise we'll use a Google reader.

Link: http://www.google.com/reader

Link: http://fastflip.googlelabs.com

Link: http://www.google.com/alerts

In the three links above, you'll find tools that allow you to discover and organize RSS feeds (Reader), read them in pages like a magazine (Fast Flip), and automate Google so that you get an e-mail alert to notify you about new content that features your chosen keyword (Alerts). Each of these items is a valuable curation tool.

You may find that you want to set up a pretty sophisticated set of saved searches on Google News, links in your RSS reader, and even searches for images on Flickr and other content sharing sites. That way, you've got a regular stream of new content that you can scan and add to your curated content offering. This is how you're helping your readers: doing the heavy lifting of finding and sorting so they don't have to.

There are lots of other ways to find content bubbling up in your area of interest. There are a number of crowd-sourced social-recommendation sites that invite voting and surface popular content. Both Digg and Reddit offer searches that will turn up all kinds of links.

Digg, for example, turned up a story about a video game company sending out a barbecue tool kit to make amends with unhappy customers. It may be a weird story, but it's still a kinda cool item for your barbecue site.

Twitter

And finally, perhaps the most timely and fast-moving source for information that you can add to the aggregation equation is Twitter. This microblogging tool, as you probably know, is the global phenomenon that has friends, business associates, and brands tweeting about topics large and small. But consider Twitter your über-aggregator: it's the world helping you find links and stories that you can add to your site. So use one of the Twitter alert searches like TweetAlarm.com to have your keywords reported to you.

Video

So now you've got blogs, news, tweets, and images all on their way to you with a bit of work each day reading headlines and putting summaries and links on your site. But what about video? There's TiVo and other DVRs. You could record and then use various tools to rip those files and put them up. But then, most likely, you'd be in copyright violation. Fair use, as it's called, is notoriously hard to define unless you're a legitimate news outlet. Your barbecue site would be hard-pressed to defend scraping barbecue videos off cable TV and reposting them.

The good news is you don't have to. There's YouTube, of course, but culling from that is going to be a very manual process. And there are a number of automatic video aggregators that will discover, embed, and manage video for you. Magnify.net, the company I founded in 2006, is blazing a new trail in the area of real-time video curation. There's no doubt that if video is core to what you're looking to feature—either making it, aggregating it, or both—then Magnify is a cool, free solution.

The power of multimedia aggregation, as opposed to text, is that choosing which videos should be categorized requires human esthetic judgment. A video curator needs to see themes and context, and order videos within that frame.

Simply put, gathering and sorting the right collection of text, video, images, and such isn't the work of a computer; there's a human required. After you've set up all your sources and a routine to find content every day, and use some trusted sources from an RSS feed to automatically fill out some content on your site, you've created a pretty detailed workflow that takes time—and hopefully a better understanding of the ins and outs of barbeque than I have. After all, if you don't have passion and knowledge in the vertical you're going to aggregate and curate, you're likely to be facing competition from someone who really loves grilling. That person is going to have the secret sauce to create a content mix that is truly special. So pick your curation topics with your head and your heart.

Step 3: Create Your Content

Now that you've found sources to aggregate content, you're halfway there. Because, as we've explored throughout this book, curation is about creating a mix—a unique blend of discovered, contributed, and created content that makes your collection uniquely yours.

The good news is that you can create some content, and you don't have to create that much. If you're comfortable pointing a Flip cam at yourself, then sure, why don't you record some videos? But don't think you need to try to impersonate the local news anchor. In fact, don't do that. Do the opposite. Be you—don't change, because your audience is coming to you for authenticity, not fake glossy production values. If you're the guy or gal who wears overalls to the barbecue, well then, strap 'em on and let's get grillin'! And if you're not comfortable turning the camera on yourself, you can still take a little video camera or still camera on location and use that video or stills to illustrate a story about the local barbecue competition.

Content creation for your site can come from three sources: content you make (both text and video), content your visitors make for you, and content you contract others to make for your site. Content you make is going to set the tone. Do you want your barbecue site to be folksy, or technical, or for a serious foodie with a charcoal fetish? The tone of your site is going to come from you; the content that comes from your visitors is going to depend on how you invite them to participate. If you want neat tips and tricks, you'll need to provide some examples. If you're looking for folks to become regular contributors to your site, you'll need to invite a handful of experts to blog for you; you might want to reach out to 5 to 10 experts to see whether a few are looking for a home. Now that you've learned the actual work it takes to find a platform, find aggregated content, build a site, and start to get traffic, you can see why lots of folks would rather just post occasionally for you rather than deal with the whole effort of building their own sites.

Shawn Collins, who runs the ad industry's biggest networking conference, Affiliate Summit, says finding the right tone in content is key. "People will follow your affiliate site as they get to know you," he says. "Odds are that you're not a journalist, so don't pretend. Just be yourself and write in your voice. It can sometimes get tough to think of things to write on your blog, so make it a practice to have an editorial calendar where you will schedule topics to write about in the future. I frequently send myself e-mail with ideas for future blog posts."

One thought you may want to consider is running a contest. Sites that value and even reward visitors for participating in competitions that make content for them have often garnered significant traffic. The handmade-crafts site Etsy asked visitors to make a video for it that it would then make into a TV commercial. The contest resulted in more than 250 entries of 30-second spots, and the winners were awarded cash prizes. The winning videos were eye-popping. The Web site of *Bicycling* magazine invited its visitors to make a video about why they deserved to win a $5,000 bike. Of the hundreds of pieces of content submitted, the winner was heartfelt, funny, and authentic.

Link: Etsy http://etsy.magnify.net/

Link: Bicycling http://video.bicycling.com/contests/win_any_bike_contest_2010/

The other emerging source of content for site curation is the trend toward content farms, which are large organizations that hire staffs of writers to continually churn out written content for the Web. Yahoo owns a content farm called Associated Content; another is Demand Media. The idea is to offer freelancers relatively low pay to create content but to let them choose the topics that interest them so that they can work on their own preferred subjects and on their own schedules.

The need to access human skills on demand was what convinced the folks at Amazon to create a service known as Mechanical Turk. The name Mechanical Turk is based on a "robot" that dates back to 1769, when a nobleman astonished Europe by building a mechanical chess-playing automaton that was able to beat human opponents. The Turk toured Europe and overcame brilliant challengers such as Benjamin Franklin and Napoleon Bonaparte. The secret behind the Mechanical Turk was a human chess master cleverly concealed inside the cabinet. It was a trick.

Today Amazon's Mechanical Turk is founded on the premise that there are still many things that human beings can do that computers can't. For example, Amazon needed to scrub through its entire collection of JPEG CD covers to make sure that the image of the Rolling Stones was the correct image on the site's item page. There was simply no way for a computer to be able to know whether the image was correct; it needed human intelligence.

Mechanical Turkers perform such acts as identifying objects in a photo or video, removing duplicate data, transcribing audio recordings, and researching data details. Traditionally, such tasks as these have been accomplished by hiring temp workers. But now with Mechanical Turk you can post a job, set a price, and pay only for work that is good quality. So, for example, you could request an article written about every keyword for barbecue that we found on Google and then ask the worker to include 500 words on the topic and a photo from Flickr that is available with a Creative Commons license that allows for commercial use. You could pay $20 an article, and for $200 you'd have 10 pieces of barbecue content that were yours.

That's a quick overview of content, but the created, contributed, and curated content is a powerful mix of sources that allow you to build a site without having a building full of writers or a fat bag of cash.

ADVERTISING

So your site is ready to go. You've got great source content aggregated. You've sorted them into relevant verticals, and you've added your own high-quality created content. You've even invited visitors to submit their own photos and video. You're ready to generate some revenue. There are four kinds of revenue you can expect from your BarbecueKings Web site: the three main models that comprise affiliate marketing (CPA, CPC, and CPS) and sponsorships.

1. *Cost per click (CPC).* These are the text ads that you see on all but the largest sites on the Web. There are two major sources of these ads: Google Ad Sense and Yahoo Display Ads. Both these services are known as search engine advertising, and, simply put, they allow you to sign up and put a bit of custom code on your page. Then, the ad network will read the metadata from your page and discern from all the keywords which ads are best suited for your visitor. In your case, ads for barbecue sauce, grills, grilling utensils, as well as other goods and services would be served up on your page. Keep in mind that the advertiser is only charged if a visitor clicks on the ad, and you're paid only per click, so the fresher and more engaging the content is on your page, the more likely you'll have visitors who found you by searching for "barbecue" and are therefore expressing *intent.* They aren't just casual visitors; with any luck, your site is attracting serious barbecue talent. And they'll see your text ads as useful, even valuable, since they need more sauces, grills, and high-tech accoutrements.

2. *Cost per acquisition. (CPA) and affiliate marketing.* This is a different kind of advertising. It gives you the opportunity to put actual offers on your site, actual ads for actual products and services where you get a piece of the action when your visitor clicks through and buys something. But sales aren't the only actions you can get paid for. If you offer registrations or subscriptions on your site, a CPA-based program can be very lucrative.

3. *Cost per sale (CPS).* This represents cost per sale, and the model compensates an affiliate on a revenue-share for referring a sale.

4. *Sponsorship.* CPA, CPC, and CPS solutions are self-serve and require little effort other than setting up an account and putting some code on your page. But without significant traffic, the dollars can be very few. If, however, you've made a good-looking site that is properly targeted, has fresh and updated content from reliable sources, and is growing both traffic and potentially registered users, then you might do well to consider selling sponsorship. This takes some effort, because you need to figure out who are the right sponsors for your site and either e-mail them or call them and propose that they take ads and maybe invest in a larger presence on your site. Sales are never easy, but if your barbecue site was in search of a sponsor, you might start by looking at a site like bbq-sauces.com.

Shawn Collins, who we introduced earlier, is a cofounder of the largest conference for action-oriented advertising. He's a blogger, Web site builder, magazine publisher, and all-around advertising entrepreneur. He's built many ad-supported sites, and he shares this advice: "When I start up a new project, I know that affiliate sites should be viewed as long-term projects and not quick hits." Collins says it all comes down to finding content you care about that can work: "When starting a new affiliate site, don't try to leverage the latest trends. Instead, focus on topics that interest you. Try brainstorming two or three areas where you are passionate and create your site based on the one that you think you'd like to focus on the longest."

Lots of folks spend huge effort on getting the right name and spend a ton of money buying a domain name from a previous owner or a domain squatter, someone holding on to the name so he or she can cash in. Collins says don't waste the money. "You can get a .com domain for around $10 per year," he notes. "Don't obsess about your domain name, I'd say you shouldn't spend more than 20 minutes picking it out. Just get something relevant to your topic, and the shorter the better. Start with a registration of one year, because you can extend it at any time, but if you decide the domain stinks, there is no use being locked into multiple years."

And finally, Collins says building an audience is going to take time. "This is the cheapest and most important part of a new affiliate site: patience," he says. "Resist the temptation to put up ads right away. Instead, focus on building content to give people a reason to visit your site. When the time comes to incorporate ads, focus on relevant ads and not those that pay the best. I'd suggest posting 10 or more times or longer to a blog before any ads are up there. When you do put up ads, go beyond the banner. The vast majority of my affiliate commissions come from text links."

When you are looking to find the right ad networks here are a few good ones to explore: buy.at, Commission Junction, Google Affiliate Network, LinkShare, and ShareASale. There are a variety of ways that affiliates can find affiliate programs. Try searching Google for ones that make sense for your affiliate sites. For instance, if I have a site about Halloween costumes, I'd search for "Halloween costume affiliate program" to find merchants to promote.

SYNDICATION

We're now at the fun part, getting the word out. Syndication is about getting your name, your links, and your buzz out and all over the Web. It means simply putting little bits of bait on other sites where folks may be looking for your kind of content, so you can lure them to you. This is where you need a bit of old-fashioned showmanship.

Think about your barbecue site and make a list of the all places that might want your content. Consider competitors, magazines, search engines, and video sites—it's all up for grabs. And if you really want to build a following, come up with a gimmick. A weekly count down of the "hottest" barbecue news. A regional (virtual) tour of the U.S.A., one barbecue destination at a time. Whatever it is, make sure it's fun, easy to understand, and something you'll enjoy doing for a while. On the Web, consistency is crucial. Your fans (yes, you'll have them) expect you to be out there and publishing every day or week—whatever schedules you set up. But it's critical that you not "go dark." The reason that readers are counting on your aggregation and curation skills is because they don't want to have to start looking for their own content one piece at a time. If you aren't consistent, they'll leave you.

And syndication isn't just limited to Web sites. Popular social networking sites like Facebook are a great way to gather groups of people and tell your story to a fast-growing network of friends and followers.

Here are some syndication tools you'll already be familiar with and that you'll need to consider if you're going to build buzz around your brand:

- Facebook

- Twitter

- YouTube

- Others include Foursquare, LinkedIn, and Gowalla

These technologies are the big hits of the moment, yet there's a risk in seeing what's happening on the Web through the filter of any single site or solution set. Curation is more of an idea than a technology. That said, certain companies and tools are leading the way. We're living in a time in which technologies seem to appear of nowhere, get so big it seems like they'll be around forever, and then fade into the background. Remember MySpace? It was the big bad social network before Facebook. Now it's a shadow of its former self. As of this writing, social media is centralized around Facebook and Twitter. They are the two big players in the content curation space, but there's change in the air as the Web evolves from static spaces to ever-changing real-time environments that require fast, fresh content rather than old, stale links.

There's no doubt that being an aggregator or curator is real work. As Collins says, "You shouldn't expect much money for months. It takes time to build up a site and an audience. It can be a grind, but stick with it." That's right: there's definitely gold in them thar hills. You just need to know how to look for it. With curation replacing search as consumers' primary source of information, learning the tools and techniques now, and testing new solutions early, could give you the leg up as more and more advertising revenue flows into curated and contextual content spaces.

7

MAGAZINES AND CURATION

At the top of the editorial food chain, the glossy magazines of Condé Nast represent the pinnacle of taste and distinction. These magazines create styles and set the agenda in their areas of focus. Historically, the company has mostly printed only those things that it has had commissioned exclusively for its pages. But even at Condé Nast, curation is increasingly becoming a useful tool. Magazine publishers are rethinking their roles and embracing their missions as finders, organizers, and publishers with content creation as only part of the mix.

Ava Seave wrote the book on media moguls (*The Curse of the Mogul: What's Wrong with the World's Leading Media Companies*), and she says the future of the magazine can be found in curation. She's a consultant to the Reader's Digest Association, whose publications are increasingly counting on consumer contributions and curation.

"Actually, aggregation is something that has been around for a long time," Seave tells me. "And it was kind of buried in strategy concepts as distribution. The book is called *The Curse of the Mogul*. In the book we make clear that there are three kinds of media experiences if you are a company. One is content creation, which is as an author, or in some cases—if you are the Bloomberg Company, for example—the content in that is stock prices or bond prices. And then there is this thing called aggregation, and that means that you collect all of the information, package it up, and actually distribute it to somebody else, so you're the middleman. And traditionally, that would be something like the big music labels, for example. When they would find artists (artists would create the music), they would package them, they would market them, then they would get them to the final distribution channel, the retail side. So, it always existed, and it was always the most profitable part of the business. So, when you do aggregation and packaging, that's really where you can put your stamp on something and keep customers close."

Seave says that media companies have always been curators to some extent, but the challenge has been to keep the quality up and the costs low. Back when publishing was highly profitable, content creation was more cost effective. But that's no longer the case. Seave says video creates new challenges and opportunities for print publishers.

"The text business is where I come from and where I live. I think that video is really the future of the Internet. YouTube is already the world's second-largest search engine. That means that people who are younger than me think of things in video, and it is really, really important for all media companies to be in video at this point."

For Seave, the difference between robotic aggregation of content and human curation comes down to trust. Readers trust human editors, not algorithms. They reward trust with attention, engagement, and loyalty. "Trust is a really highfalutin way of thinking about it," she says. "What it really is, consumers say, 'Oh, I like what you do, I like the voice, I'm used to this.' In the parlance of strategy, this becomes customer captivity, because customers make small decisions—I'm talking about readers or users— every day or twice a week, or a few times a week, to go to the Web site. And they look at it and say, 'Oh, this appeals to me, I understand what this is and I am going to watch it,' or 'I am going to read this recipe,' or 'I know that chicken recipes from this site that say they have no cream still taste okay.'"

So it all comes down to judgment and this idea of curation once again. But from the standpoint of customers, it is very subtle. They don't know that they are basically becoming more addicted to the viewing taste. An easy example: let's say you read a particular reviewer of movies, and you always agree with that reviewer; you will eventually always go to that reviewer because you know your taste and his taste are the same.

NEW YORK MAGAZINE

While the magazine business is engaging curation in different ways, there may be no more successful curation mix than *New York Magazine*'s NYmag.com. Michael Silberman is the general manager of NY Media, the parent company that runs both NYmag and its growing collection of blogs and Web sites, including Vulture and MenuPages, and Grub Street.

"Magazines as a concept, an interesting package of content that appeals to a particular audience, I've always thought translates really, really well to the digital world," Silberman says. His career, like that of many people now innovating in media curation, began in television. He spent 10 years at CBS News and then made the jump to digital as one of the key members of the launch team at MSNBC.com. Then he moved to magazines, at the niche lifestyle publisher Rodale, and ultimately arrived at NY Media.

New York Magazine has long been known as having a listing section that is essential for New Yorkers. But interestingly, it has always been curated. "I think that the curation point is a good one, which is it's not just every single restaurant in New York," Silberman notes, "it's the restaurants that we think are the ones worth having in the database."

On Silberman's arrival, a new focus on growing both the scope and the depth of the content destination made it clear that NYmag .com was going to be in the curation business. "There's only so much news that you can gather yourselves when you have a small operation," he says, "and so inevitably that meant that we were going to be doing a mix of original reporting and aggregation. There has always been an element of curation in the editor's job."

The dramatic growth in the past two years has been in video curation, where NYmag.com has extended its editorial worldview with video into entertainment, fashion, the arts, and politics.

"We were creating a certain amount of video ourselves, but we were also finding all kinds of video on the Internet that we thought was interesting and worthwhile to point out to our readers, and so we were doing our job as editors, which is not just finding the stories that we were telling exclusively or had a particular point of view on," Silberman recalls. "We were also finding stuff that we thought would be interesting to our audience that somebody else might have done, and either writing up a paragraph and linking to it if it was another story that existed someplace else on the Web, or if it was a video, taking that video and embedding it in a blog post with some sort of a lead-in and saying, 'Hey, this is why we think this is interesting. Check it out yourself.'"

The amount of video on NYmag.com that is created in-house is, of course, very small when compared with the video on the Web. And its editors were often pointing its visitors to video that was interesting or topical. So after some consideration, it made far more sense to bring the "discovered" video onto the pages and mix created and collected video into an integrated collection.

The results have been measurable. Web site sales have doubled since 2007, and digital sales are up 70 percent over 2009 and are now 35 percent of the revenue. The MenuPages app has been downloaded from Apple over 160,000 times. And, most important, 75 percent of visitors to its various sites come from beyond the New York market. NYmag.com is hardly a "New York only" site; it has a global brand and it's growing. And perhaps most tellingly, this year the National Magazine Awards bestowed by the American Society of Magazine Editors awarded *New York Magazine* with the coveted "best digital" publication for two years' running.

MAGAZINES EMBRACING CURATION

Magazines, it seems, have the ability to encourage innovation and provoke notable and outspoken critics. Jeff Jarvis was the former television critic for *TV Guide* and *People* magazine, creator of *Entertainment Weekly*, and Sunday editor and associate publisher of the *New York Daily News*. Jarvis bailed out of mainstream media almost 10 years ago and now he's a founder and investor in Daylife, a media aggregation and curation platform that's selling its services to sites that he used to work for. "Death of the Curator. Long live the Curator," Jarvis writes on his blog Buzzmachine.com: "For a long time now, I've been pushing hard the idea of journalist as curator. It appears that curators are looking at journalists and worrying about their loss of control, as evidenced by this post about the death of the curator, inspired by journalists (http://newcurator .com/2009/04/the-death-of-the-curator). Except the irony in this comparison is that journalists need to learn better curatorial skills. Yes, in a sense, they've always curated information, collecting it, selecting it, giving it context in their stories. But now they have to do that across a much vaster universe: the Internet."

Jarvis continues: "I hear all the time about the supposed problem of too much information online. Wherever you see a problem, I advise, seek the opportunity in it. There is a need to curate the best of that information (and even the people who gather it). We have many automated means to aggregate news (including Daylife, where I'm a partner). Curation is a step above that, human selection. It's a way to add value."

Across the publishing world, the emergence of new platforms such as the iPad, along with declining advertising revenue and increased costs for paper and production, are forcing venerable publications like *Forbes* magazine, founded in 1917, to embrace a new way to make a publication.

Forbes magazine's new chief product officer, Lewis Dvorkin, has said he is "re-architecting" the publishing model. "The goal is to tear down the walls between content creators, audience and marketers," he told DailyFinance. "How do you get those three voices talking to each other so that everyone knows who's talking? To me, if you can do that with transparency and legitimacy, that's the future of the free press."

Dvorkin is a lifelong journalist who spent the last big chunk of his career at AOL before deciding to go the entrepreneurial route with a blog network called True/Slant. But before you go searching for it, it's gone—purchased along with its management team by *Forbes*, which gave Dvorkin the top job to rethink the Web site and the digital publishing model.

"On one side is low cost, low quality," Dvorkin explained. "On the other side is high cost, high quality, and they're so calcified they can't change. What you need is high quality, efficient. You need to be a scalable content-creation force."

But before you think that everyone is a fan of magazines embracing curation, there are those who would say that magazines are destroying their core vale proposition by engaging curation.

Dvorkin's innovations have drawn fire from, of all places, the blogosphere, where TechCrunch writer and former magazine journalist Paul Carr flamed the changes to *Forbes*. He wrote that the *Forbes* decision would result in the magazine suffering the "Death of a Thousand Hacks." It seemed worth asking him what he meant by "hacks."

"It has two meanings." Carr told me. "The first, much like the death of a thousand cuts, is that they're chipping away at everything they used to represent by replacing real reporting with SEO-driven bullshit and an army of unpaid amateur hack bloggers. The second meaning is that those thousand hacks are going to kill their brand." Now, to be clear, Carr isn't against what he considers expert curation, just the kind that he says is done indiscriminately.

"Curation is what museums do, what encyclopedias do, what travel guides and experts do," Carr said. "Unfortunately in recent months, it's come to mean something else: lazily cutting and pasting and quoting from other people's hard work and calling it content. Curation without expertise is just scrapbooking." But, of course, expert curation isn't scrapbooking; it's creating contextual content.

Carr isn't one to mince words about what he sees as the scam and as low-value curation. In his mind, it's just free labor. Theft.

"No, not everyone will get paid," he said. "That's just bullshit peddled by sites who want people to curate for free in exchange for the promise of money if you're good enough at driving traffic. It just rewards SEO attention-seeking with false promises. It's evil squared."

Yikes! Evil squared. So, who is evil squared, exactly? Carr takes aim: "Newser.com has always been shit, and I'm disappointed in Michael Wolff for creating it. I used to like him. He used to care about content. Huffington was great, but now they're chasing traffic and SEO and filling up their pages with slideshows and sex tapes and horseshit."

Just for some balance, let's see if one of the magazine world's most respected and well-known innovators can put this whole make-versus-gather debate into some perspective. *Fast Company* was launched in 1995 by founding editors Alan Webber and Bill Taylor. The magazine became the fastest growing, most successful business monthly in history, and has gone on to win two National Magazine Awards. Webber and Taylor were even named *Adweek's* Editor of the Year in 1999. It's safe to say that Alan Webber knows his stuff. Oh yeah, and by the way, Fast Company was the single media source to predict a whole lot of the trends about distributed workforce, crowd sourcing, listening to customers, and of course *Speed*.

"The problem with the Web is that the Web is its own worst enemy," Webber says. "Since there's so much stuff on it, it is all mostly unedited. So rather than calling it editing, which is what it needs, people have invented the fancy word *curation*."

And while the word may be fancy, the need for it seems critical, almost desperate.

"When I was a young person, I did not respect editors. I thought editors were kind of a second order of humanity. It turns out the world needs editors. Writers are great; editors are essential.

They organize information in ways to help make it either exciting to figure out how the person organized it, or it becomes a magazine, which is an entire concept organized around the way the editor sees the world."

And while none of the leaders in magazines are willing to bet on the future of "ink on dead tree"—that's digerati-speak for printing—they're all pretty sure that the future of content curation looks a lot like the practice and worldview of magazines.

Says Webber, "It's not about 'magazines,' it's about 'magazining'—a fun reading experience with great design and all the audio and video links that the Web makes possible. It means differentiation is possible, which means that readers will be attracted to great design, which means that design is going to make the Web a fun place for readers, for writers, for art directors, for advertisers, and for publishers."

And news gathering and reporting, at its base, has always been about curation, or something much like it, reasons Robert Scoble, a tech blogger and reporter. He says he's always been a curator: "When you look at a newsroom, a newsroom is a curation engine. You have groups of editors who go through the Associated Press wire feed. I did this in college. I watched the wire feed, and if something interesting was there I would pull it out, and I might even assign it to another reporter to go follow up, like 'Hey, there's this interesting article about our mayor; why don't you go and follow up about that and write your own story based on what you read on the wire?' That's curation, but part of it was just picking one article out to put in the newspaper."

And in fact, Scoble points out that choosing which coverage to print, like a predigital Re-Tweet, is also part of the system: "I remember when O.J. Simpson was found not guilty, in an hour there were something like 650 different news stories filed, and the *Mercury News* guys had one . . . the local news, the *New York*

Times, and I had to pick one to publish in the paper the next day. So you're watching that flow of news and you're trying to figure it out from all different angles and you're trying to pick the best article, or you might even be writing your own article based on five separate articles and join them all together: that's curation."

Beyond the broad strokes, our view of the future is exciting but blurry, which sounds a bit like the way folks describe an e-ticket ride at Disneyworld.

"Fasten your seat belt, things are about to take off," Webber says with unmistakable glee in his voice. "But still, we're in the infancy of this stuff. I think it's very raw and very crude, and when people find something that works, they'll go look at it, and then everybody goes and does that. But nobody has figured out a killer model of what exactly is exciting about a wonderfully produced movie, magazine, book, record." Webber's point is clear: creating unique, memorable content isn't a formula—it's a happy accident. In the same way, as publishers struggle to figure out curation, there will be a few leaders and lots of followers searching for the future economic model for content.

THE FUTURE OF JOURNALISM

Every formerly powerful editorial structure, it seems, is having a fit over loss of its centralized control: how dare people without history degrees pick what they like, or how dare those without journalism degrees share what they know! The nerve!

If you are wondering why there's so much hand-wringing over the future of journalism in a curated world and less Sturm and Drang over, for example, how Etsy is disintermediating the local arts and crafts fair, there's a simple answer. Journalists who see themselves as victims of technology have the currently dominant media outlets to broadcast kvetching. Clay Shirky is the ideal observer of all this noisy change. An actual adult who's almost preternaturally youthful, he teaches at New York University's interactive telecommunications program (ITP).

"I'm a hybrid," says the writer, thinker, and professor. Sitting in a chaotic classroom at NYU's IPT program, he explains the dichotomy of his world this way: "From nine to five, I can act like I'm 22. After five o'clock I have to go back to being middle-aged."

Shirky spends his days with people who he says don't have to unlearn anything. They didn't learn that newspapers come from newspaper stands and plane tickets come from travel agents and books come from bookstores. For Shirky the future is surely bright if you're beginning your career. But if you're middleware (middle age, middle management), you may be in for a bumpy ride, he says: "The really important fight is between the 60-year-olds— whose bias is 'if I can just hold this together 5 more years, I get to cash out'—and the 30-year-olds who are looking around thinking, 'There's no way this is lasting 35 years And if those guys push off the changes another 5, I'm done for.'"

Shirky describes himself as a news junkie but makes it sound like it's more of a mainstream behavior than an outlier. There's a whole group of overwhelmed news junkies who are mainlining information 24/7 and grumbling about information overload: "The news used to be over. You turn on the news, and then there would be some news and you'd watch it for an hour and then the news was over, and that was it for news. And then there would be more news tomorrow . . . Now there's a 24/7 stream of news you can put right in your vein and never unplug, that you actually have to choose when the news is over—the news doesn't tell you when it's over."

Part of the reason for the overwhelming volume of news is the sheer volume of content makers; Shirky says that today "everyone is a media outlet."

"We can all put things out in the public view now," Shirky says. "And when I talk to a room full of smart 25-year-olds living in a media-saturated environment, one of the hardest things to get across is what it was like to grow up in an environment when, at 6:30 in the evening, your entire range of choices of video was which white man was to read you the news in English. You couldn't not watch the news. You couldn't not watch white men reading it to you. You couldn't hear it in any language other than English. That was it. That was what I grew up with. And in that world, if you were a civilian and you had something to say in public, you couldn't. Period."

So, what to do? News is never-ending, volume is increasing, sources are growing exponentially. Shirky says find filters—or *else*: "People see the Web as chaotic and bookstores as not chaotic. What filters give us is the ability to ignore the 99 percent of the environment we don't care about. It's those filters that broke because they were operating in a world in which the volume of available content was limited by the economics of content production. It takes a lot of money to put out a book or a magazine, or it takes a lot of money to creative a minute of video. It does not take a lot of money to do a blogpost or a podcast."

Certainly, smarter machines will make for better algorithms, solving what Shirky calls today's "filter failure." He says the algorithms will get better. And a lot of things we used to rely on humans to do will be done by machines. So, new filters are emerging, and that means more rather than better technology around search. When people are frustrated with search, they go searching for human curation: "Curation comes up when search stops doing everything people want it to do, when people realize that it isn't just about information seeking, it's also about synchronizing a community," Shirky says.

He gives an example: "Like a book club, that's a place where, again, humans do that better than machines. And I think the job of curation is to synchronize a community so that when they're all talking about the same thing at the same time, they can have a richer conversation than if everybody reads everything they like in a completely unsynchronized or uncoordinated way."

So people are begging to adopt sites that manage to filter the flood and that organize material around their worldview. Finding filters that work, voices that help separate signal from noise, is something that Shirky says will be essential as everybody becomes a content creator and starts to add voices, facts, reviews, opinion, and data into the sharing ecosystem. People "have to confront the fact that they're going to be curating their own lives. Instead of ABC News telling me when the news is over, I'm going to rely on some other source to limit what I'm exposed to."

Every day, Shirky stands in front of the kids who are building the future of media, technology, communication, and computing. He's smart enough to be able to point the way toward the future and agile enough to adjust his thesis as he is able to see around the bend. But he's also honest enough to admit that what he knows about the past obscures his vision of the future. He counts on the students to help him achieve a clearer picture. And he says that we're still at the early stages of creative destruction, watching the forest burn before the new growth emerges: "We still have to see a lot of edifices crash and burn before we see what the new world really looks like."

What's clear on the horizon is that for every print publication that embraces new curated editorial models, many more will struggle and fade away. Shirky's students may not harbor any romantic notions of ink and paper and the historic snapshot of the Paper of Record, but surely their parents do. Don't expect old media to go down without a fight.

8

NAYSAYERS

For all the buzz and momentum around the concept of curation and the emerging consensus of what consumer curation is, not everyone thinks it's such a grand idea.

The critics of the curation economy tend to fall into two categories: those who say it's immoral, and those who say it's illegal. The legal issues are murky at best, and the issues around fair use and copyright are very much the kinds of things that get decided in court. That's why aggregators, bloggers, and publishing platforms all watched with considerable interest when Viacom filed a one *billion* dollar lawsuit against YouTube for copyright infringement. The case was filed in 2007 and moved through the legal system at a snail's pace. And during those three years a lot happened in Internet land. YouTube had just been purchased by Google, so now Viacom was forced to sue Google, which had considerably more cash than YouTube, and a huge interest in defending the practice of user-submitted unfiltered content, and, in particular, a piece of legislation named the Digital Millennium Copyright Act (DMCA).

Wait—don't skip this chapter! You *care* about this, because the DMCA is the law that created a framework for you to build a business around aggregation and curation of links and content. And just so you don't take my word for it, I went to one of the best-known attorneys who defends this kind of stuff, Rick Kurnit, a partner at the New York law firm of Frankfurt Kurnit Klein & Selz, PC.

"In the simplest terms what the Digital Millennium Copyright Act does is provide a safe harbor for people who distribute content so that they don't have to investigate and be clear about the rights, provided you comply with the requirements of the act, which essentially is that you register so people can send a takedown notice to you and you take these things down when properly requested, so you won't be liable for all the initial publishing," Kurnit explains.

Let me decipher: *safe harbor* means you're protected if you inadvertently post content that you don't have the rights to, as long as you respond to a legitimate takedown notice and remove the material when you're properly asked to do so. This is what YouTube was doing when Viacom sued, saying the law wasn't affording it enough protection.

Kurnit says the problem is now in the hands of the copyright owners, who must find places where they don't want their content to be and then request its removal. This is a shockingly pro-Internet law, in fact, and it lands squarely on the side of the aggregator.

As Kurnit explains, "From a legal standpoint, the crucial notion is that the technology moves faster than the legal system. And so what interestingly Congress, the government, seems to have recognized about that, is that very premise, that by the time somebody says you violated my intellectual property rights with what you've done with digital capabilities, the digital capabilities and the communications have moved on."

The law encourages sharing, Web-wide distribution and, by extension, aggregation and curation. The DMCA allows content to spread across the Internet, either because it wants to share, or in pursuit of fame, or for some future economic gain.

So Viacom led the charge, claiming that "YouTube's brazen disregard of the intellectual-property laws fundamentally threatens not just plaintiffs but the economic underpinnings of one of the most important sectors of the United States economy." The suit claimed "immediate intentional copyright infringement," and had it been successful, it would have had a massive chilling effect on the emerging Internet content sharing ecosystem.

The complaint claims 160,000 clips of Viacom content had been posted on YouTube and that these unauthorized clips had been viewed more than 1.5 billion times. "YouTube appropriates the value of creative content on a massive scale for YouTube's benefit without payment or license," Viacom wrote in its complaint.

So what happened? U.S. District Judge Louis L. Stanton of New York disagreed with Viacom's assertion that YouTube had exceeded the protections of the safe harbor protection under the DMCA.

The judge wrote in his ruling: "Indeed, the present case shows that the DMCA notification regime works efficiently: When Viacom over a period of months accumulated some 100,000 videos and then sent one mass takedown notice on Feb. 2, 2007, by the next business day YouTube had removed virtually all of them."

Open Web advocates cheered the decision. "Without this decision, user-generated content would dry up and the Internet would cease to be a participatory medium," said Center for Democracy & Technology lawyer David Sohn.

Kurnit, somewhat gleefully, explains, "Much was made in the YouTube lawsuit of the fact that YouTube argued that Viacom tolerated a fair amount of the use of their material because it was promotion. So if people were doing a blurb from Jon Stewart the next morning on YouTube, that was going to build the audience for Jon Stewart and they weren't going to object. So the argument that had some impact with this judge was, we can't know whether somebody who owns something objects to it—you know we live in a world today where if you look at the music industry, the idea is put your music out there, become famous, don't charge anybody, and make the money off of the tour—so it's fair for someone to say, 'Until I get an objection, I don't know that you object.' The Google decision is very helpful to the [aggregation/curation] business model."

For lawyers the whole area of Internet rights, sharing, linking, and royalties is what's known as *unsettled*, which means it's too early to make law because things are changing too quickly. To make that point, Kurnit reminds me of the world of CD-ROMs. (History lesson: these were CDs with read-only memory that had content on them, like a tiny Web site on a CD. Now they're extinct.)

Kurnit says CD-ROM rights were a blip in legal history. "By the time we could figure out whether CD-ROMs were included in the rights that you gave to a publisher or didn't give to a publisher, nobody was doing CD-ROMs," he points out. "And so the Digital Millennium Copyright Act was rather insightful in recognizing that providing some protections for the digital media, and some safe harbors, and some ways for it to develop was really the only way that the legal system could even begin to cope."

It's not often that legislators and regulators err on the side of not regulating something. But Viacom's claim that YouTube might destroy a vital part of the nation's economy was clearly a cry for the court and Congress to defend the controls and revenue streams of old media.

Kurnit explains it this way: "What Congress was doing with the Digital Millennium Copyright Act is admitting that they can't establish regulations. If Congress tried to sit down and write a copyright law for this medium, it would be out of date before it got enacted, and they essentially recognized that. So one could posit that Google's response was, 'We just want to proliferate content because we're the curator; we don't even care about being paid for content, we give away our content.'"

Google is, after all, free. It gives away links to content that it aggregates via Web crawlers and curates using its page rank algorithm. Free content curation is at the core of Google's business model. And by all accounts, it's doing pretty well. Viacom is now appealing the judge's ruling.

But, in the industry broadly, the claim that aggregation is stealing seems to be fading into history. There are plenty of skirmishes about where the lines should be drawn, with folks like Nick Denton claiming that Huffington is stealing from Gawker, or the Newser versus The Wrap kerfuffle that I wrote about in chapter 3. But overall, the Web's sharing ecosystem seems to be in place for entrepreneurs looking to build niche-content businesses.

But what about the moral question? Is aggregation immoral? On that, the results seem less clear-cut.

THE MORALITY OF AGGREGATION

One of the most vocal critics of the emergence of Web content is Andrew Keen, author, pundit, and publishing curmudgeon.

Keen's book, *The Cult of the Amateur*, set the Internet world on edge. A self-described polemic, it took aim at the sheer volume of "amateur" content on the Web. Keen argued, as I have in these pages, that the sheer volume of unfiltered content left readers unable to find contextual editorial. (Of course, I have found what I think is a better answer than banishing amateurs from the Web.)

Today Keen remains passionate about professionalism and expertise as it relates to both content and curation, saying, "I still have faith in the meritocracy, that most things require training and require hierarchy. And most people can't do most things, so you need to examine systems and professional organizations, and gatekeepers, and all the other infrastructure that is necessary for meritocracy to operate. For people who fly planes or people who are heart surgeons, or journalists, or film directors, in a professionalized, industrial—particularly a postindustrial—economy, there is a need for some sort of collective agreement on what determines expertise."

The irony of Keen's rant is that while we all agree that airline pilots should have training and expertise and licenses, it's hard to see how those same concerns or agreed standards should be held up by journalists or film directors. For example, some would say that Keen shouldn't have an author's license. Others would strongly disagree. But Keen continues taking aim at the adoption of curation and the lack of an agreed-upon professional standard for this new breed of curators: "What you're doing is you're making a mockery of the word," he declares. "I mean, it becomes an entirely meaningless word. Then everyone has always been a curator, because when people sat in pubs and they said, 'Oh, you should go and see that movie' or 'You should go and try that restaurant' or 'You should have that beer,' then they're a curator. And the word is just so meaningless—it becomes absurd."

Is a curator an organizer or a guard at the castle gate? Keen says that you can wrap curation in a democratic fiction, but in the end it's about making choices and as such is exclusionary: "*Curator* is a euphemism for *gatekeeper*, it's a liberal euphemism for the NPR crowd who aren't willing to utter *gatekeeper*. That's what a curator is. A curator doesn't say yes most of the time; a curator says no. A literary agent is a curator. A literary agent gets 1,000 requests a day saying, 'I'm talented; you should represent my work,' and he may take one of those. Maybe in NPR-speak, a curator says yes and a gatekeeper says no, but they're doing the same thing."

In Keen's world, a curator is an obstacle, a barrier, a human shield. Of course, this misses the point that in a world of unlimited bandwidth, the fact that anyone can publish doesn't mean anyone gets heard. "To me the curator is someone who stands between the person who's creating the music, the movie, or the writing and the audience. So it's the editor, it's the literary agent, it's the newspaper publisher, it's the recording engineer, it's the A&R person."

So, trying to get Keen to acknowledge the value of the emerging role of finding and filtering, I set a trap and invited him to curate the barbecue site from chapter 6. No dice. "If you want to talk about barbecue sauce, you can always be the de facto expert if you want to be," he says. "All you need to do is print out a one-pager and send it around, and that would make you an expert, right?"

In Keen-land, guilds, professions, and organizations have developed to set professional standards. Today the Internet runs roughshod over those institutions, replacing them with what he calls "radical democracy." For him, it's not technology; it's politics. And curation doesn't solve it. He says, "I don't think you're using the word correctly, because if I stand in my yard and kick a ball against the fence, does that make me a football player? If I strum a guitar in my bedroom, that doesn't make me a rock star." Point taken.

How does the Huffington Post fit into this? "[Arianna Huffington] is an example of a super creative," Keen says. "In the twenty-first century in the created economy or the knowledge of economy or whatever you want to call it, super creatives are very, very powerful.

I'm a wannabe super creative. She's a real super creative. In the old industrial structures of the twentieth-century meritocracy, which was siloed, you could either be a journalist or a lawyer or a doctor or an astronaut or a plane pilot. My core argument is that the new meritocracy is even narrower and more elite than the old one. I think the fundamental difference between what I stand for and, say, someone like Jeff Jarvis, is I acknowledge the economy is changing. I'm not a reactionary. I understand the economy is changed. But their argument is, it's making it more democratic. I actually think that the creative economy and the new kind of meritocratic structure is even narrower. So to become an Arianna is really hard. The old version of Arianna is she would have been a newspaper publisher; she would've been a Sulzberger or a William Hearst. But today, she's different; she's crossing over silos. She's sort of a political activist/publisher."

Is Huffington Post "democratic"? Clearly not. The site isn't a meritocracy; it's edited to her tastes and political persuasions. The fact that it's curated doesn't mean that it doesn't have a point of view; in fact, very much the opposite. But unlike journalists' enterprises of yesteryear that were built on the presumed basis of balance and objectivity, Huffington's choices are transparent and subjective.

So is the Web and the shift from old industrial publishing to new low-cost meritocracy truly more or less democratic? Andrew Blau, copresident of Global Business Network and a partner at the Monitor Group, says we may have the word wrong: "It occurs to me that maybe the word that throws us off here is *democratization* or *democracy*. It's a word like *motherhood* and *apple pie*—now who could be against democracy, right? Democracy is good. It's actually a bit of a distorting thing."

Having put aside for a moment the politics of the change in publishing, Blau says that there is a meaningful transformation under way: "What is clearly happening is that there are many, many, many more people speaking in public or some version of public without having to ask permission, some of whom seem to be able to accumulate large audiences, some audiences, the scale of traditional broadcast television or feature films."

But, of course, Keen doesn't agree. "The reason why the Huffington Post is growing is because specialization is changing, and because of the existence now of more and more personal brands," he argues. "The Huffington Post works because people get their stuff for free because they're promoting themselves, their expertise; it reflects a free-agent nation. So again, it's a new kind of meritocracy. The old kind of meritocracy would be you publish yourself and you sell it as a journalist, or you'd publish it in one of your professional guild magazines or publications. The Huffington Post reflects a meritocracy where we're all peddling ourselves. And Arianna is, you know, the supreme self-promoter, a peddler."

Says Keen, "I believe that throughout history there have always been elites and there will always be elites; and democracy is just another smoke screen to use by small groups of people to justify their own power."

So is Jarvis preaching curation and democracy while crowning himself and his cronies the new keepers of the curatorial flame? When I pose that very question to him, he has a lot to say in response. "What Andrew complains about is amateurization. What he wants is professionalization of the world. So actually what he is arguing for is an elite," he answers. "He wants an elite and a hegemony to take control of the world." For Jarvis the future is about a loss of control by the former controllers, and he is quick to point out that Keen is the old controllers' ally.

"What annoys me though is their language, their dishonesty, whether they know they're doing it," Keen says in disagreement. "Arianna is the classic example. She launches a supposed platform to democratize media, blah blah and blah. And what she is doing is she's creating—first of all, she was an immensely powerful person in the first place, and the only way she's able to do it is by having this remarkable network, and secondly, she's made $20 million, $50 million, maybe $100 million dollars out of this deal already. Chris Anderson of Wired Magazine talks about free and sells a book called *Free* for $500,000. So I just like people to be honest about what they're up to, not to dress up their own appetite for power and wealth in the language of democracy. I mean, it's that kind of level of absurdity and dishonesty. It's just a fraud."

Keen's fundamental issue is that a new class of elitists are becoming the powerful filters, the über-curators if you will, and doing it under the guise of a populist movement. He spares no one in the new literati of this criticism, least of all Google: "All Google does is reflect the will and the interest of the crowd and the mob, firstly. And secondly, it's very easy to game. So when I enter something into Google, of the top 10 things that come up, some of them are advertising, some of them are lame, some of them are irrelevant. Google isn't very good."

The shift from professional to amateur is one of Keen's most well-worn bugaboos, and he laments the democratization of the professional curator. "I don't think it's a good thing for anybody," he says. "Firstly, the librarians lose their jobs; but secondly, the kids now that use Google think it's intelligent. I mean I was talking to my 12-year-old son about Google. He'd bought something online, and I said, 'Well, why did you buy this from this particular store?' And he's pretty smart, I mean for a 12-year-old, especially on the Internet stuff. He said, 'Well, it came up first out of Google.' I said, 'Well, that doesn't mean it's good.' He said, 'Yes, it does—Google is very reliable.' So I think the 12-year-olds, even the smart 12-year-olds, today believe that Google is intelligent. And they believe it's a replacement for librarians, which isn't a good thing, because it isn't intelligent and often it reflects, you know, commercial interest or something else."

With folks like Keen on one side and Jarvis on the other, the debate seems to be drawn across content-creator party lines. Old-school makers see sharing as theft; new-school bloggers see the linked economy as a bonanza waiting to be monetized by forward-thinking media companies. It's hardly a balanced debate.

But folks like Clay Shirky say that the shift toward collaborative content creation and sharing are more fundamental than just new technology and low-cost content creation. "Arguments about whether new forms of sharing or collaboration are, on balance, good or bad reveal more about the speaker than the subject," writes Shirky in *Here Comes Everybody: The Power of Organizing without Organization.* "Every webpage is a latent community. Each page collects the attention of people interested in its contents, and those people might well be interested in conversing with one another too."

And while Keen sees the amateurization of content creation as a sign of society's drift from quality to mediocrity, Shirky sees no problem between mass participation and high-quality professional quality content. As he told Andrew Keen in a recent interview, "When I say, 'Publishing is the new literacy,' I don't mean there's no role for curation, for improving material, for editing material, for fact-checking material. I mean literally, the act of putting something out in public used to be reserved in the same way. You used to have to own a radio tower or television tower or printing press. Now all you have to have is access to an Internet café or a public library, and you can put your thoughts out in public."

As Shirky sees it, we're approaching a moment where participation and sharing isn't a trick, it's simply how it's done. "It's when a technology becomes normal, then ubiquitous, and finally so pervasive as to be invisible, that the really profound changes happen," he says.

And Esther Dyson, whom I'm sure Keen would call an elitist as well, says that community-connected content, sharing, and crowd curation aren't going to be scared away by professionals with pitchforks and torches. She's certain that sharing will require civility and some trust that people will do the right thing.

"If you put this stuff out there, by and large, it's out there for other people to use," Dyson says. "You can't offer free content and then get upset if someone points or links to it. People will realize the aggregators that simply link with no curation aren't adding a lot of value. If you take someone's content that's advertising supported and you sell ads around it, at some point you're stealing, but 9 times out of 10 you're bringing them more traffic than you're stealing ads."

For Dyson, it all comes down to being rational, and reasonable: "The reality is, life is too short. I can put this stuff up there, and people's opinions vary. I call it informal Creative Commons. If I think someone is getting rich off what I do, I try to get paid. If someone uses my stuff in a manner I don't like, it's a free world. They can say rude things about me, and many times they have. People do act badly, but you can't launch a lawsuit every time somebody acts badly."

9

WEB PLATFORMS EMBRACE CURATION

 e're living through a funny time in history. Machines are making content creation easier, faster, and noisier. At the same time, battle lines are being drawn between the folks who say that machines can become publishers and the folks who say machines need humans behind them. It's the battle of the machines versus the humans. And it's just getting interesting.

MACHINES VERSUS HUMANS

There are some obvious reasons as to why content creation is exploding. The tools to make content are ubiquitous: handheld mobile devices with cameras, recorders, and keyboards are now in the hands of high school students, housewives, and freelance reporters alike. The explosion in content creators has built a demand for new solutions and content platforms. Nationally, a number of brand-name media companies are making bets that they can source, edit, and publish crowd-created media—and build big new brand-name businesses around the trend.

The issue comes down to this: can Google News replace the *New York Times*? If an algorithm knew enough about your interests and your history, and could find all the data—what used to be called news—and put it in a readable format, that would be YouNews. News for and about your life may be what is delivered for you to read every morning in the future.

Machines

In order to explore this, let's start with the machines. The machine of the moment is Demand Media, the most visible, and some say evil, of the so-called content farms. The "evil" designation came from New York University journalism professor Jay Rosen. He recently narrowed his criticism, downshifting from *evil* to *demonic*, explaining, "A demon is someone extremely focused, diligent and skillful. In that sense, Demand Media is demonic at assessing demand from the live Web and producing 'into' it, and of course in the sheer volume of stuff it makes daily."

So what exactly does Demand do? Well, simply put, it reads search data coming from Google that is available to the public information from Google Insights for example. Then, it offers up writing assignments to freelance writers, and it pays on a pretty basic per-piece basis. Seems harmless enough, and Demand's CEO Richard Rosenblatt is careful to make it clear that he doesn't want to do "journalism." So why are folks so freaked out about the Demand model?

"There has been so much misinformation about our model and what we actually do," said Rosenblatt in an interview with Kara Swisher from All Things Digital. "I thought it was a good idea for our company and those who work for us to lay out our principles. We are so different from traditional journalism, which I have nothing but admiration for, so it was time to make people understand that." He goes on, asking, "What is wrong with coming up with a way for thousands of writers—who have been laid off, by the way, from news organizations—knowing exactly how much they make, selecting their own topics and publishing when they want? We're trying to find a new and innovative way to make content."

What's wrong with Demand is that the assignment "editor" deciding what writers will get paid to write about is an algorithm. So that means that if people are searching for "how to fry an egg," Demand will assign a post about it. Google will index and link to it, and a Google ad will show up next to it. But, of course, far fewer people seem to be searching for difficult subjects about poverty, war, and world hunger. Simply put, this is media being created by the largest needs of the largest audience at a time when the Web was promising to be about empowering new voices, smaller niches, and more knowledge and understanding. It's the needs of Google's aggregated audience rather than the passion of a publisher or a group of individuals.

Robert Scoble, noted tech blogger and video maker, says the Demand model is just plain wrong: "When I was a kid, I had a job on an assembly line, put in the same part in the same motherboard over and over and over again. That job will never pay more than minimum pay. Even if it did, it's so mind numbing after a while. It's not interesting, it's not good for you, it doesn't help you get to a new level. So, that might help pay the bills while you're trying to do something else, but it just doesn't seem like something that adds a huge amount of value."

Scoble says factory work editorial isn't going to be where talented creators end up. "You have to write a post every 10 minutes to make enough money to matter, because they're only going to pay you a couple of bucks per post. You can't spend any time doing those kinds of articles. Certainly, it won't be something that will let you build the brand that you can build on later on. It's a quantity game, not a quality game. Quantity games are profitable for the guy who owns them, but not very profitable for the people who do them."

The danger of this, content advocates say, is that there's only a financial incentive to make content about things people en masse find interesting. Search drives creation rather than merely discovering things for searches, which is why I'll argue in these pages that search is broke and unfixable, and will be replaced by a human-and-computer partnership. It's a vision AOL's CEO Tim Armstrong has put front and center in his rebuilding of the AOL service from a company that dominated dial-up to the world's best content company.

To do this, Armstrong, a Google veteran and charismatic leader, has been driving hard to invent and test multiple ways to create, aggregate, and curate content for the AOL platform. Just a few weeks after taking the helm of AOL, Armstrong lured away a high-profile technology reporter from the *New York Times* to head up one of the company's core initiatives. Saul Hansell had spent more than 20 years at the *Times*—a lifer by any measure—but he claims that the chance to be part of the future made the AOL offer hard to ignore. Hansell is now the chief programmer at SEED, another of the services looking to reinvent how content is created.

In a blog post entitled "Borg Master," Hansell said of his new job: "The thing that most excites me about AOL is that it isn't devoted to one method of producing content. It has full-time journalists, wire service and syndicated content, bloggers, freelancers, input from the entire Web community, and all kinds of automated ways to find interesting stuff. Our challenge is to create the right blend of information from all these sources for each page that will be the most interesting, accurate and engaging for readers and to do it at a cost that can be sustained by the revenue available to Internet media."

SEED, like Demand Media, may assign content jobs to an army of freelancers, but Hansell is quick to point out that SEED is very different from Demand. While Demand is driving content by mining search results, Hansell is using the needs of AOL's dozen's of content sites and content hubs like to fill the pipeline. Hansell explains: "Our best opportunity to making SEED work is to fish through the people who are already passionate about the topics who are on our sites."

Can AOL be the six trillion dollar editorial machine? Lee Majors, watch out: here comes Bionic Journalism. "We are trying to take the best of a machine, which does lots of things over and over again, and a person," Hansell says. "Because another way of describing what we're doing, what journalism has always done, is separating signal from noise, and that requires both man and machine."

Is AOL trying to beat Google at the news-gathering game? Hansell says it's far more than that: "Google News will give you a whole clump of things that are, probably, about the same thing with a reasonable degree of accuracy. But it can't tell you what it's really about. It can't summarize it. It can't translate it into people language. That's what we're in the business of. The essence of journalism has always been separating signal from noise. I have to go someplace and listen to all the boring bits to find the things that are worth two minutes or five minutes of somebody's time. It's all judgment. It's all selecting the best bits."

So what about costs? Some freelancers are complaining that the Web doesn't pay a living wage. "That is not my problem," Hansell says. Then he rephrases his response. "It is my problem, but I didn't create it, the world did that."

He is, however, trying to sort it out. As Hansell sees it, the issue is that the Internet has changed the fundamental economics of freelance work. His solution is to give work in bundles—10 tasks rather than 1—hoping that freelancers will improve their speed over time and make up for the low pay by producing volume.

The idea of leveraging writers and technology didn't start with Demand Media or Yahoo's Associated Content or AOL's SEED platform. In many ways, though, it did start when AOL, under Jon Miller, discovered the nascent WebLogs Inc. platform.

Cofounder Brian Alvey explains that it was post-bubble, the Internet economy had crashed, and mainstream journalism was beginning its painful decade of "creative destruction." "So here's what happened: all these great journalists were out of a job," he says. "And by journalists I even mean people who were not working at *Forbes* and the *Wall Street Journal*. But they were working on small newsletter publications too. So really, I think there were two reasons why the blogging movement took off. First: everybody's unemployed so they have plenty of free time to invest in creating paid content. You have 24 hours a day, you're sitting in an apartment, you have all these skills, and you can't use them. So that was number one. Number two was that the technology actually was usable. The Movable Types of the world could just walk up to something for free and start a media empire. I could publish, it would go out in seconds, all these things were free and I had all the time in the world and these skills were languishing in my apartment."

So he and Jason Calacanis built a network of blogs that were curated. Both the topics and the writers were chosen and focused. Some sites were talent-driven, like Engadget, which was edited by former Gizmodo gadget wiz, Peter Rojas. Other sites like Joystiq and TV Squad, however, were more classic blog network creations, with unknown writers and a changing cast of characters.

Scoble says the early success of Engadget is a clue about the power of curation and special skills humans bring to the game. "Bloggers are the first curators, and when you gather information on a very specific topic and put it in one place that creates huge value," he explains. "I mean look at Engadget for instance, which is a gadget blog. They go through the world and look for the best gadget information and curate it and put it together in one place so people who are interested in gadgets can know where to find it. And the advertisers love that because they know that the people reading are interested in gadgets. So if you're gonna try to sell a new gadget, do you want it to be on a toy site or do you want it to be on Engadget?"

Humans

It seems as though we're witnessing the classic battle between robots and humans. As Alvey says, "People ask me all the time about companies that just bubble a bunch of crap up into a tag cloud, and I say, 'I would never use that site.' I walk up to that site, I get on that site, I look at it, and I go, 'Oh, this is built by robots. I can smell the metal.' And I hit the Back button. I'm gone."

But if sites can't smell like they're created by algorithms, content robots, if you will, then how can content leverage technology and still feel human? Alvey says the answer is curation.

"I think curation is the evolutionary leap beyond blogging," Alvey says, recalling the human editorial team that ran the relaunched Web site Netscape at AOL. He describes it as Digg with an editorial team. Humans were essential.

So what exactly do they add? Is it magic, or something more quantifiable? Taste, judgment, serendipity? Scoble says what they add is uniquely human. "Algorithms are good at picking the big stuff, because it's easy to count how many views an item has or watching on Google how many people are clicking on an article or how many people are playing a video," he explains. "Computers are good at counting numbers or links or numbers of clicks or numbers of re-tweets. Humans aren't going to compete with that. But as humans, our brains are pattern recognizers. I can look at the tree across the street, and in a microsecond I know it's a tree. A computer has to look at an image of a tree for hours and spend a lot of processor time to figure out it's a tree, when I can explain it's a pine tree and it's dying."

Scoble says humans can also see emotional patterns and organize unusual content, even humor. It's impossible to program a computer to find the weird stuff. Weird is about interesting anomalies. He explains. "If you try to program it to artificially pull in weird stuff, it'll pull in noise that doesn't make sense. So I think the best new systems are going to join humans and machines."

While Alvey was busy building the future of aggregation and curation technology, there were a few media outsiders who were toiling away inventing content curation businesses that big media just couldn't seem to fathom. In hindsight it all seems clear, but back in the day the content entrepreneurs who were working like mad scientists were just figuring it out.

For 16 months Jason Hirschhorn was the CEO of the once-groundbreaking social network MySpace. Now he's out—on his own—and building his next big thing. He's done it more than once before. Hirschhorn has always been a bit of a media-giant outsider, more of a start-up entrepreneur whose creations and vision have drawn him in time after time. So jumping from one of the largest media jobs in the business without a clear landing space doesn't seem to faze him. If it does, he doesn't let on.

Hirschhorn's story starts, as with most modern-day computer nerds, in high school. He had an Atari and was hacking away in BASIC. At the age of 15 he was a club promoter, and so the mix of music and technology was, early on, one the things that connected for him. While getting his BS at New York University he was an intern for Warner Brothers Records, and as the Internet began to grow, he took interest in the Ultimate Band List (ubl.com), which eventually became Artist Direct. Ultimate Band List was a database with info on over 600,000 artists, concerts, record labels, and other music-related resources.

"I always thought I could do better," Hirschhorn says. He hacked together some sites, using Perl scripts to search the Internet and bring in music headlines and sort them. This was before RSS. Hirschhorn built his own hand-coded aggregation site. Back then it was called scraping. Then he found a site called RockOnTV and bought it and hired the developer. His plan: to look at every TV schedule and find and catalog all music references. "That was my first stab at curation," he says.

Hirschhorn scoured TV listings, looking for patterns that would trigger musical connections. "The *Brady Bunch* is on today, the *Brady Bunch* episode with Davy Jones [from the Monkees], but that should be a music episode too, because Davy Jones is an artist. So we started to basically cherry-pick every show, regardless of whether it was a performance or not, and make them into music listings, and then link them up with the data provided by Muze, a music data reference company and we built a big Web site."

As Hirschhorn's network of music site grew, industry heavyweights took notice. And before long, executives at MTV came and knocked on Hirschhorn's door. But to their surprise, there was no huge team of editorial workers behind it, just an Upper East Side apartment in Manhattan and a bunch of computers. They bought the company, and at 28, Hirschhorn's Mischief New Media was inside the belly of the beast, as he tried to be an entrepreneur at Viacom. Hirschhorn says big companies can operate better than they can innovate—a clue about the challenges of running MTV's digital assets for six years.

"I was a kid of pop culture, and I knew every movie and I knew all the music and when I thought about things, I thought about arranging them," Hirschhorn says. But his vision was always more than robotic aggregation. "An algorithm couldn't tell me why I should like music; I needed to know that an artist was influenced by this, or that an artist liked a certain guitar line in a song and that influenced them for another song.

"And curation came out of, really, artists liking one another—that was how I discovered things, not through algorithms—so it was a very human thing, not a technology, so to speak. So, you'd read an article where Diddy said his favorite band was Coldplay. Now, an algorithm would only put Diddy with other hip-hop artists, and now you're reading between the lines of what artists like about each other and how they influenced one another.

"At the end of the day, I love Pandora, I love Amazon—all those things are phenomenal—but what they don't give me is context, or context that I can understand. So, you're suggesting music because it has a three-chord progression or it has woodwinds in it—that's Greek to me. But if you tell me that I would love this song and you're able to write something about it in a headline, or the subhead makes a connection, that's curation."

Hirschhorn is back in entrepreneur mode, thinking about what's next—and what's next may just be the thing he did first: finding, filtering, and recommending. Curating content.

"In the early days, you had this tremendous amount of emotional connection," Hirschhorn says. "The emergence of MTV was very much a trend magnifier, they took trends the masses did not understand and curated them and magnified them and made them big. And then when the Internet arose, filters like Boing Boing or Google became sort of the loved brands, the ones that sort of made sense of all of it for you. But when you get a lot of text back and it's just samplings of a page, it's not the same as someone that you trust telling you which one you should go for. Because there's this infinite amount of content out there on the Internet." After MTV, Hirschhorn took a gig as president of Sling Entertainment, the company responsible for Sling Box.

"When I left MTV, Sling was a technology that allowed me to watch all the TV I loved outside of my home, but there was so much video on MTV and other channels and there was so much video on the Internet, what we aimed to build as entrepreneurs was a place where we curated. So Sling.com was a beautifully built video Web site that was programmed on a daily basis. Curation was a huge part of that in a world where Hulu and YouTube did almost no curation.

"I believe in curation, and I'm always amazed but also incredibly suspect of algorithmic curation, because I think sometimes it can implode on itself, meaning it thinks it knows you, and therefore never introduces anything new to you.

"One of the ways that MySpace stood apart from other social networks is that we had broadcasting mechanisms. If you look at other social networks, no one has them. Facebook doesn't because it's very one-to-one. We had your home pages and hubs. That we all felt, should be programmed." Today, MySpace has been relaunched with a focus on social curation. The technology gathers and connects content, but the real power of MySpace is what

MySpace Music Chief Courtney Holt calls "Social DJs." Holt explains: "We have a lot of people every day that are young and come through the front doors of our network. I'm really trying to pay attention to what they're doing, because even someone who is just passively consuming is effectively curating."

Hirschhorn's roots, from his days at MTV and through all of his gigs, reflect a core belief in content curation. He is now the sole curator of an influential industry newsletter called Media ReDEFined (or @mediaredef on Twitter). The 5,000 subscribers are a who's who of media moguls and managers, with names like Quincy and Rupert. You figure it out.

Hirschhorn explains how it all began: "The history of Media ReDEFined began when I got to MTV and Viacom. No one likes a preacher—they don't want to be yelled at or preached to by you about what they don't know about technology. So I went back to how I learned about what was going on with media, marketing, and technology. I read and I asked questions. And I started forwarding articles around, and by the time I left Viacom there were a couple hundred people that I was forwarding to. Then I left, and I got e-mails, 'Oh please don't stop doing it.'

"Now I wake up at about six o'clock in the morning, and I star the articles that I like in Google Reader. I have about 160 sources that I go through on a daily basis, I read about a third of the articles that I choose beforehand, I read all the blurbs entirely. And because it's mobile, I've got access on my iPad and iPhone, so everything's hooked up to it.

"Media ReDEFined is truly a trail of my reading and what I'm interested in. I put it into a form that others can then follow. The feedback has been from big executives and regular people who just read stuff: 'We feel that you know what's going on.' And it tells me that curation has a huge part to play in the future, and I believe that for all the searching, for all the browsing, the human element

of programming and curation is still going to be the major component of the experience."

But even Hirschhorn sees that he needs to keep up with the ever-
growing volume of data. The newsletter comes out once a day—but
Media ReDEFined on the flipboard is updated as he finds material.

"I've had heads of media companies tell me that Media Re-
DEFined gives them anxiety," says Hirschhorn. "There's so much
they want to read in there and there's not enough time for them.
And that's been curated! Some of them even print out the articles,
which I find hysterical. That to me shows you that even more
hyper-curation needs to go on."

What Hirschhorn has discovered is both the appetite and the lim-
its of his audience. They want him to filter the information he finds,
and narrow down to meet their specific needs and interests. Here
technology and human editorial are likely to work hand in hand.

"A lot of people, including Rupert, think I need to curate even
more," Hirschhorn notes. "He says it's too much! I said, 'Rupert,
you're probably right, but there's so much going on right now, it's
truly a golden age of change, you don't have to read everything.' And
you know, it's got about 5,000 subscribers now, but it's the heads of
most of the media and tech companies, all the media journalists,
analysts . . . tremendous amount from start-ups as well as large
companies. It's become their go-to thing to read on a daily basis."

Hirschhorn considers his next start-up: "As I was thinking about
leaving MySpace, I thought about starting a new company; it's really
going to be all about curation, and maybe I'd bypass the Web altogether and do newsletters and apps. When it comes to music and
movies and fashion and all these different areas, I think there is room
for ReDEF-like curation. Obviously some have been done before.
And there are great tools that enable quick, hand-done curation."

For Hirschhorn, an executive who could actually have almost
any job he wants, the return to a one-man-band curation operation

is a huge clue about where the world is going. He quit his first job at MTV at 28, after six-and-a-half years. At MySpace, he stayed just shy of a year and a half. He says innovation in content is going to come from the outside, from small start-ups, not from inside big media.

So, as he returns to work, Hirschhorn is building a new company. It would be a curation, newsletter, content offering. Think fashion reDEFined, music reDEFined . . . with a whole bunch of verticals swirling around in his head. Can it be that the idea he had in his East Side apartment is more valid than ever? Maybe so.

"I think this idea of the demise of the actual human as the programmer and curator is just not going to happen. There's something that a computer can never re-create—a human element, a human take on something," says Hirschhorn, with some degree of satisfaction. Humans win.

BALANCING OUT CONTENT CREATION AND CURATION

For Alvey, and Hirschhorn, and Scoble, the man-to-machine interface may get new tools from developers, but the need for humans to find themes and patterns, and add their curatorial context can only grow as the sheer volume of created content increases.

"I think curation is seeing a pattern in the world and telling someone else about that pattern," Scoble says. By way of explanation, he tells the story of how he broke the news of the Chinese earthquake 45 minutes before CNN. "I was one of the first people to see the Chinese earthquake happen, and I was the first American to tell someone else about it. And why did that happen? Because of a pattern that didn't exist before, and I understood that pattern, and then I told somebody else about that pattern on

Twitter." That pattern was a series of tweets reporting the tremors. Scoble explains, "That was 5 minutes before the USGS Web site said there was an earthquake and 45 minutes before CNN or the *New York Times* said there was an earthquake."

If Scoble is a human aggregator and curator, then Alvey is the modern equivalent of a blacksmith, making tools so that folks like Scoble can be more efficient and effective. He's taken all he's learned about high-tech aggregation and human-driven blogging and curation, and put it into a new software start-up called Crowd Fusion. Crowd Fusion is growing fast, teaching big media folks new tricks. It's already powering sites like TMZ, and Alvey and his team are the wizards behind much of the new MySpace relaunch that's under way.

"Crowd Fusion has the ability to link to Facebook Connect or tweet stuff out or pull in tweets," Alvey says. "Who does Crowd Fusion compete with? It really competes with your best in-house content management system that's perfectly tailored to your site. We can do the job of a whole bunch of humans with one human, but there still ought to be . . . what we call curation is not a technology. Curation is a human process."

Scoble notes, "Robots can help you, they can go and find everything about the Chinese earthquake and bring it to you, but you have to go through there and see a new pattern in the data that the algorithms collected for you and explain what you saw. Like, hey, the government ignoring this region. Why? A computer isn't going to always be able to see those patterns." He believes a human being who has training, work experience, life experience, contacts, context, can see a patterns that a computer simply can't. The ability to organize, comment, or even simply add captions to a picture make humans increasingly important.

The moral of the story seems clear here: computers can only see patterns after humans discover them, find key elements in them, and create patterns from them. By definition, new patterns can't be evaluated until they've gone through a human filter. Content farms fail because they only create content to fill known demands. But becoming a content creator *and* curator—using the tools, talent, and leverage the Web provides—could well be the way to balance the effort of original curation with your deep knowledge and passion for your chosen subject. Humans prevail over the robots because of the things that make us uniquely human.

So what is Alvey's advice to would-be curators? Focus. "I'd suggest do one thing well before you go into the others, because it's not guaranteed to work," he says. "You want to focus. You can't do eight things: you do eight things one-eighth. You lose to everybody. You do one thing well, you can succeed."

So, for writers, this means you need to wear a lot of hats. Alvey says you need to be able to market your work, so that means Facebook, Twitter, and maybe even a bit of HTML.

And while making money is important for the first-time curator, Alvey says don't let money be the only metric for success early on: "Whether you're getting a $1,000 AdSense check at the end of the month or a $3 AdSense check, there are other benefits of getting out there and doing this stuff. So in terms of specific skills I think it's changed. I think it's not technical anymore. It's definitely social."

Social networks of all shapes and sizes are the new marketing landscape for content creators and embracing those tools is important if you want to create, curate, and succeed.

10

BRANDS: CURATING YOUR CONSUMER

There's a famous proverb about putting a frog in a pot of boiling water. If you try to just toss him in an already boiling pot, he jumps out. But if you put the same frog in cold water and turn up the heat slowly he slowly boils to death. Which makes one wonder: why aren't brands jumping out of the pot? After all, it's pretty darn clear that the good old days when money and media reach ruled the world are over.

Just take a look at who is on the rise. Craig Newmark, who founded Craigslist, has now taken away from newspapers their one sure profit center, the classified ads. Newmark, who's famously eccentric, told me that he loves the Web because it's a place where one can look at sexy aliens. Hmm . . . I guess if you're into *Deep Space 9*, but not the old *Star Trek* episodes. Okay, Uhura maybe. But I digress. Craigslist isn't slick or fancy, or even tidy. It's messy and noisy—and *free*. And so are lots of other things that used to cost money.

So why isn't AT&T saying, "Yikes! This Web thing could crush our network and put us out of business?" Instead it seems to hand the keys to Steve Jobs, who's already got the music industry under his thumb and is fast at work to own the emerging world of tablet computing. The point is, big, old companies can't be small, nimble companies—their sheer size requires them to move slowly. It's hard to turn the *Titanic* on a dime. So this is where you get to come in and take the premium piece of the old big business and have a great success with your new, zippy, nimble curated thing.

HOW BRANDING IS CHANGING

Steve Addis comes from the grand old world of consumer packaged goods—CPG. He started his career at Clorox, but along the way he decided to take a journey into branding, and now he's proud to call among his clients Lego, Intel, and Smith & Hawken. When I talked to Addis, the first thing he told me is that his branding firm curates its clients, focusing primarily on those who are interested in doing things that are "socially good and environmentally responsible." This is mind-blowing stuff—an agency that has set up rules about who gets the most valuable precious resource: its time. Of course it makes sense, because an agency that has a mission can hire better talent, keep people motivated, and maybe not use money as the only thing that gets its employees excited about coming to work.

Now, Addis/Creson is in Berkeley, so maybe you could expect a bit more of an agency with an attitude, but Addis isn't that at all. He says the future is about curation, and he's put his blog posts where his mouth is to prove it.

"We're overwhelmed. There's simply too much choice and access to information to manage on our own," Addis blogged. "As a result of this new changing reality, we now live in a curator economy. Businesses that understand, embrace, and harness the power of the curator have the opportunity to tap into newfound loyalty." Okay, so the good news is that he's smart. But the bad news is that very few clients seem to have gotten the message. Addis wrote his first "curation economy" post back in 2005, like a freight train's engineer laying on the air whistle from miles away. But despite all the warnings, it seems Addis's arm waving and blog writing went unnoticed. Today, he says brands have to play catch up with the fast-moving trends of social media and real-time aggregation and curation. "For brand managers to think of their role as curator rather than marketer is to define the brand's point-of-view, reason for being, needs and desires it fulfills—brand essence—and then to stick to the rational and emotional benefits that make the winning brands unique," he reasons.

Consider Whole Foods. One of the touchstones of the company is its "whole philosophy." As a curator, Whole Foods carefully screens the products it carries and shares this standard with its customers:

> We carry natural and organic products because we believe that food in its purest state—unadulterated by artificial additives, sweeteners, colorings, and preservatives—is the best tasting and most nutritious food available. Our search for quality is a never-ending process involving the careful judgment of buyers throughout the company.

Shopping at Whole Foods is, therefore, fundamentally different from shopping at a typical grocer that does no screening. And as the benefits of natural-food products continues its rapid move to the mainstream, more and more consumers will seek nutritional curators such as Whole Foods. But Whole Foods' curator philosophy goes beyond products: it endeavors to be the curator of the shopping experience itself. The result is a far more emotional and satisfying connection versus typical grocery-store experiences.

New brands, born in the past 10 years, have a curation equation baked in, Addis says. They don't have to "get it"; they *are* it. They came into being after the power and influence of network TV began to wane, and they cut their teeth on social media. So brands like Google, sites like Etsy, or companies like Starbucks don't have to reinvent themselves. But that may mean the large packaged-goods companies are on the long slow slide down the tubes. It's simply difficult to teach an elephant to dance. Getting brands that are used to buying their way to the front of the line with media dollars to understand that being transparent and responsive wins the day is very hard. Shouldn't their trusty friends on Madison Avenue be able to ride to the rescue?

Here is where the notorious and ubiquitous media analyst Bob Garfield gets to sound off, predicting that there will be a dark age of dead old media that will cast a shadow across brands, advertising, and media long before the new Web world emerges. "Alas," he says, "the future—near or not—doesn't happen till later." He continues his gloomy prognosis: "In the intervening years there are three more initials to consider: SOS. Because revolutions by their nature are neither seamless nor smooth. There is no reason to believe the collapse of the old media model will yield a plug-and-play new one." Simply put, old institutions were built on their control of distribution channels and shelf space. Now, in a world of unlimited distribution and virtual shelf space, their power and dominance is very much in jeopardy.

The shocking thing is that he too wrote about this in 2005. And just so you don't think it was ignored by brands or advertising agencies, it was published in *Advertising Age*. On its front page! And, just in case folks didn't get it the first time, he updated it again in 2007 with the now dire warning that companies were entering: "a post-apocalyptic media world substantially devoid of brand advertising as we have long known it."

Garfield and Addis may never have met, best as I can tell, but they've both lived the life of a one-eyed man among the blind. They've seen the future, and it's not about advertising. It's not about telling or yelling or carpet-bombing a market with messages about your product. It is, shockingly, about listening. Garfield explains in his book *The Chaos Scenario*:

> Mass media, of course, do not exist in a vacuum. They have a perfect symbiotic relationship with mass marketing. Advertising underwrites the content. The content delivers audience. Audiences receive the marketing messages and patronize the advertisers, and so on in what for centuries was an efficient cycle of Economic life. The first element of Chaos presumes the fragmentation of mass media creates a different sort of cycle: an inexorable death spiral, in which audience fragmentation and ad-avoidance hardware lead to an exodus of advertisers, leading in turn to an exodus of capital, leading to a decline in the quality of content, leading to further audience defection, leading to further advertiser defection and so on to oblivion.

The refugees—audience and marketers alike—flee to the Internet. There they encounter the second, and more ominous, chaos component: the Internet's awkward infancy. The online space isn't remotely developed enough—nor will it be any time soon—to absorb the advertising budgets of the top 100 marketers, to match the reach of traditional media, or to fulfill the content desires of the audience.

A collapsing old model. An unconstructed new model. Paralyzed marketers. Disenchanted consumers. It's all so . . . chaotic.

The thing about all this chaos is that it has an impact on far more than just ad agencies or consumer packaged goods. Advertiser chaos has an impact on newspapers, local radio, television, magazines, and all the consumers of media that have enjoyed the subsidized existence of high-quality media.

Addis says that while he saw the trend early, two major events have made the likely into the inevitable: "First, we discovered that we can't always trust what companies tell us. And, secondly, the tools of mass communication are now in the hands of anyone with an Internet connection. The contemporary marketplace of infinite choices and instant access to resources has bred a generation of educated, skeptical, and resourceful consumers."

The idea is that brands, both old and new, need to stop ignoring the emergence of consumer power and instead embrace it and accept it. They must channel it, and in turn change how they think about customers. Humans, formerly known as either consumers or couch potatoes, are now creators and thought leaders, passive no more. "Finding and cultivating consumer trust in this economy of abundance means businesses need to understand, embrace, and harness the shift to become a curator brand—a brand that engenders such a level of trust and advocacy that it rises to the level of a peer," Addis says.

So, with the water now boiling and the ad agency frog still able to hop, are agency creatives and ad wisemen finally taking Garfield's message to heart? "Brands have hitherto been able to dictate their entire stories," he told me a few months ago at the South By Southwest conference, as he stood a bit too close to a man in a Cookie Monster costume. "They've been able to craft it from beginning to end and put it on your television machine. What they're scared about is that they don't have control of their own stories. And they have no control over what is being said about them. Moore's law will influence the amount of content that is out there. And so that's not going to change. The question is by what mechanism does the cream rise to the top?"

The secret ingredient is, to borrow from the Charlton Heston movie *Soylent Green*, people. In order to collect the best content and put it together, someone's got to figure out what's best. That's what curators do; they bring their judgment and experience and taste to bear on the question of what you and I should look at next. And we cannot survive without them.

So is this really a fundamental shift? A shift from big national brands being able to beam their message into your head via mass media to a curated future where consumer conversations and niche-content aggregators rule the world?

Well, simply said, yes. The nexus between big media and big brands is broken. And in between the message and the people formerly known as the audience are curators, whose motivation can't be assumed to be simply monetary compensation.

HOW BRANDS CAN ADAPT

Chris Brogan is perhaps the best-known leader of the social media–conversational marketing revolution. He started early and created a human, funny, honest persona in his 11 years of sharing, blogging, and eventually tweeting. He now has earned a powerful amount of attention, attention that he says equals cold hard cash.

"Attention is a currency, just like many others," Brogan says. "We understand time and money as two interchangeable things.

But attention is just as much something that needs to be arbitraged and disconnected from a 1:1 value. Said another way, attention costs me time and time is worth money, so attention by extension is worth money."

And Brogan doesn't just preach the gospel of free content; he puts his content up for grabs. "I give away all the content on chris brogan.com for free, provided *you* don't use it commercially, and provided *you* give me link backs to my original posts," he says. "So, a curator who wants stuff about human business and social media and marketing can use my 11 or so years of experience for free as material they share with their customer base. How do I make money from that? People send me messages once a week (or more, when I'm lucky) that say, 'I saw your post over on BlahBlah Site .com and I want to know if you're free to speak on December 4th.' Money, baby, and I didn't even have to work for it."

Brogan says that curation is an essential new tool in the marketers' toolbox. "I think brands have a great chance to be a thought leader, should they choose that opportunity." In fact, having just bought his first fancy-pants car—a shiny new black Camaro SS— he suggests that he's a prime target for marketers to engage him with curated content.

"I'd love to read all kinds of curated information about Camaros and especially by other owners, and by people who make accessories for the car," Brogan says. "Think about it. I'm fresh meat for buying accessories and aftermarket parts."

So what about the brand that says, "Nah, I don't need to be the thought leader in my space"? Can it afford to sit this one out?

Brogan says, "I think brands have a choice. They don't have to do anything. Oh, wait. Were you asking me whether that was a good idea for brands that wanted to stay alive and make money?" That's sarcasm, kids—sarcasm.

Of course, curation doesn't solve all the needs of all marketers. Brogan points out that you must create content, or brands won't be able to express their own voice. "Collecting recipes isn't cooking in a restaurant," he says. "You need to make a few dishes of your own."

It turns out that the Web, and all the noise and funk it brings, is both a blessing and a curse for brands accustomed to the power and control of mass marketing. As potential customers read, link, and "like" content on the Web, they're leaving breadcrumbs for markers. That content has to come from somewhere. For PR gurus like Steve Rubel, put a few extra checkmarks in the blessings category.

"On the blessing side, we have a million places where we can go to tell our story. It's infinite, we can create our own content," says Rubel, while seated in the ultra-swanky Soho offices of Edelman PR Worldwide. "I like to say that we rain on people every day, and we hope that eventually we drop enough rain to cause a behavior change and somebody says, 'I gotta buy an umbrella.' It used to just take a drizzle; it now takes a monsoon."

Monsoon. Tsunami. Avalanche. Use whichever weather metaphor you like. The simple fact is we're drowning in undifferentiated data. And the guys at Edelman are counting on the fact that they can do more than simply pitch bloggers to write about their clients. The old rules about clients creating content are long gone. Edlelman is in the publishing business, hiring Richard Sambrook, the former head of content at the BBC to come in and run an operation that will help such clients as the American Heart Association, eBay, Unilever, and HP make, gather, and curate content for the Web.

Sambrook left the BBC as he saw the balance of power shifting from journalists who wrote stories to the big brands who *are* the stories.

"Media companies are struggling," Sambrook says. "Spot advertising is recognized as less and less effective and, therefore, in that gap lots of companies and organizations are looking for new ways to engage consumers. Of course, digital provides them with an opportunity to go direct to the public rather than wait to be mediated by journalism."

Now firms like Edelman are hiring a new generation of digital storytellers, people who understand how to curate content, generate content, and create content. Increasingly an employee will walk in the door with a Flip cam, knowing how to edit, shoot, and write. That's a whole new ballgame.

Rubel explains, "We think that where PR is going involves three things: getting other people to write content, curating what's there both with a client and in a broader environment, and creating your own content—and sometimes those are all connected. Content creation now is part of the PR process because we can now go direct to audiences in ways that we could not before."

Is this good for folks in the public relations game?

Rubel says that PR is poised to be the leading discipline in next the five years, because it is increasingly focused on social media, not mass media. He says the future is all about social connections.

"It's not a matter of 'create content and they will come'; it's 'create content that gets socially connected and they will come,'" Rubel says.

But Rubel is quick to point out that curation is about more than automated aggregation or a spiffy feed-reader that's sweeping the Web looking for links. It's about curating quality. "A good curator is somebody who is able to separate art from junk," he says. "You go to a great museum in New York City, my finger paintings are not there. But a Monet is there. Somebody is able to look at that with a discerning eye and say this is going to fit the tone of our audience, the tone of our museum, and our budget. They make a decision; say they're putting together an exhibition. That's what a curator does." In fact, Rubel, whose official title at Edelman is senior vice president, director of insights, says he sees himself as a curator for his clients.

"I actually see what I do as threefold: I curate, I incubate, and I communicate," Rubel says. "So on the curation side I am out there trying to understand what are the key trends, talking to CEOs to emerging companies to thinkers in the space, and just reading a tremendous amount of information and parsing it all down and saying, 'Okay, what are the big themes that I need to be helping our clients on a global level understand?'"

And Sambrook goes even further, saying that companies have a *responsibility* to tell their own stories, be it product launch, brand proposition, or corporate point of view. Companies need to insert themselves in conversations that they have a stake in—or risk being left out.

But if the folks in so-called earned media are feeling new super powers, don't write off the folks on Madison Avenue. Things are changing, as advertising agencies look to add community content to the mix, but they're still working to figure it out.

"How do you create content, accurate content, that is much more conversational in nature? What surprises me is that I think the industry still doesn't have a recipe for that," says Jean-Philippe Maheu, the CEO of Publicis Modem. As the former CEO of Razorfish, a groundbreaking digital media shop, Maheu is perhaps the leading innovator from the early days of digital to now be working with large brands and agencies.

Maheu joined *Publicis* from his job as the head of digital at Ogilvy Interactive. *Publicis* begins with the mission "Contagious ideas that change the conversation." The idea that media can impact conversation is a clue about just how prevalent and powerful social media has become. Maheu says his job is to develop ideas or content that is contagious. Ideas that are interesting or useful or provocative—ideas that are going to be shared. His job is to create or change conversations.

Says Maheu, "The empirical evidence is that when the brand changes the conversation to its benefits, sales accelerate."

And what about the whole idea that consumers are talking about brands like never before? Maheu says consumers have always talked about brands in both a positive and negative light. But the Web has dramatically changed the volume at which this discussion occurs. "The big difference is that now they have huge microphones and podiums to do that and really create a movement, so that's a huge difference, obviously. So, that is a huge shift, there's no question."

"For a media brand, the concept of curating content becomes an important component of your strategy for connecting with an audience," says Dan McCarthy, CEO of NCI, one of the United States' largest local media companies serving the housing market. "People have a large appetite for content; the increase in the proportion of content that they are accessing through trusted connections suggests that people are looking into their social graph to ensure a good content experience. When a consumer includes a media brand in their social graph, they are inviting that brand to help guide their exploration of good content. It doesn't all have to be original. It does all have to be useful and relevant to the brand experience."

So you can see that the PR folks and the advertising folks don't look at the world the same way. Maheu points to campaigns like the Old Spice Man, which was done by a competitive agency, as evidence that broadcast television still drives buzz and starts consumer conversations. But no one denies that the social Web was a massive accelerant for Mr. Spice. While Rubel talks about raindrops, Maheu still wants to seed the clouds. There's a difference in worldview.

"I think marketing has evolved into two tiers . . . one which means you still need a campaign, you need points of view," Maheu says. "You need brand to have the courage to say something and to engage with consumers on something that's going to be interesting." Not surprisingly, he still sees mass media as the key fire starter to a campaign. But the new piece of marketing is what he calls "always on," the engagement of what was formerly known as word of mouth.

But what Maheu and Rubel agree on is content and the need for brands to take control of the conversation and curate.

Says Maheu, "You need a point of view. And you need content that enables you to communicate your point of view, and engage and respond. The question is to what extent the brand, the marketers who create and produce content are serious about finding content partners. And curating content from others."

Now this gets interesting—and tricky. Because brands have always wanted to wrestle control from media companies and become their own networks. Now with the tools at their disposal, brands toy with a new kind of control. And that, Maheu says, may be overreaching: "There is no way that the brand can control all the content and can be the sole producer of the content. So there will be a huge hole filled with curation. Content curation is critical, and it's something that I think marketers are starting to understand."

The passion to bring curation to brands is based on some core values that seem either obvious or inevitable, depending on your point of view.

BRANDS AS PUBLISHERS

Brands begin with the need to lead, the expertise to tell their story, the skill to attract intent, and therefore the ability to be trusted within their community. Because brands have access to both paid and earned media (advertising and public relations), as well as their own brand space, they are inherently publishers. The big change for the brands that have been built in the post-millennium world is that they *are* media, rather than buying media. For example, Starbucks sees such remarkable foot traffic and return visits through its doors that it doesn't need to buy television advertising to reach its customers. Its stores, its signage, its window displays are all media that lets it tell its story to customers.

Increasingly, customers are in control of the brand story. This can be both good and bad. As a simple example, on a recent summer evening I ended up with tickets to see a terrific performing artist on stage at a venue in Manhattan called City Winery. The performer was Marshall Crenshaw, and he and his band put on a remarkable show. Everything was great: the food, the wine, the service, and the music. I looked around and saw that other folks were taking pictures and Flip cam videos, so I decided to join in. I'd brought along my Canon 7D and walked up to the edge of the stage. I recorded an amazing rendition of his hit song "Mary Anne" with good sound and HD video. I wasn't sure if the venue or the artist would mind, but there wasn't any mention of not recording video, so I figured it was okay. Back home, I posted it on my Facebook page and sent out a tweet on Twitter: "Great night at City Winery; Marshall Crenshaw performing 'Mary Anne.'" Then I posted this link: http://bit.ly/curationnation14.

I didn't think anything about it. In fact I was totally surprised when hours later I found this tweet responding to my post from the CityWineryNYC account:

CityWineryNYC@magnify Thanks for your support—come by tonight and get 2 ticks for the price of 1—show tweet at the door

It's a great response.

I didn't know that I was supporting them by recording and posting, but of course I was. I had endorsed both the venue and the artist, and they were repaying my endorsement with an offer, and some warm feedback. My immediate reaction was that I want to go there again, post again, and become an even more ardent supporter of the venue. That's good marketing. The tweet response is a new kind of marketing called a "loyalty-based social media offer" powered by a service called buzzd.com.

In fact, brands may have no choice. They may *have* to become publishers and take control of the conversation that swirls around their space and the product, such as contests that invite creative contributions, with customized printing like the M&M's with a personalized message on the back, and even by bringing fans into product development, as Lego does.

"In the past, brands went to publishers because they have distribution channels for delivering messages. It's kinda like the rest of us going to UPS or FedEx or USPS to deliver a package. We pay for the use of their delivery channels," explains Joseph Rueter, one of the founders of the Minneapolis software start-up CurationStation, which powers Web-based brand curation. "Brands pay publishers to buy space and/or time in their distribution channels to send their ink splatters and light rays to segments of people. Those channels have been built over time in breadth, depth, and trust. Trust leads to loyalty, recommendation, consideration, engagement, preference, action and so on. This sounds like what brands do. Now brands can be their own publishers."

Rueter describes good curators as having a clear set of attributes that includes building trust, awareness, conversation, community, participation, interaction, engagement, and affinity. Somewhat paradoxically, Rueter suggests that well-executed brand curation can be "noise canceling," which is to say that when customers search for answers and information arrives at their front doors with a trusted brand-published offering, they tune in to solve their problem or answer their question and tune out the extraneous noise and content. This is a powerful brand opportunity but also a complex one. Building trust with a customer is more than offering a biased, positive, brand-centric view of the world—that's the fastest way to convince customers you're not an honest broker. Cultivating trust will force brands to develop an honest and sometimes self-critical look at their practices and products.

So that leaves brands having to face critics like Bob Garfield, whose customer service frustrations led him to launch Comcast MustDie. Garfield's advice? Embrace your most unhappy customers and face the harsh music that you hear when your brand has a weakness. "My advice to brands would be to look for their own Bob Garfields out there," he says. "You attend to their issues as rapidly and transparently as possible. And here's what happens: the squeaky wheel is not only silenced but seduced, whereupon they go out and become your greatest evangelist. You already know they're not shy. Well, now they won't be shy about telling the world how great you are."

In a transparent world, engaging an unhappy customer has a twofold win. You get to learn from a critic with a megaphone and you get to turn a foe into a friend.

"It's jujitsu, and it's just so basic and so obvious—but it is also so contrary to all of the instincts of every corporate PR person who has ever lived," Garfield says. "Their instincts are to deny, to deflect, and to quash. In the connected world, you can't do that, and so that's why you should cultivate even your worst critics."

And this is hardly limited to service brands. Branding expert Steve Addis says consumer packaged goods can get in on the curation meme as well. His firm Addis/Creson has been doing brand work for the natural food brand Kashi.

Kashi is hippy granola all grown up. Kashi is healthy and whole-grained, and consumers know that any subbrand like GoLean is going to share in the parent brand's mission and message of sustainability and healthy living. In order for brands to be present and participate in the new "social" world, they need to have a voice. And a voice that is more than a monologue. A dialogue. And that requires that they develop a curatorial context for the space they're in—and a way to share ideas that come from their areas of expertise, but not necessarily from their own content creators.

Rueter concludes, "Brands have the expertise, the time, and the money to be great editors and curators of digital content. It seems reasonable to conclude that one part of being a great brand is now also being a great curator."

This whole new world can't be easy for brands or their creative partners. It used to be so easy when dollars equaled dominance, but now there's a digital fly in the ointment. Curation can give brands a way to convene a conversation, keep the tone appropriate, and create a safe space for customers to learn and share. But brands that ignore the need to embrace an editorial voice are bound to be unhappy when consumers use their newfound power to talk about them—whether they like it or not.

11

NETWORKS: WRITING INSIDE A CURATED COMMUNITY

If the first curators were bloggers, which seems likely, then blogging is very much on the early side of the curve in terms of where media is going. Blogging and curation are like parts of a set of Russian nesting dolls, with individual bloggers increasingly becoming link gatherers and curators. And on the network side, the emergence of both blog-content networks and blog-ad networks are providing new sources of revenue for bloggers and new aggregated-advertising opportunity for marketers.

BLOGHER

Early on, back in 2005, three extraordinary women noticed that something was missing from the Internet. They knew that women were blogging, but there wasn't a central organizing place for them to meet, share ideas, and build a community.

As Lisa Stone remembers it: "Elisa Camahort Page and Jory Des Jardins and I originally suggested the first BlogHer Conference to answer a very simple question. People were asking, everywhere we turned, 'Where is a woman who blogs?' And we thought, 'Oh, this can be answered.'"

The mission of BlogHer was at first community, and as it grew and evolved with the Web, there was an economic mission as well. The world of BlogHer is separated into two areas: BlogHer.com, which anyone can join and participate in; and the BlogHer network, which is a collection of the best women's blogs and includes an advertising component and revenue share. The network is curated: only sites that meet the published community standards are allowed to join. And that, Stone says, means advertisers know they are appearing only on sites that have signed off the shared standards for credibility and quality.

Since the launch of the BlogHer Network in 2006, Stone and her partners have seen exponential growth by all measures: traffic, bloggers, and revenues. BlogHer is now reaching over 20 million unique women each month. The network feeds 25,000 blogs that have been reviewed by editorial team members and has a publishing network with more than 2,500 affiliated bloggers.

Says Stone, "Blogging and social media are fantastic opportunities for the entrepreneurial woman, whether she's a specialist in food, family, or in technology itself. And a cornerstone of her strategy really should be a blog, because as much as I love Facebook and Twitter, and as much as most women in the blogspace do,

140 characters is just not the place where you can provide or exchange the kind of advice and insight that keeps people coming back every day."

BlogHer's unique offering to advertisers is its curated network, which is based on a very specific set of published criteria. The following is a portion of the site's editorial guidelines:

> We embrace diversity and expression in all blogs; however BlogHer declines to include blogs with unacceptable content in the BlogHerAds network. We define unacceptable content as anything included or linked that:
>
> Is used to abuse, harass, stalk or threaten a person(s).
>
> Is libelous, defamatory, knowingly false or misrepresents another person.
>
> Infringes upon any copyright, trademark, trade secret or patent of any third party. If you quote or excerpt someone's content, it is your responsibility to provide proper attribution to the original author.
>
> Violates any obligation of confidentiality.
>
> Violates the privacy, publicity, moral or any other right of any third party.
>
> Contains editorial content that has been commissioned and paid for by a third party, and/or contains paid advertising links and/or spam. Every opinion expressed must be the true opinion of the author.

Beyond those standards, BlogHer has some additional editorial requirements. Eligible blogs must have some history and be live for more than three months. They must accept comments, updated preferably twice a week or more, and have no advertorial or sponsored posts. BlogHer doesn't want any blogs with profanity in the title, and the blogs must be written by women. If these standards sound familiar, they should. This is BlogHer curating its network, creating a consistent quality offering for advertisers.

Beyond the rules, Stone says BlogHer blogs have one thing in common: passion.

"When women ask me what to do with their blogs," Stone says, "I say first of all write about what you passionately love. Because if you truly care about the topic, are you going to be willing to dig into the day-to-day workload and minutiae that come with being your own columnist? Because really this is about taking the values of a traditional media columnist into the social media space. If you care what you are blogging about, you have to go off and read other columnists and communicate with them on their site. You absolutely have to dig into the latest techniques, whether it is writing or technology, and that's the reason that BlogHer.com and BlogHer publishing network has a whole 'how to blog better' series of conferences and articles on our site. It's a major part of our mission, educating the community."

Stone says that bloggers can reveal their personae with both what they write and what they share with their readers via curation. "The bottom line is that it's your blog. It's your voice," Stone says. "If you found something that is so funny, so valuable, so insightful that you say the value that I can give for you today, reader, is for you to read this. Isn't that value?"

HOW GLAM ARE YOU? ASKS GLAM MEDIA

If BlogHer was built from the ground up, as a community first and an advertising network second, then its chief rival is precisely the opposite. Glam Media was founded in 2005, at almost the same moment as BlogHer. But Glam, unlike BlogHer, isn't about community; it's about creating the world's largest ad network targeted at women.

Founded by Samir Arora, the site was created with a clear plan and venture capital to build "a better way for premium brand advertisers to connect with audiences on the Web. With over 90 million unique visitors a month and a network of 1,500 publishers, Glam now describes itself as "the #1 web property for women and #6 in the Top 10 Media Companies in the US."

But Glam's growth hasn't been without some controversy. In 2007, as Glam was out looking to raise $200 million in private funding, its private placement memorandum made the rounds in Silicon Valley and ended up in the hands of the blog TechCrunch's Editor in Chief Michael Arrington. He wrote a now-famous post titled, "Is Glam a Sham?" and went on to call Glam's claims of being the number one site for women "nonsense."

"A cornerstone of the company's argument for raising such a large round is their tremendous growth over the last twelve months," Arrington wrote. "They boast of faster growth than MySpace, and claim to be the no. 1 women's website on the Internet with 19.1 million unique monthly users."

Arrington digs into the Glam private placement memo and doesn't like what he finds. In particular he says that Glam's claim of dramatic growth is based on selling advertising for sites like My Yearbook and Kaboodle, sites that don't really reflect Glam's promised target audience of woman or style-conscious readers.

The debate is important here because Glam is clearly a network of blogs, not a community in the way that BlogHer is. But Glam's traffic across its properties can't be ignored. And in fact, as VentureBeat reported, continues to grow. The battle between the two largest women's networks took a turn in 2008—when iVillage invested in, and acquired, an interest in BlogHer—at least in part to hedge against the fast-growing Glam.

And while BlogHer has a narrow focus and clear editorial guidelines, Glam's broader reach is clear in how it describes its network:

> The Glam Vertical Content Network is not your typical web property. By combining our owned and operated sites with sites like yours we can leverage your contextual content, audience, and traffic for the mutual benefit of our publishers and help you monetize your site with a broader audience and premium brand advertisers . . . All publishers from Glam.com Women's and Brash.com Men's Networks, GlamTV, and BrashTV will be a part of the Tinker Network. Accredited professional journalists and news editors as well as magazine and TV organizations are pre-qualified and invited to join the network, along with bloggers in networks such as Federated Media, BlogHer, TotalBeauty and others.

Arora is clear about the size of the venture capital investment—$130 million dollars so far—and the reason he chose to target women first: "Our main focus is servicing large, saleable audiences that advertisers use. The spenders are the women. No question. Eighty-three percent of consumer spending is women. Ad money goes where the spending goes, and women are the decision makers in the buying process."

And while Glam is clearly a media company, it's a new kind of media company: one focused on aggregation and quality. For that, Arora says, he's got a core team with a singular focus: "We have a team of curators who look for good talent who deliver consistently over time."

BlogHer and Glam each has the same offer to advertisers: to be "the" way to reach women and to provide income for women bloggers along the way. But each has gone about it in totally different ways: BlogHer by serving women first, and Glam by seeing its primary customer as advertisers. But neither is fundamentally in the content creation business.

SB NATION

A third blog network, also large and growing quickly, has taken a very different approach. Rather than aggregate and curate sites, SB Nation is using new tools and techniques to create and replicate sports-oriented blogs in a repeatable, low-cost, quality-templated fashion. SB Nation embraces content from outside, using curation and the Huffington concept of the linked economy to build robust sites with low overhead.

The network is run by former AOL executive turned content entrepreneur, Jim Bankoff. While at AOL he embraced the power of blogging and led the acquisition of Weblogs Inc. He now runs SB Nation, one of the fastest-growing content networks on the Web.

"The history of media has been always framed in terms of content and distribution. Now everyone is able to become their own media company," Bankoff says.

So Bankoff set out to become his own media company and build on what he saw as three emerging trends. The first trend was the fragmentation of media. If old media was mass broadcast, then Google and the Web turned bit topics like sports into microniches: local, narrow, personal. After all, most people attending a basketball game at Madison Square Garden don't identify as sports fans, the logic goes; they consider themselves Knicks fans.

So with the concepts of "sports" and "fragmentation," Bankoff began to build a network of blogs. But rather than aggregate existing blogs, as other networks have done, he wanted to "own and operate" much the way a chain of retail stores might set up shop in the local mall. Today SB Nation owns 270 sports sites, and each focuses on a team, one for every pro and most major college teams. While SB Nation is the owner, the individual sites have their own names, logos, and URLs. Bankoff says, "The New York Yankees' brand would be Pinstripe Alley, and the San Francisco Giants' brand would be the Covey Chronicle. And by having specific brands for specific topics, we think that we're being more authentic and more genuine with the audience that cares about them. But it's all playing into that fragmentation."

The second trend that Bankoff targeted was socialization. Learning from what was arguably AOL's greatest win in content, SB Nation puts a premium on inviting and managing high-quality community content. Fan posts, comments, and submissions are all curated. "Spectator sports are all about the conversation," Bankoff explains. "That's pretty much the whole reason it exists. And so it's important for us to have high-quality conversations when you're talking about your favorite sports team."

And the third trend that Bankoff built his network on is the rapidly emerging real-time nature of the Web. "*Real time* has become a buzzword," Bankoff says. "But what it means in our case is really reducing the cycle from the moment an event happens to the moment we make it available for our audience. We put emphasis and investment in curation and publishing and getting things out there fast."

For a site with breaking news like professional sports, being able to crowd-source content gathering from multiple sources and then use curation to filter and transmit real-time information is core to Bankoff's vision: "When something happens, an athlete tweets something or there's a press conference on YouTube or the *New York Times* reports something or one of our own editors or writers creates or reports something, no matter where it happens, when it happens, we make a promise to the audience that we'll have it up within moments of the events' actually happening. And we'll put our own spin on it, and, of course, we'll link to the primary source if we're not the primary source. That's the way we created our product. And I think it's because these news cycles have become instantaneous and curation is really the way that we deal with it."

SB Nation is a modern variation on what used to be mass media. Using technology, a distributed workforce, and a mix of aggregated content, unpaid fans, and commentators and paid bloggers, SB Nation has created a new way to do sports journalism. It's a Web-centric view of content creation, community, and consumer broadcasting.

As former mass media is broken up in to smaller and smaller pieces, folks in old media are scratching their heads, trying to sort out how to build a business model. SB Nation is building scale by reaggregating a fragmented market. It is able to launch a new site for a team or region with very low incremental cost. Then, it is able to offer advertisers scale with a single buy across many niche team sites. By cross-promoting the sites across the network, it has found both efficiency and scale. Finally, it is able to leverage large relationships with Comcast, Yahoo!, AOL, and USA Today across the platform. It is truly the future of microniche publishing.

As bloggers look for new gigs, some will decide that they want to build their own brands and their own sites and their own networks. But for plenty of writers with a passion for a particular subject, a full-time or freelance gig writing about a team they love is a dream come true. As Bankoff explains, "We've gone out and recruited someone who is a diehard fan of their team and who's also an expert at engaging an audience around the topic of their team. And we pay that person. In most cases, it's kind of like a freelancer relationship, where they're under contract and they work for us. In some of the bigger sites, it's a small team of people, but there's always one person in charge. And that person is in charge of creating content for the site and managing the community."

HUMAN REPEATERS ARE THE NEW BUILDING BLOCKS

Three blog networks. Three different approaches to finding, curating, and monetizing content. But in one way or another, each network is looking to turn the power of community into a coherent and economically rewarding new spin on social media. Readers, content creators, and an emerging army of retweeters, recommenders, and rebloggers are amplifying audience and providing what Jeff Pulver describes as "human repeaters." Says Jim Bankoff, "Word mouth has given way to word of mouse."

User-generated content may have been the revolution of 2008, but for Bankoff, user-generated distribution is the next big thing. "User-generated distribution enables users to virally share content that they find appealing with one another," he says. "Certainly, looking at modern media company SB Nation, but just about everyone else I've talked to as well, the biggest growth and maybe, in some cases, the biggest absolute distributors are now these user-generated distribution channels, namely Facebook, Twitter, or even e-mail."

It used to be that what we thought of as networks were webs of technical capacity. NBC, the National Broadcasting Company, reached the country with an over-the-air signal. Now you can do that from your living room or your cell phone. Bankoff has proven the new model is less about hardware and more about something more human; a human network able to rebroadcast in real time and transmit to its network, and so on, and so on. It's a whole new way to imagine distribution.

The next generation of media moguls may not be content creators at all, but rather networked content curators.

12

THE
MICRONETS

In order to set the tone for this discussion, let's flash back to 1993. Are you there? If so, then you should notice there's no such thing as a Web browser or broadband or WiFi, or any of the digital plumbing that we now take for granted that's fueling so much of what is now roiling the "old media" world of television networks.

What *did* still exist back in those dark ages was storytelling. And in my pre-Web days, I was in storytelling full-time. Back then I owned a production company that had broken into big-time cable TV programming by creating and producing series and specials for networks such as A&E, History Channel, CNN, and HBO.

But something was bothering me. As video was moving into the mainstream and camcorders were getting cheaper and better, the stories that we were telling for cable and my syndicated news program *BROADCAST: New York* were all starting to blur together. In a world of complexity and diversity, the handful of folks making TV was just too small, and the stories too much the same. I wanted to break out of the box and get more people into the network. I wanted to open-source the content creation ecosystem. And I needed a partner to help me do it.

THE ORIGINAL MICRONET

The concept was called Viewers News Network, or VNN, a consumer reported 24-hour cable channel dedicated to first-person storytelling with handheld camcorders. I presented the idea with a great deal of enthusiasm to the CEO of Viacom, Frank Biondi. Sitting in his office on the executive floor of 1515 Broadway, we dialed into our toll-free number and played call after call of passionate storytellers pitching their stories. With his encouragement and a tape full of ViewersNEWS, I made a pretty elaborate presentation to MTV. I presented to executives Joe Davola, Linda Corradina, and Dave Sirulnick, and to their credit they were immediately enthusiastic about embracing consumer-created content. Yet they had questions. Would people *actually* call in? Would the stories be interesting enough? They wanted to test the concept before they signed on.

And so weeks later, we put on a 30-second promo for a pilot series called *MTV Interact* and invited viewers to suggest stories they would like to report. The promo played just three times, and the calls were delivered to our toll-free numbers to be tallied and transcribed. Forty-eight hours later, we had 5,000 calls.

The series was given a green light to go into production. *Interact* became *MTV Unfiltered*, and MTV assigned Rob Barnett to produce the pilot. *Unfiltered* was an extraordinary experience. The core staff, the evolving editorial philosophies, and some of the hard-fought internal battles all served to teach me about the opportunities and complexities that lay ahead, as user-created content moved toward the mainstream. Little did we know that the emerging Web would lay the groundwork for YouTube, and then the emergence of micronetworks like My Damn Channel and blip.tv.

What exactly is a micronet? Well, it's kind of like a beer microbrewery. Local, high-quality, and focused on a community rather than a market. For what would become the micronets of video, it was important that they could be delivered over the Web and not broadcast or cable networks.

But back to *MTV Unfiltered*. The process of creating the show was quite specific. Each episode we would invite viewers with a story to tell to call our toll-free number and pitch their story to *Unfiltered*. Alison Stewart, the show's first host, had a remarkable way of exuding both trust and passion, and she seemed to be able to reach through the TV set and coax audience members to dial the phone. The calls were transcribed, and printouts of the day's calls were distributed to the show's associate producers, producers, and executive producers. Early on we decided to let associate producers "adopt" stories that caught their eye. Certain APs tended toward more visual pieces, adventure sports, and stunts, while others were drawn toward socials issues and injustice, and others gravitated toward personal stories and journeys. As the show's lead producer and executive producer (along with MTV's Dave Sirulnick), I would make sure that good stories all got adopted by someone. I was curating from the story proposals, looking for new subjects, new voices, and new memes to embrace.

It's important to remember that back in 1994, when the series premiered, few viewers had a video camera. We lent people cameras if their story was chosen. There was no Web access, no e-mail, and certainly no cell phones with cameras, so all communications were on landline phones and fax machines. These were truly the early days of first-person media. Everyone who called with a thoughtful proposal got a call back though. Having humans connect with humans was critical.

The entries were as diverse and different as you could imagine. A girl from Penn State wanted to document, and object to, an annual male streaking ritual on her campus. Skateboarders felt the cops harassed them. A boy painted his room and windows black—he was afraid to go outside. A teen father complained there were no baby-changing tables in men's bathrooms. A cross-dressing student graduated from Florida State in drag (Tweeka!). And then there was Shaun.

Shaun was 15. He seemed like an average teen. He had friends. He was funny and popular. And then he shocked his friends and family by committing suicide.

His best friend, a 14-year-old girl, called the toll-free number, sobbing. She was angry. Angry with Shaun for the pain he'd caused. Angry that he'd left his friends to deal with the grief. She wanted to record her anger so that any teen thinking of suicide would know the pain it caused. She wanted us to send her a camera to tell her story.

At that point we had 30 cameras. They were Sharp Hi8 Viewcams, and they were constantly on the move, shipped from one storyteller to another. Each person was allocated just 10 days to shoot, but people often kept them longer. And as tape came in, we would often send a camera back for additional shots or new interviews, coaxing the tale from the storytellers in little bites.

Each week we met and discussed stories, and associate producers lobbied for access to the few cameras that had freed up from the week before to start their stories. The Shaun story had been adopted by Dina Kaplan (who had left the Clinton White House to join *Unfiltered*). She wanted this story to be made.

Others weren't so sure. Was this really the right show to do such serious material? What images could actually be photographed? The story had already happened, so it seemed likely to be a waste of precious camera resources. Kaplan was adamant. She wanted a chance.

It was a pivotal moment for *Unfiltered* and for user-generated content as well. Kaplan won, and the camera was shipped. The result is a story that haunts me to this day. The piece featured home videos of Shaun both happy and deeply depressed. Interviews with his father, mother, sisters, and his friends. I never forgot Shaun, and I always remember to hug my kids and tell them I love them. There is no doubt that suicide was a touchy subject. And that's why it deserved to be explored by people who'd earned the right to talk about how it feels to lose someone you love. To view this story and other segments from *Unfiltered*, go to http://www.unfiltered .magnify.net.

Not every *Unfiltered* story was that important or successful, of course. Lots of viewers lost interest and didn't finish their pieces. Our associate producer walked a tricky line in building bridges without crossing them. Each camera that got sent out included a recorded introduction by the associate producer who would work with the storyteller. When the camera arrived, a note would say "press play," and a prerecorded introduction from the *Unfiltered* staffer would play. "Since we're going to see video of you and your life, we figured you should be able to see what we look like," the tapes always began.

We broke ground with new tools and new technology. We'd be the first show at MTV to be cut on nonlinear Avid editing equipment, in large part because the stories came together in a nonlinear way. And once the first crop of DV cameras came out, we shifted slowly from Hi8 to DV, immensely improving picture and sound quality. In hindsight, Hi8 was just barely broadcast quality.

But *Unfiltered*'s most important innovations weren't technical; they were philosophical. We thought what people had to say was more important than what *we* had to say. We thought our role was to create a framework, a support system, and a community.

This is worth a moment's consideration.

When consumers shift their function from consumption to creation, the impact is significant. And for content companies, the results will be earthshaking—and potentially disastrous. And so, we stand at a content crossroads: not a moment driven by technology, but rather a moment powered by technology. Human beings tell stories. They gather and share knowledge. They entertain. They teach. There have always been gating factors that have separated community speakers from amplified speakers. The printing press, the radio license, the TV transmitter.

But those gates are gone.

Now the flood begins: content made on the fly, content made by professionals, content created by communities for communities. The impulses that drove people to call our toll-free number back in 1994 are, if anything, more prevalent today than they were back then. The world has become more complex, the news media more consolidated in its ownership and its tenor. And the economics of cable and broadcast forces them to reach for broader and more disposable programming choices at the moment when media consumers are increasingly looking to highly specialized niche-content sources, including Web sites and blogs.

Which brings us full circle. *MTV Unfiltered*–style crowd-sourced content replaces centralized content creation. People replace search. We're standing on the eve of new era in person-to-person storytelling. It is an era in which institutions that have for the past 50 years been at the center of mass media may find that they need to rapidly reinvent themselves or slip into obsolescence.

WEB VIDEO 2.0

In February 2005, Chad Hurley and Steve Chen started a Web site to solve a problem they were having. Video sharing was difficult, and they thought a public site was the solution. It was called YouTube, and it was neither slick nor complex. In fact it was pretty bare bones. But in the aesthetic of Web 2.0, it was extremely open and provided few barriers to upload and storage. It's pretty clear that the guys at YouTube didn't expect that they'd be lighting the fuse on the final explosion of conventional television as we know it. But that's exactly what happened.

People formerly known as content consumers began to turn their thoughts, hobbies, humor, and voices into a massive content-creation engine. And the discussion of "exploding TV" became the hottest topic on blogs that debate the evolution of the Net from text and pictures to full-motion video.

Fred Wilson—who's influential blog AVC.Blogspot.com had been a bellwether for music technology and personal media—turned his attention to television. For him, technology was changing the way people both made and shared media. The nature of the open Web made the economics of past, with closed networks and walled gardens, impossible to sustain. He saw ubiquitous, open, sharing networks like BitTorrent as the future of content.

Says Wilson, "I think the advent of the media-centric PC will cause this trend [BitTorrent-downloaded TV] to accelerate. If my family room is driven by a PC with a DVR, set-top box, and Web browser built into it, connected to cable for both programming and high-speed data, and then connected to a nice big flat-panel display, the option to watch a show via live TV, VOD, DVR, or BitTorrent is just a click of the remote. And when it's that easy, why will my girls choose to watch *One Tree Hill* via DVR when they can just as easily get it via BitTorrent?"

And Jeff Jarvis, the founding editor of *Entertainment Weekly*, has pretty strong feelings about TV as well.

Jarvis sees the "exploding" of TV in a number of critical ways. First, he proclaims, "At some point, soon, content producers will get rid of all middlemen," and there's lots of reasons to believe this is true. After all, the Web is disintermediating lots of businesses that used to have middlemen. But Jarvis goes on to connect all this to Madison Avenue, seeing a battle ensuing between old-media companies moving online and emerging complete new-media outlets.

Says Jarvis, "What excites me most is that reduced cost of production. That's really what drove Weblogs: history's cheapest publishing tool reduced the barrier to entry-to-media and allowed anyone to produce and distribute text content. Now this will come to video . . . A half hour of how-to TV that now costs X hundreds of thousands of dollars to produce can be done quite respectably—and probably with more life and immediacy—for a few thousand dollars. New content producers will pop up all over, just as they did in blogs, and now they can distribute their content freely thanks to BitTorrent. That is where I want to play."

Jarvis sees a future in which citizen journalists and consumer content creators become central figures in the creation and consumption of editorial material. What makes his perspective so rare, and refreshing, is that he had a full-on membership in the ruling media elite. For him to step outside and go from a TimeWarner–Condé Nast creator of MSM (mainstream media) to a blogger, a position of some less authority and power, is a sign of just how intoxicating the promise of personal publishing is.

Both Jarvis and Wilson are on the money: the transformative changes that are roiling the media industry go deeper than technology or personal expression. At the core of the growth in first-person media is a passion that challenges the promises of the democracy.

Big media, like big government, thrives on being able to monopolize the conversation. Media companies need to be able to control the conversation, set the agenda, and manage whatever role community members may want to have in the conversation. But consumer-generated media isn't a parlor trick that's given credence by corporate media; it is in fact a peer-to-peer system that flourishes on networks that fall below conventional radar.

In May 2010 YouTube announced that was serving more than two billion videos a day, which it described as "nearly double the prime-time audience of all three major U.S. television networks combined."

YouTube is notable in a number of ways. Its fast start is both remarkable and inevitable. From November 2005 until June 2006, it launched and grew with an adoption curve unlike any other software product, Web site, or piece of consumer electronics in history.

Today cofounder Hurley's six-year-old site is the third-largest site on the Web, just after Google and Facebook. He told the *Financial Times*: "We wanted to create a platform for everyone, a level playing field. We wanted to democratize the video experience."

THE EMERGENCE
OF MICRONETWORKS

So, along the way there were a handful of us who were exposed to a glimpse of the future and weren't able to forget what we saw. One of those people was Rob Barnett. Barnett is honestly the rain man of music. He has an encyclopedic memory for all things pop culture and a genuine and deep-rooted love of talent. He'd already had a dazzling career in rock radio before he arrived at MTV to help the channel build its long-form documentary business. He had been at MTV for four years back in 1993, when his boss, the head of MTV News, Linda Corradina, said, "I want you to meet this guy and produce a pilot for a show that we think could be really great." The idea was *MTV Unfiltered*, and the guy was me.

As Barnett tells the story: "That was the first time that I remember hearing an idea that literally put the brand into the hands of its audience. That's what captured my attention. The idea that you would take the world's arguably most important pop-culture brand and put it physically into the hands of its audience was a revolutionary thought, and one that I hadn't considered until it was introduced to me."

To me, democratization of media was inevitable, and I wanted to be first. Tools were getting cheaper and smaller, and people were going to use them. MTV's audience was young and willing to break the rules, so it only made sense that they'd be the first folks to turn TV upside down and make it rather than watch it. But they wouldn't be the last.

The idea emerged as the technology for content creation was crossing the chasm from highly complex and professional to low cost consumer devices. MTV was also making a conscious decision to put not just people in the driver's seat, but technology too. Barnett produced the pilot for the series and then went on to great things at MTV and VH1. He eventually ended up as the president of programming for CBS Radio.

But the way Barnett tells it, he never entirely forgot that spark that he saw at *Unfiltered*—the idea that content didn't need to be made in big buildings, with layers of executives and endless pages of notes that were demoralizing to talent and didn't make the music or storytelling better. "Anyone in the largest possible job at an old-media company got there originally because they got their minds blown by a rock and roll record, or a movie that they saw or a television program that infected their DNA," he says. "But when someone rises to the top of a major media corporation, the creative gig is constantly attacked by the political realities of managing your manager and the layers of executives that you have to deal with on a daily basis end up taking up most of the time, making it almost impossible to spend the maximum amount of time needed on creativity." After MTV, Barnett had a meteoric career in media, ending up as the president of programming for *CBS Radio*.

Finally, Barnett had had enough. "I opted out because I got tired of being told to sit down and get cut out of some corporate plan that I had absolutely no input in," he says. "One of the most important reasons for me jumping out of a big media gig was to move away from the myriad of layers of management that stand between the artist and the audience."

In 2007 it all came together. The tech, the passion, and glimmer of hope that an independent company had a shot. It's just about impossible to stop working *for* a big media company and build a small media company—a micronetwork, from the ground up. But Barnett was going to try.

Barnett explains, "I've loved working with talented artists for my entire career, and I named the company My Damn Channel to be able to go to people that I loved, trusted, and respected and put them in a position where, for the first time in their artistic lives they had some of the power that Sumner Redstone, Les Moonves, and Jeff Zucker have had." What Barnett was doing was answering the rant all creative people have after a network meddles in their creative process. The find themselves saying, 'I wish I had my own *damn channel.*'" Barnett continues, "I might have been a little early, but I saw the moment coming where they had the ability to distribute as powerfully as Sumner could, and that's what got me really excited."

To make My Damn Channel work, Barnett figured he'd need some amazing talent. The only problem was, he couldn't pay them anywhere near what they made in Hollywood. So he'd offer the one thing he, and the Internet, could: freedom. He headed off to go big-game hunting and set as his first goal the voice of Principal Skinner from *The Simpsons*, the legendary Harry Shearer.

"I met Harry in 1979, and I was a little snot-nosed kid trying to elbow my way into rock and roll radio," Barnett says. "The guy who was mentoring me at the time was the real life character that Dr. Johnny Fever was based on in the show *WKRP in Cincinnati*. This guy's name in rock and roll radio is Steven Clean. Steven and Harry were, in the 1960s and early 1970s, two of the original free-form FM disc jockeys." Radio fans know that back then, in the golden age of rock radio, Steve and Harry were people who could say anything they wanted and play any song they wanted from any genre of music. They would blow people's minds with the sets of music they put together. Barnett needed Shearer for his star power, yes, but he also needed him to believe that Web video could recapture that creative passion.

"I knew that if I could get Harry to understand the vision and business model of My Damn Channel, then I would have one of the smartest comedic minds in the country to help us," Barnett says.

So Barnett reached out to Shearer and said, "I will give you money and 100 percent total artistic freedom, with no notes, to do exactly what you want to do. It took him exactly half of one millisecond to say yes."

Once Shearer accepted the offer, My Damn Channel began to invite talent to join the fun and do work they could be proud of. Here's a short list of who's on Barnett's A-list speed dial: Tom Arnold, Jon Bon Jovi, Coolio, Rob Corddry, David Cross, Andy Dick, Illeana Douglas, Will Forte, Ed Helms, Keanu Reeves, Paul Rudd, David Wain, Don Was, Kristen Wiig, and Fred Willard.

But don't think that Barnett is an old-media wolf in new-media clothing. Far from it. He's hardly about big names—he's just about what he cares about and curates: "I'm one of these guys that really doesn't use the terminologies 'user generated' or 'professional.' I think there's some kind of elitist thing going on in that. We're looking for the best. Often, we find that the best stuff in the new world is made by the same people who made the best stuff in the old world, but we've also found people who previously had absolutely no audience, no track record and somehow these people were able to create content for My Damn Channel that got 20 million views. In the case of the show *You Suck at Photoshop*, these two guys really figured out how to tap the zeitgeist of the moment and blow people's minds with something that was completely original."

BLIP.TV

Barnett's micronet isn't the only one. In fact, he's one of a number of TV execs turned entrepreneur who've decided it's time to build a new curated paradigm for TV distribution. The largest and fastest growing of the micronet distributors is blip.tv. Blip.tv has become the Web's largest home for long-form Web series. Not short clips, real Web video shows. Now, I've got some history with blip.tv.

You see, back in the old days—before the Web, before e-mail, before broadband—there was this president, Bill Clinton. And back then, college students would give up their weekends, evenings— heck, everything—for a shot to work on the Clinton campaign. Dina Kaplan was a young campaign worker, and she had a dream. But she had to settle for her backup dream, which was a job at the White House. She explains, "I had worked at the White House as a backup when my internship at MTV fell through." Okay, read that again. You read it right. MTV was her *first* choice. "[MTV was] the only place I wanted to be, I talked about it nonstop, my family wanted me to say enough with this talk about MTV," she says, "but I absolutely believe that MTV had this huge impact on young people and what they were interested in and passionate about."

So, when Kaplan arrived in my office at MTV—having been hired by the head of news and told to report for work on a new show called *Unfiltered*—well, let's just say we were both a bit suspicious. "At the moment that I heard about *Unfiltered*—and please understand that I grew up in awe of Whitney Houston and Madonna videos—I thought, 'Wow! This is a real cheap way to make television. Interesting!' I'm not sure any of us had any idea of the cultural importance of what we were doing. We all thought no one would call. And we were all huddled together when the number went out on MTV thinking that the lines were going to be dead for months."

Okay, you've figured it out by now, one of the cofounders of blip.tv got her first TV job at *MTV Unfiltered*.

"At the time that the number from *Unfiltered* 'submit your stories' flashed on MTV, we all sat huddled around the phones," Kaplan says. "We were floored at the response. Calls came in immediately. The story ideas that were suggested blew us away. And in fact we learned that the stories that everyday people had were far more interesting and more relevant—in short, better—than what we could come up with as MTV producers."

Back then, Kaplan was an associate producer. Today, she's the COO and a cofounder of her own micronet. But the roots of what is now Web video can be found in those early Hi8 tapes and the toll-free number at 1515 Broadway.

For Kaplan, the early lessons learned at MTV both inspired and haunted her. "The one I can't forget was the suicide story about Shaun," she says. "I can remember these stories as if they were yesterday and I can remember the pieces, and I can remember what the people involved were saying. These stories stuck with you because they were authentic and, that is also what does well with Web video content. What translates in terms of both views and dollars."

So in May 2005 Kaplan and her partners launched blip.tv. This was as early as it gets for Web video.

She recalls the time like it was almost before Web video existed: "There were two series at the time really, and there was one that no one ever heard of called Rocketboom. Another one emerged called Tiki Bar TV, and that was pretty much it. So, we took a bet. We made a gamble and part of that is the blue ocean theory—fish where no one else is fishing. We started at the same time, the same year as YouTube, as Metacafe, as many of the other video sites that people are familiar with, and we saw YouTube emerge, and it became very clear to me that this company or a company like it would do extraordinarily well focusing on series, though maybe not right away."

Blip.tv took the bet that Web video technology would improve and be able to support longer streams. It also bet that lots of creative folks from TV would look to the Web for creative freedom and the ability to attempt to build their own audiences. Of course, in 2005 YouTube was taking off too—but Kaplan and her partners felt that they could stay the course. Their idea was to support the program length market and embrace program creators.

The bet blip.tv made is the same one that Whole Foods made: to find a focus and a mission, and do that one thing very well. To make your customers feel welcome and appreciated when they enter your world. Kaplan's customers were nascent program producers, short-form Web video makers who were aiming to give the future of cable TV a run for their money.

Today blip.tv hosts and delivers 50,000 Web series on its network. But Kaplan says that it isn't the most highly produced shows that connect with the audiences. "We are sitting with a bird's-eye view of 50,000 shows on blip," she says. "What translates is not the most highly produced shows. What translates are stories that are authentic and told in an authentic, honestly in-your-face fashion and the same was true of *Unfiltered*."

Blip.tv has data that shows that Web video consumption is emerging with real revenue. Back in 2009, Web video viewers were snacking on short form segments. The average running time for blip.tv's top 25 shows was just 4 minutes; one year later blip viewers are watching an average of 14-minute-long clips. That's a huge jump, and it starts to look more like folks watching shows than clips. Second, blip.tv's peak viewing time used to be midday, lunchtime, as folks at work used the boss's broadband to munch and watch. But one year later the peaks have moved to what was conventional TV prime time, 8 p.m. to 10 p.m. Folks are watching blip.tv at home rather than watching network or cable TV. Uh oh, here comes Web series to start nibbling into mainstream media attention. And not surprisingly, Kaplan says the advertising revenue she's seeing and the revenue sharing checks she's cutting for producers is ramping up steeply as well.

"We sent a check to one of our shows last month for $123,000, for their share of revenue from just one quarter, Q2," Kaplan says. "That check will go up significantly in Q3. It will go up a lot more in Q4. I would be surprised if we don't make well over half a million dollars for one show produced independently by some guys who live in the south. Okay, half a million dollars for the creator share of a Web video series is serious cash. It might be that micronetworks are ready to step front and center, and take the lead in how content is created, sold, and viewed. That would be cool."

What does all this mean for traditional media companies? Kaplan says there's only one thing for them to do: curate—and quick.

"I absolutely believe that traditional media companies will succeed if they think about themselves as curators and not simply content creators," Kaplan says. "Here's why: on the Web there's a great meritocracy, and so content that does well will take off and attract a lot of viewers and advertising attached to it; therefore, revenue for the producer. And content that isn't good won't do well unless you put a lot of marketing dollars against it, and that's very different than television."

Kaplan thinks that networks will shift away from a hit-driven model and focus on creating verticals with a curated content mix. She explains it this way: "If you're *Glamour*, you can decide to go after high-end, beautiful-looking fashion, even if it takes eight hours to prepare, and you can then bring in videos, photos, and text from anyone and everyone that has content along . . . that fits with your vertical, bring that all into your *Glamour* brand. Also, produce some content, whether it's text articles or blog posts, video shows, photos, et cetera, and bring those all together and try to own that vertical."

So Barnett and Kaplan are living the dream. They're helping the creative people they admire build the roots of a new business model. Which means we'd be crazy not to ask them for some advice.

Kaplan says we can look to the music industry for clues as to what's going to happen to digital media. She says the reduced cost of creation and distribution haven't hurt musicians but instead has hurt the middlemen, distributors, and the record labels.

"There are more musicians than ever who are making a living. However, it's much harder to get really rich. And the institutions behind the music industry with a capital *I* are hurting. It's a great time to be a musician, and it's a great time to be a fan. This is just starting to happen with video and we will all benefit from this."

So for video folks, is there an economic model? Is it finally time for them to quit their day jobs?

Kaplan says not so fast: "We definitely tell people don't quit your day job. To the point with the media companies—you can't bet on hits, we also can't bet on hits, especially when you are starting a new show—should not bet on a hit. So keep a day job . . . I would wait a year until you see what your revenue is and then maybe think about quitting your day job."

So now that Barnett isn't getting "meeting'd" to death or tortured by the claws of corporate bureaucracy, he's ready to share some of his wisdom and give advice to fellow content entrepreneurs. He's developed a set of rules for how he runs his mini empire:

> *Rule 1.* Try to work with the best people we can possibly get in front of the camera and behind the camera.
>
> *Rule 2.* Quality, quality, and quality.
>
> *Rule 3.* Don't try to be a Web site that throws every single video in the world at the audience, but be extremely selective and curate only the best of what you're able to get.

And while big media spends time, money, and effort trying to bar the door and keep out the hoards of network wannabes, Barnett says that the future network creators are all working out of their garages just like Bill Hewlett and Dave Packard did when they founded HP and planted the seeds of what would become Silicon Valley.

"I was talking to DJ Adam Carolla," Barnett says. "Adam is now doing a podcast out of his garage where, on average, 200,000 people are downloading his show on a daily basis. Technically anyone can start a podcast; technically, anyone can start a Web site; technically anyone can be in the NFL. Technically, anyone can win an Oscar. But in the end, it's always going to come down to who's got the best stuff, who's got the content, who's got the quality—and it always comes down to your ability as an individual content creator to break through the noise and find an audience."

Find an audience. Have a voice. And have the guts to put yourself out there. These are heady times for creative and passionate creators and curators.

So entrepreneurs, take a look at Rob Barnett, He isn't on-camera talent. His talent is finding talent and building a system that supports creative talent and makes them feel appreciated and loved.

Barnett says that now's the time to build your dream content business: "Anyone can now light up a company exactly like My Damn Channel, and the only way you can attract artists, audience, advertisers, and other revenue streams is by cutting through with the best content."

It may not be that anyone can build what Barnett has, but for the first time in the history of the entertainment business, the tools to create, curate, and transmit audio and video begin at the entry price that is just slightly north of free. If that isn't an incentive to give it a try, I don't know what is.

13

WHAT IS YOUR CONTENT STRATEGY?

t's rare that you get to meet someone who's actually in-

venting a practice that's changing the world, one Web site at a time.

But with her spiky hair and her disarming Minnesota mid-

western charm, Kristina Halvorson has been giving the Web de-

sign community a pretty swift kick in the ass. So, if you're feeling

a little sore in your hindquarters, you might be able to blame her.

Pointing her finger at Web-consultant colleagues Halvorson

asks, "Who among us is asking the scary, important questions about

content, such as, what's the point? Or who cares? Who's talking

about the time-intensive, complicated, messy content development process? Who's overseeing the care and feeding of content once it's out there, clogging up the tubes and dragging down our search engines?"

Halvorson thinks content is the *most* important thing on the Web, and it's the least cared for. In talking with her, one quickly realizes she's more than a consultant; she's a content evangelist. As she says, "We appear to have collectively, silently come to the conclusion that content is really somebody else's problem—'the client can do it,' 'the users will generate it'—so we, the people who make Web sites, shouldn't have to worry about it in the first place. Do you think it's a coincidence, then, that Web content is, for the most part, crap?"

She may be blunt, but she is also right. Content has, for the most part, been left as an oversight after the technologists have built the platforms, the designers have done the wireframes, and the Flash designers have made everything all so . . . flashy. Content, therefore, is often just an afterthought. It is—to use Halvorson's word—*crap*. Such crap might come in the form of random press releases from corporate communications, dull CEO interviews, and marketing materials dropped into the corporate CMS to masquerade as content.

So, Halvorson created a new discipline: content strategy.

If you want to know what content strategy is, ask Halvorson. She wrote the book on it. Literally: *Content Strategy* is available on Amazon.com.

She explains what CS is in this way: "Content strategy plans for the creation, publication, and governance of useful, usable content. The content strategist must work to define not only which content will be published, but why we're publishing it in the first place. Content strategy is also—surprise—a key deliverable for which the content strategist is responsible. Its development is necessarily preceded by a detailed audit and analysis of existing content—

a critically important process that's often glossed over or even skipped by project teams."

So, where did this come from? How was it that a plan to make, gather, organize, and present content on the Web was essentially an oversight until 2007? Well, it turns out, as long as content was scarce and readers were hungry, visitors were willing to find content with a hunt-and-peck method. And there was Google, after all. But today, and certainly tomorrow, the noise will overwhelm any site that doesn't have a clear, sustainable, coherent content strategy.

Halvorson explains, "As a freelance copywriter, I really loved writing for the Web. I loved the information architecture component, I loved learning about usability, I was fascinated by how people went looking for information and how they used that information once they found it, I loved figuring out what worked and what didn't. And so, I decided I was going to start calling myself just a Web writer. Which everybody thought was a stupid idea because I was pigeonholing myself."

As a Web writer, Halvorson was getting invited into larger and larger projects, but that just meant bigger and bigger train wrecks. At the eleventh hour there would be brainstorming on a white board, and all the various clients in the company would bring in their "content" in a virtual shoe box and toss it to the information architect. And then it would get slotted in the site. No one was thinking about the strategy of what content should be on the site and what purpose it served.

Until the emergence of content strategy in 2007 with the publication of Rachel Lovinger's article "Content Strategy: The Philosophy of Data," content was the thing that got left to fill the hole that Web designers, information architects, and content-management systems thought of last. Content was easy; Web design was hard. In the article, Lovinger writes about "how content is getting done, the work flow, how it's being cared for and measured, and the standards by which it's being judged. Nobody has been really responsible for that, or wanted to be responsible for it."

No one was responsible, it turns out, because content is a subjective judgment. Who gets their content on the home page? The CEO? The marketing department? Public relations? What about user-generated comments or tweets or photos or even industry content that's aggregated from across the Web? These aren't easy decisions.

"People see content as this magical thing," Halvorson says. "They just tell people, 'We're going to have the users generate the content for our site' or 'We already have all this content that's been generated by marketing, and we'll just get it online.' That's all just lies that we tell ourselves because we don't want to look really closely at the complexity of the situation."

In the end, as with so many things, it just comes down to guilt. "So the guilt factor is 'Oh my god, everybody else knows how to create this amazing content on a regular basis that I don't, and I don't have the time or inspiration,'" Halvorson says.

But fear not, content strategy doesn't mean making more content. In fact, Halvorson says, perhaps we should be making less. Her theory is best demonstrated by a cupcake analogy: Halvorson says that content, like cupcakes, comes in all kinds of flavors. For the baker who is not necessarily a great writer but who needs to promote her cupcakes, maybe blogging isn't the best format. Maybe it would be easier to take pictures with a digital camera and post a cupcake a day online. Halvorson says content needs to fit your site and your brand. It shouldn't be painful. "There are just so many different options beyond this really high, intensely laboring tense way of getting good stuff on your site, and it makes me crazy," she says.

Just to be clear, if you're building your own site from scratch, in your garage, you probably don't need to hire Halvorson or one of a growing number of folks who are now practicing content strategy. But if you're a corporation or a brand or a large site and you've got content coming at you from marketing, sales, research, the CEO's office, the PR department, as well as vendors and now your customers—well then, figuring out how to prioritize, organize, and present that material in a way that meets your visitors' expectations and needs is no simple feat. In fact, you may need what Halvorson calls content governance.

Now content strategy is moving to brands, and folks like Erin Scime are helping brands navigate the new fast-moving world of Web content. As she puts it, "The constant strategist as a digital curator can help a site develop a personality and make sure that you know they're connecting with their audience, they're extracting ideas from their audience, and they're driving the brand forward. They're the center of the keystone to all content on the site."

Scime says the first thing a content strategist has to do is take inventory of what clients have to work with. It's important to look at competitors to see where they are playing in this content space. The next step is coming up with of a grand vision of what the site and the product is going to be going forward. After that's locked down, then there are two ways of interacting with a client:

1. The content strategist can step in and fill the lead editorial role as the content assets are evaluated and the content plan is put in place. Then once the client hires a full-time editorial resource, the strategist can hand over the editorial role and strategy.

2. Alternatively, if there's an editorial team in place, they may have great ideas. Then the strategist can help create

workflow and templates to organize and deploy an editorial strategy. Here the content strategist's role is more of a facilitator. He or she works with the client to determine what the priorities are, where the focus is, what the client wants to accomplish, and what can be accomplished six months down after postlaunch.

From Scime's perspective, a content strategist can become a digital curator, in particular by creating governance rules around submission and publishing. It's all about establishing standards for user-gen. "The content-strategist-as-curator must balance user-generated content with editorial content," Scime says. "This means balancing the great work writers, art directors, and editors produce with the best user-generated content and activity—the 'best' means the content that's most useful and supports your thesis and brand."

How can content strategists create a curation mix that includes users? Well, the first thing is to look at the taxonomy of the client's site and structure user-generated submissions around existing content categories. The contributions that users add to the client's site should align with the client's topic areas. Why? Creating structure for conversation and contribution gives users clear opportunities for participation and creates a coherent experience for visitors.

And finally, user-generated material is, just like any other material, another publisher in the content workflow—nothing less, nothing more. As Scime says, "Think of your users as 'free' freelancers who provide and catalog unique content on a minute-by-minute basis. This gives you better content that you can repurpose editorially or feature with minimal reworking." It is important to give user-generated material the framework to succeed. Scime explains, "User-generated content still needs to be checked, edited, and managed differently from editorial content. User-generated content is not exactly perfect—but there is a payoff. For the digital curator, well-structured user-generated content upfront means reaping material that meets metadata and quality standards."

EVERYONE'S A PUBLISHER

So, just how prevalent is this gig? Is "content strategist" going to be on the Forbes list of fast-moving jobs? Maybe so. Content strategist Jeffry MacIntyre says that today everyone's a publisher: "If you are putting content onto the Web, there is an expectation that the content must reflect your organization, your brand. And in the world of the real-time Web, in particular, if your homepage has not been updated in the last week, month, quarter—depending on the type of organization you have—users find that flaw. That is now considered a bit of what we call 'rot,'—or redundant, outdated or trivial content—because, again, you're expected to reflect your activities as an organization on the Web, particularly on your Web presence."

And so, if the future of content requires a strategy, the question is, whose rules apply? There's no consensus among thought leaders.

Erin Scime, of HUGE design, starts from her background in library sciences. "I obviously come from free content," she says. "Free access to content coming from libraries. But I know that there is the argument the press have about the stealing all of the articles from the *New York Times*. Their situation is that they gave away their content for free initially. Now they don't have any online subscription model that is working, On top of that, people are linking to them and they're not getting the ad revenue." But Scime says that linking to content provides value to both the content owner and the link distributor.

Halvorson nails it as she lays out the various stakeholders in content strategy. "Because everything that content strategy talks about touches so many different areas and functions of an organization," she says. "It touches IT, marketing, public relations, subject matter expertise, and content creation; it touches the Web team, the relationships you have with your external agencies; it touches legal, so you have to engage all of those people."

The trick is to mediate the needs of this diverse group of stakeholders. These content microcosms all need to be managed under a central set of rules or governance. Organizations are starting to understand that content is a shared responsibility and a team sport.

"The deeper they get into strategically considering their content, the more they're going to realize how complex the effort is," Halvorson says. "Content is going to require reallocation of resources and new definitions around what governance means to them to be able to really do it effectively."

What is clear is this: curation is definitely an element of content strategy. For some clients it's a central focus; for others it's a bit of a sidebar. But considering and setting in place a curation mix is critically essential, whether you're a big brand or a start-up cupcake company. Insert bakery metaphor here—it's all about the mix.

There is, of course, for clients of big-time content strategists like Scime, the other lurking emotion: fear. If the rules aren't yet carved in stone, what if we make a mistake? *Gasp!* "That's the scariest part for our clients because legal red flags go up," Scime says. "We have to have heavy moderation or outsource moderation. For example, one of my clients had a very large discussion board community, and that was the root of their brand. What we did was try to construct their taxonomy so that it matched what the people were talking about. Then editorial content was also structured in the same way as the discussion boards."

Scime says properly moderated and organized discussion boards can help shape editorial, even using the user conversation to get to honest, unvarnished customer research.

CONTENT CONSUMERS

The Web is about content. And any brand, site, or community that doesn't think of its visitors and content consumers is going to miss a critical understanding of the major shift now underway. The volume of content on the Web is rising rapidly, and visitors are coming to each site and asking just one simple question: "Are you a content source I can trust?" If the answer is yes, they'll be back to read, contribute, and purchase. If the answer is no, it'll be the last stop on their Web checklist, a place that may offer information but that doesn't do so in a way that is clear, accessible, and fresh.

Embracing and enhancing your content mix and thinking about your content as a critical resource to attract and retain visitors and customers is going to be a litmus test of who emerges as leaders and who fades in the background as the real-time, always-on Web presents itself as your front door to the world. Content strategists like Halvorson, MacIntyre, and Scime are quickly going to find themselves in great demand as companies with no internal sense of content curation find that it's become a front-burner issue.

The one thing that Halvorson cautions is this: don't believe the hype about social media solving the content equation for brands. In her mind that's a dangerously simplistic worldview that the social media gurus are preaching. In the end, free consumer-created content is valuable, but it can't be counted on, scheduled, or expected to arrive with any regularity or consistency. After all, social media content is being created for free, by unpaid volunteers. The simple fact is that you can't reliably expect them to do anything. They'll do what they want.

"You can't just let people loose creating content on social media without having some level of governance that you ensure is consistent with what's being said elsewhere," Halvorson cautions. "The pundits make it out to be the corporation's fault: 'You have to find your passionate employees, let them blog!' But just because that works for Dell does not mean that it's going to work for 3M or General Mills." Halvorson isn't against user-generated content; she simply rejects the idea that it replaces content created by professionals to meet communications objectives. "It just makes me insane . . . what they're saying is, then, 'Don't worry about the wild wild west component, don't worry about the governance, because the lawyers are just going to get in your way. Just run with it.'"

There's no right answer here. Certainly social media is the new hip thing, and good old-fashioned copywriting and content creation isn't as cool. Halvorson says that companies are committing content malpractice if they turn over their sites to social media sources entirely though: "It just makes me crazy that the social media advocates have the attitude of 'Do this or you will be left in the dust.' Because you know what? It's a lot better not to do it at all than to do it sort of recklessly and as a knee-jerk reaction."

Content isn't the stuff you use to fill up your wonderfully designed Web site. It's the voice, the message, the meaning that your customers come to engage in. Content curation centered on a clear set of content policies, with orderly governance, means using all your enterprise's resources in a holistic way. Your sources, your mix, your community all are powerful tools. Content strategists can be the ringmaster in your three-ring content circus. It's all about knowing when to send in the clowns.

14

FACEBOOKING
THE FUTURE
AND TRENDING
TOWARD
TWITTER

Plenty has been said about the emergence of professional curation as an occupation. The pioneers in this new field are content hunters and gatherers who are increasingly scouring the Web for contextual content to publish and amplify.

But curation is a trend that's rapidly on the rise for more than just professionals. Chances are, you're already a curator and you may not even know it. New mobile applications, sites, and consumer-driven content discovery are feeding the emergence of what could be called the accidental curator.

ACCIDENTAL CURATION

We're becoming a Curation Nation, a place where abundance is assumed in the world of content. There's no shortage of content makers of all shapes and sizes. But the avalanche of content makes finding the content you're looking for significantly harder. Accidental curation is passive, anonymous endorsement. It's curation for the crowds. Share your location? Share your favorite bar or restaurant? Share your credit card statement? Share your stock trades? Are you ready to share your naked data with the world?

The chances are—with Facebook, LinkedIn, Twitter, and blog posts—you are already an accidental curator and just don't know it.

FACEBOOK

Here's a personal example. My younger son decided a few months back that he wanted to learn to play the trumpet. I was tasked with finding a trumpet teacher. So, I did what we all do: used a search engine. I found a number of names in my city, and then I was stuck trying to find out which one would be the best fit with my son. A list of names, and no way to know which of the many trumpet tutors were skilled and well liked.

I did something I'd never done before and put a number of names into Facebook. Sure enough, one of them was a friend of a friend of mine. I reached out to my friend: "How do you know him? Is he good with kids? Would you recommend him?" What came back was a glowing recommendation for a great guy. I was sold. As you might expect, he ended up being a great fit and teaches my son to this day.

What happened there? Is my friend a trumpet expert? Clearly not, nor did he "friend" the trumpet tutor expecting to become a recommender. Yet there he is, the accidental curator, helping me sift through a list of choices to find the right one. Social media as a curation mechanism is both accidental and purposeful. Facebook's Like button, both on and off the Facebook site, is quickly becoming a powerful tool for both recommendation and profile building. Each click of the Like button is both an endorsement and a statement of your preferences and interests.

We're witnessing the beginning of Facebook's Open Graph, a piece of technology that allows Web sites to embed a Like button on pages that don't have a direct business relationship with Facebook. The apparel brand Diesel has created what appears to be the first Like button in a dressing room. Diesel stores now have a Diesel Cam, where fashion-conscious buyers can try on jeans and then instantly take and upload photos to Facebook. Diesel calls it "The first 'mirror on the wall' that works in social networks." The question is, do your friends "like" you in those skinny jeans? It's the power of what blogger Jay Baer calls "friend-curated information" that could be the next big shift as curation takes hold in social media. "Instead of you having to go to Facebook to see what your friends are up to and what they think, that information can be exported and embedded so that it becomes omnipresent," he says. You can see the Diesel demo video here: http://bit.ly/CurationNation4.

Just what does the future of a Web-wide Like button mean? Well, first of all, it gives presentation software like Flipboard—what tech blogger Robert Scoble calls a paginator—a powerful source of data to help sort content from your friends. It's as simple as this. No longer do you have to grab a line, bring it to your Facebook page, and share the link. You simple click "Like" on any piece of content, blog post, photo, or brand or e-commerce offering. That expression of your support is now linked to your profile and shared with your friends. From a content consumer's perspective, it allows them to view aggregated recommendations of all their friends within their social graph. For a look at what that might look like, start here: http://likebutton.me/.

Social media is both the source of much of the increased volume of data and increasingly the tools to empower curation, both accidental and purposeful. Simply put, we're each making more data and recommending more things. The data we make comes from our posts, pictures, location data, and recommendations; the data we curate comes from what we link to, recommend, and endorse.

"Social media curators direct the audience toward important information, provide context and commentary, authenticating claims, and indexing information," says Jamie Beckland, who describes himself as an "emerging media strategist and digital roustabout." "The only difference is that the process happens much more quickly now."

Now that you're thinking about your actions as endorsements, the number of emerging applications that capture and aggregate your behavior starts to make it clear that you're putting data into curation patterns whether you want to or not. The world of curation will have lots of brand-name, well-known curators you know and trust. The new media moguls won't be makers; they'll be finders, endorsers, and presenters. But you'll be a curator too. You'll find that you're endorsing products, places, and people in both public opt-in forums and in a crowd-sourced anonymous data-driven, click-stream stew.

Here's a way to think about it: have you ever had a great meal and posted about the occasion to Yelp? What about getting slimed by a hotel on a vacation and ranting on Trip Advisor? If you've added either positive or negative data to the Web about a book, a movie, a restaurant, or an airline, then you've added your curatorial two cents to the wisdom of the Web. For lots of folks, adding this data is a rare experience. It will take an experience that is either exceptionally great or terrible for you to add your vote.

But there are other, less-purposeful ways that you're already an accidental curator. If you tag a photograph in Facebook with any of your friends' names, you're building their collection of photographs and their Web reputations. If you post photographs on Flickr, allow sharing, and include a location or keyword, you're building a public database of images that helps the world see more clearly.

In fact, any time you provide an implicit endorsement to a person, place, or thing, you're building not only that place's digital identity but your own. In a manner of speaking, you are what you tweet. The trend of wearing Nike logos and other symbols of your tribe on your clothing has now entered the digital realm.

It all comes down to the role of humans in your trusted relationships. Jeff Jarvis says the difference between aggregation and curation is prioritization. "The power of the human link is gigantic and could well challenge the size of Google and search," says Jarvis, who authored the book *What Would Google Do?* "Eric Schmidt [the CEO of Google] tells publishers that Google causes four billion clicks per month to publisher sites, one billion of which comes from Google News. [In May 2010], Bit.ly surpassed four billion clicks a month. And not all that is publishers and news. A lot of that is cat videos, but it shows only a portion of Twitter, and Twitter is only a fraction of the size of Facebook, and Twitter alone has a lot of human links, which is a form of curation, so that becomes a factor in the ecosystem of discovery of content."

Jarvis's point is that Bit.ly, the link shortener, is driving essentially as many clicks to publishers as Google. Bit.ly is primarily a source within the Twitter ecosystem, where people you know and follow provide you with curated links. If this data is to be believed, Twitter is delivering as much traffic as Google, and Twitter is on the rise.

And in real-world terms, the results of this human-centric alternative to searching can be dramatic. As blogger Dan McCarthy explains, "An underlying premise of social networking is the authenticity and credibility of your social graph. When people who you have networked with digitally recommend information, experience, or products, you are likely to lend their recommendations more credibility than someone you don't know. Facebook and Twitter make this kind of socially curated content sharing incredibly convenient to do."

Google News has about 63 million visits a month, but commands just 1.39 percent of upstream clicks to news and media according to Hitwise. Facebook has 2.7 billion visits—and it's members socialize more than 3.5 million pieces of content—Web links, news stories, blog posts, each week. As a result, 3.52 percent of all upstream clicks come from Facebook. The data seems to point to the fact that people are filtering content, and are looking for content filtered by the members of their social graph.

FOURSQUARE

The urban game of human bingo known as Foursquare is the red-hot center of accidental curation. Less than two years old, the New York start-up Foursquare became "the thing" at the 2009 South By Southwest Internet Conference. Part game, part social tool, and part low-profile advertising engine, Foursquare is a mix of media, community, and commerce. It's a location-based game that allows mobile phone users to check in at locations like restaurants, bars, workplaces, and other public spaces. Users earn points and badges as they alert friends to their current location. The goal of the game: to get the most points at a location, so that you can become the "mayor" of your favorite bar or restaurant until someone else checks in even more times than you have. It's kind of like the Amazing Digital Race.

The result of this change in consumer curation is a shift that puts power back in the hands of the people and no longer allows products or brands to ignore unhappy customers. Each time you log a return visit to an establishment on Foursquare, you're registering a de facto vote in favor of the business's goods or service—an endorsement. Chances are you're not checking in at a restaurant that served you undercooked chicken last week. So establishments with the highest ratio of return visits by the same person are being collectively curated as well liked. Subtle shifts for a national chain or brand will surface quickly, in the form of declining return visits on Foursquare. Other unhappy customers will vote with their feet or their wallets.

Here's just one example of how Foursquare's mix of location and endorsement is changing both commerce and community. Harvard University, where Facebook was born, made the decision to be the first university in the nation to embrace Foursquare, giving students the tools to explore the campus and surrounding businesses. The program allows students to create an up-to-date online rating guide of stores, restaurants, and businesses around Harvard Square. The importance of embracing location-based ratings and curation in the Foursquare game format is that it gives students a way to both explore and share a newly discovered college community and provides an easy way for the students to contribute and crowd-curated experiences.

"Harvard is more than classrooms and buildings. It is an interconnected community of people, ideas, and experiences, and we are actively pursuing ways to enhance those connections," said Perry Hewitt, director of digital communications and communications services for Harvard Public Affairs and Communications. "We believe that Harvard's participation [in Foursquare] will allow our community to engage with friends, professors, and colleagues in new ways. We also hope visitors and neighbors will benefit from the platform as it grows through use."

Foursquare turns social networking into a game, creating digital badges as incentives for students to explore neighborhoods, discover new venues, and make recommendations to the Harvard community. Social networking sites, such as Facebook and Twitter, can be used to share information generated from Foursquare.

And of course, Foursquare isn't alone in the race to own and engage in the future of location-based curation/recommendations.

In the summer of 2010, Facebook added a "where" to the who, what, and when questions that have powered extraordinary growth for the service. Facebook Places lets you tell your friends where you are, in real time, using the Facebook app on your mobile device. The "checking in" behavior that fueled the growth of sites like Foursquare and Gowalla may become just another feature on Facebook, or they may remain stand-alone. User behavior is hard to predict, but one thing is sure: *checking in* isn't going away.

THE RISE OF TWITTER

Twitter was born on July 15, 2006, when a handful of managers from a podcasting company began to test a SMS group-messaging service that would allow broadcasts of short messages to a defined group of friends. It's fair to say these managers probably didn't have a big idea that would transform communications and media. But innovation often happens that way. What software architect

Jack Dorsey said about the title of this venture was that they came across the word *twitter* whose definition was "a short burst of inconsequential information," and "chirps from birds," and it was perfect. Twitter was a work in progress until it found itself in a place with a large number of digitally connected, data-hungry early adopters.

Twitter had been growing slowly, populated mostly by relatively trivial information about people's daily doings. Then at the 2007 South By Southwest conference, Twitter exploded, tripling traffic from 20,000 tweets a day to 60,000. It was the hit of the event, in large part because it solved an immediate problem at the event itself. Attendees at the large and noisy conference were looking for information in real time. They wanted to know what panels were interesting, where the good parties were, and what was hip and happening now. Twitter came to the rescue, created an instant phenomenon, and put tremendous strain on the AT&T network that was powering wireless connectivity for the mostly iPhone-toting crowd. The 140-character revolution was born. What Twitter was able to plug in to was the massive growth of Web-connected devices and the stunning lack of real-time information or broadcasting tools. As technology history has now been written, Twitter ushered in the era of the real-time Web, but it did far more than that.

In a flash, two things happened that forever changed the world of digital information. First, Twitter put power in the hands of the content consumer. Receivers could subscribe and unsubscribe to sources at will. These sources include anyone with a Twitter account—individuals, brands, or news organizations. It is a level playing field for brief real-time publishing. This behavior, known as following, gave content consumers never-known-before power to opt in and out of sources. It also put new pressure on old-media content makers to consider the needs and appetites of their audiences. In old-world TV, networks were famous for saying "If you don't like what we have on, just turn the channel." But in the new Twitter world, turning the channel would mean "Stop following me." As the signal-to-noise ratio increased, no content maker wanted to invite its audience to unfollow it. The result of losing a listener is terminal. Lose too many and you're simply no longer significant.

The second change was even more world-changing. Anyone could become a broadcaster, and, given the viral nature of sharing, there was for the first time a real opportunity for new voices to catch fire and build a new audience. The bite-size nature of tweets and the "push" technology allowed new content creator candidates to become habit-forming, without asking readers to have to remember to check in to a blog or add a feed to an RSS feed.

But perhaps the most significant thing Twitter did was legitimize the practice of curation as a meaningful and important practice. Within the Twitter world, a retweet is the act of a broadcaster simply sharing a link or another member's post with proper attribution. This amplifying of information, often without any editorial comment or additional remarks, validated the action of recommending links and other members to your followers. Retweeting is curating.

Initially Twitter prompted users to share information with the question "What are you doing?" Eventually, though, Twitter began to encourage a shift toward more sharing of news and links. The company emphasized its news-and-information network strategy in November 2009 by changing the generic question asked of users in the space where they wrote their tweets from "What are you doing?" to "What's happening?" The result, as media publishers and mainstream celebs began to use the service, was that growth continued at a super-linear rate. The number of unique visitors using Twitter grew from 40 million in May of 2009 to over 80 million in May 2010.

For Tim O'Reilly, the founder and CEO of O'Reilly Media and a coauthor of *The Twitter Book*, it's all about emerging new forms of distribution. "What's so interesting about Twitter," O'Reilly says, "is that it reflects all the many, many use cases, including spreading misinformation as well as being the first alert of new information." No longer is a source trusted because it has the power or money to access the publishing ecosystems of TV, radio, or print. Anyone can use Twitter—there's no barrier to entry.

"I know people like me who are using it as a way of sharing my thought processes—what I'm learning, what I'm reading, what I'm caring about. I'm using it as a publishing medium really," O'Reilly says. "And I've described my own work with Twitter as being the most minimal newspaper. A publisher pays attention to a community, whether it's a community of authors or a community of newsmakers. And they then curate it. They decide what's important. And then they share that with their community of readers."

What Twitter did was dramatically increase the number of people who were making microcontent and publishing it, therefore increasing the amount of unfiltered data (noise). It also created a brand-new way for publishers to add value without adding any original content. So curators can now find, filter, and publish pointers (retweets) and tweets that followers use to find useful content.

In many ways Twitter is the first medium created entirely for curators and micropublishers. The nature of short bursts of information lends itself to links and thoughts rather than demanding the time and effort of long-form editorial content creation.

While lots of people can claim they saw it coming, only Jeff Pulver can talk about the history of Twitter as it impacted him as a nine-year-old boy back in 1972.

"If you can imagine somebody who's nine years old today spending three-and-a-half years studying Morse code, and the rules and regulations of the amateur radio operator, that's dedication," says Pulver, who now chairs the fast-growing and influential 140 Conference for Twitter users. And so, at 12 years old, he had the treasured ham radio license and the federal approval to broadcast to the world, to connect, to communicate.

"I grew up with a license to communicate and the ability to, and I started to connect to people randomly around the world but there was always this underlying theme of connecting people with people and to be able to just have a conversation," Pulver says. "And this continued until . . . my early twenties and there were times, not every week, but there were times when I used to be on the radio 40 or 60 hours a week and go to school. And that's what my life was and it was just part of who I was. And I think I learned a lot about maybe everything I ever needed to know about social media by the time I was 15 or 16 based on my own experiences as a ham operator just connecting and communicating with people."

As Pulver describes it, the real-time Web and Twitter are just the natural evolution of the connections he began to see as a child: "I see the future because I feel and see things that other people just don't. I feel and I see things that are just literally in front of me, not necessarily in front of anybody else. It's been like that forever."

From ham radio, Pulver saw the early day of voice-as-software and was able to help shape and grow the Voice over Internet Protocol movement (VoIP), the shift from old-fashioned landlines to the often-free calls you can now make on Skype. He built a series of companies, including Vonage, and time and time again knew how to bet early and get out when the time was right. So when Pulver saw Twitter, he knew there was a need for a community, a conference, and a brand name: the 140 Conference (since 140 characters is the maximum you can use in a Twitter message).

For Pulver the power of humans to connect to other humans began back in his earliest days as a ham radio operator. In amateur radio lingo it's about being a repeater. A repeater is a piece of equipment that takes someone's voice and retransmits it so that it can be heard by other people outside of the person's local listening audience. In many ways, a retweet is a human repeater.

The idea that Twitter is a platform of human "repeaters" is hard to ignore. The Web is not a network of terminals; it is a network of humans, with technology as the facilitator, but not providing any value or data of its own. In fact, the power of humans to curate and broadcast will likely be one of the greatest impacts of Twitter on the Web. As Pulver explains, "One of the serendipitous and randomness effects of Twitter on society is the fact that people's voices are no longer repressed. The fact that there is a platform that if you say something and I say something and someone else says something then there is a layering effect and all of the sudden while individual voices may be muted when everyone is saying the same thing, stuff rises to the top."

How powerful is a retweet from someone like Jeff Jarvis? Well, just consider that he's followed by legions of other Twitter members, thousands of whom hang on his every word. That's a powerful broadcast platform for anyone with a computer and a free Twitter account.

"In terms of retweets there are lots of different ways or reasons why someone might retransmit some else's voice," Jarvis says. "They may be trying to build awareness for a charity or for a cause, there may be an emergency, someone might be engaging in self-promotion, someone might have written a really interesting blog post, had a great photo, had an experience, an observation. It really doesn't matter."

Pulver says you have to respect your followers. You have power by virtue of the fact that people trust you, and if you betray that trust with links or retweets that aren't well curated, then you'll lose your followers and your power to drive audience. "It's a very interesting world we're living in, one where you can discover information about someone's something at a moment's notice and it could affect your mood and get you to actually effect change," he says. "I've donated money because of tweets I've seen, I've helped others out I never would've known about."

So, to recap: ham radio led to Voice over IP, which led to Twitter. In each case, communication innovation was driven by the power of human connections. As the technology became less complex and more widely distributed, the number of repeaters continued to grow. Which is why the power of the *NOW* Web— the real-time Web—is so critically important. We've arrived at a moment where large sections of a community are connected and transmitting almost all the time.

MAGNIFY.NET

Now, I don't claim to have the X-ray vision to see the future that Pulver has, but in my own way I've been seeing and sketching this future since the days of OurTown TV in 1983 in Saratoga Springs, New York. OurTown was my first company, started just days after I graduated from Skidmore College. It was a local, almost real-time, community-based TV program. A local newsmagazine of community happenings and events, cablecast five days a week. Back then, it was clear to me that content creation was going to shift from the hands of specialists to the hands of storytellers. From scarcity to ubiquity. Anyone with a story would have the tools and the bandwidth to put it out into the content cloud. This would solve one problem and create a new one: no longer would public speech be limited to those who could afford a TV broadcast antenna or a printing press. The sheer increase in content made every moment would create an urgent need for both alpha organizers (curators) and curation tools.

My first attempt to share this vision was hardly encouraging. I traveled up and down the infamous Sand Hill Road of Silicon Valley with a PowerPoint under my arm. I was out raising money for a curation solution, a technology-enabled human-powered series of filters. Quickly, the best and the brightest in Valley venture funds reviewed the idea and found it out of sync with the future. *Curation* was a bad word because it suggested humans, and the Valley isn't about humans; it's about using microprocessors and heavy iron to replace human behaviors with content-publishing robots. I suggested then, with little success, that content wasn't well suited to be automated, because there was an element of esthetic choice that required a set of subjective choices. The year was 2006, and YouTube was just getting off the ground. Blogs were little more than a hobby, and Google was building a massive business by indexing the Web and providing an essential and elegant search experience.

So, I took my quest back East, where humans are highly valued for their ability to embrace and even enhance randomness and subjectivity. Magnify.net was born when I pitched the idea to New York's leading angel investor, David S. Rose, saying, "Web video isn't about storage and delivery, it's about curating and giving an emerging class of publisher/curators powerful new tools." Rose said simply, "I get it." He did—and still does.

Magnify is a megaphone. It is software that helps humans find and organize the content equivalent of needles in haystacks. It is a turbocharged search engine that powers the Web site of the Big Apple Circus so that its digital team can find, sort, and publish circus videos without the pain or cost of having to make all the video that they share.

I confess, in the early days this wasn't an easy to idea to sell. Content creators would say, "You mean, I can just post other people's video on my site? Isn't that stealing?" I've answered this question a million times.

Here's how I answer it. Let's say you make a video about something you're passionate about. A song you've written. A house you want to sell. A business you're promoting. A way to prune your rosebush. Then you put it up on the Web. Why? Because you want people to share it. So, they do. They find it, link to it, embed it, promote it. They pay you with *attention*. And you have a fair deal. The only folks who complained about sharing were folks who were being paid in cash (not attention) back when content was scarce. But those days are gone, and cash is no longer king. Content is no longer king. Curation is king. And having a curator see your video and decide to value it with attention means that you are being paid in the economy of the new Web content world.

Once you see where all this is going, the number of publishers who need a coherent solution to find, sort, and publish video is massive. Magnify.net began with an idea that finding, sharing, and presenting video didn't need to be hard anymore. And we gave away the service for free for almost two years. Then, as we began to grow and add more complex tools, we added a pro and an enterprise version. And we added a "freemium" solution, so you could start at free and then grow into pro. Today we've got more than 83,000 channels on the platform. And amazing choices of channels for the arts, music, theater, computer, and created-by-content curators around the world.

There's a sweet pleasure in being able to look back on those meetings on Sand Hill Road and know that I was right and they were wrong. Computers will win in data processing and e-commerce and lots of things. But for content creation and content curation, humans will win. It will be a man-and-machine partnership for sure. Magnify makes it possible for channel creators to be alerted whenever a video appears on the Web that could be appropriate for your site. But once you're alerted, the next step is up to you: publish or delete, curate for the right fit—that's a human job.

FLIPBOARD

So how do these things all come together from overwhelming sources without any filtering or qualification, to useful, organized, trusted content from new emerging sources? Blogger Robert Scoble, who often breaks news on the Web, was the first to report on a new piece of software for the iPad that brings together links and pages in a whole new way. The next phase in the evolution of the real-time Web: after curation comes presentation. And for a glimpse into the future, Scoble discovered Flipboard. "When I first saw Flipboard, I thought this showed me Twitter and Facebook in a way that I hadn't seen it before. I don't know if I said it was curation at first, I just said it was beautiful," he says.

Flipboard is an aggregator of curated content. What it does is take all your trusted sources—folks you follow on Twitter, friends on Facebook, sources you trust—and brings them together in a format that is beautiful to look at and easy to scan. So when Scoble says Flipboard is sea change in how content is displayed, people take notice. (You can see Scoble's demo of Flipboard here: http://bit.ly/Curate11.) Scoble calls it "repagination," comparing the "curated" Flipboard with the "chaotic" Tweetdeck. "Tweetdeck has columns of stuff, there's a hundred items on my screen right now, and each has equal weight," he says. "You look at that and you're confused. Your pattern recognizer is struggling to see a pattern in that noise, so you have to look closely and pay attention, and it's hard. It's draining. My brain has to work harder to see a pattern in this."

For every person who's scanned pages of links and with a massive inbox full of e-mail, Scoble extols the virtue of the layout of the daily newspaper. Newspapers evolved for a reason, he says. People like a page with big pictures and small ones, big headlines and small ones. There's a pattern in the page, a way to scan for information that is made more pleasurable when a page is presented in a way that can be browsed without being overwhelmed.

The power of new aggregator/curator presentation software and devices like the iPad is that they put together the noisy data feed that is our world and begin to make sense of the overwhelming amount of information at our disposal. "Underneath, Twitter is just a pipe for information and Flipboard is a paginator, a displayer of that information and a filter as well," Scoble says. "Everything that gets onto that Twitter list doesn't show up in Flipboard. Flipboard's doing some filtering and trying to do what algorithms do well. This article got a lot of retweets, let's display that instead of the one where some politicians talk about lunch."

THE NEED FOR HUMAN FILTERS

Often the people who are paying attention to Web trends can be divided into two camps, like left- and right-brained people. The people who write code and think in math, and the people who write poetry and think in pictures. Of all the people I know who can spot trends on the Web and develop a picture that encompasses both the social and the technical changes, there's no one smarter than Esther Dyson. Dyson has lived in both worlds, starting life as a journalist at *Forbes*, where she was a fact checker after graduating from Harvard with a degree in economics. Since then, her life has been an eclectic mix of exploration, early-stage investments, and technology. So when one of the world's best-known technologists says the future is about humans—well, that's worth noting.

When I first met her, she was already something of a curator, although she probably didn't use that word back in 2004. What she did was bring together a remarkable mix of speakers, guests, and attendees at what was perhaps the most groundbreaking technology conference of its time: PC Forum. Now Dyson is focused, mostly, on two areas of interest: space exploration and in the related fields of health care and genetics. But she remains one of the most thoughtful participants in the emerging social Web.

"There will be so much content that people will need it filtered: by topic, by whether their friends liked it, by popularity," Dyson says. She is seeing the innovation shifting from searching to filtering: "Overall, there will be some recognition that filtering by humans—they used to be called editors—can be a useful function.

"Journalists, the best of the best, will be recognized because they do more than filter content," Dyson explains. Journalists "actually transform it into meaning—will leave their institutions and become brands themselves."

I wondered if she was willing to go out on a limb and say that search, as we know it, will either need to evolve or be overtaken.

She says that topics are easy for computers to detect. Quality is much harder. Artificial intelligence should be able to evaluate context and quality, but that's still very much theory. Being able to distinguish between a genuinely new idea or approach and the same old thing is a skill that is likely to be uniquely human for some time into the future.

As Dyson sees it, more people will create data, which she calls stuff. And the more *stuff* there is, the more there needs to be human filters. As an example, she has added to her peripatetic travel schedule the practice of photographing and publishing images of hotel swimming pools. It is both a hobby and a service. "I'm a content creator," she says. "On Flickr, I create the content, I put in the data and I think I provide a valuable service." If you're a fellow traveler and swimmer, you appreciate the service she's providing.

Looking toward the future of search, Dyson says that people do it with an intention. And she repeats what Bill Gates told her at a private dinner: "Bill Gates uttered one of the smartest things he has ever said: 'The future of search is verbs.'"

As Dyson explains, when people search, they aren't looking for nouns or information; they are looking for action. Whether they want to book a flight, reserve a table, buy a product, cure a hangover, take a class, or fix a leak—they want to find something in order to *do* something.

"A lot of the social Web is or will be directed toward helping people select things for other people, because the automated search engines get the topic but not the meaning," Dyson says.

We're entering a world where curation will be the critical differentiating factor in purchases, preferences, and identity. Curation, whether accidental or intentional, is rapidly becoming the future of media, commerce, and community.

15

ARE CONTENT AGGREGATORS VAMPIRES?

kay, let's get this part out in the open: creators don't like coloring inside the lines. They're fueled by a passion to make original work. But there's a reason why painters don't rent a storefront, hire a staff clad in black clothing, and throw endless cocktail parties with white wine and fancy hors d'oeuvres. That's called a gallery, and a gallery owner is a curator. These are the people who enjoy the process of choosing what to hang, how to price it, and how to keep painters with enough income to pay the rent and buy more paint and canvas. Hopefully.

The Web doesn't work that way. At least not yet. The folks who run the online galleries, the curators, aren't asking permission or giving a revenue share. Which means that content creators need to get comfortable with the idea that in the new world of the link economy curating and creating aren't mutually exclusive. Exhibit A: Seth Godin. He is one of the best-known marketing wizards in the world. He's a speaker, author, Web site owner, and entrepreneur. And he says that content creators can't ignore curation any longer.

"We don't have an information shortage; we have an attention shortage," Godin told me. "There's always someone who's going to supply you with information that you're going to curate. The Guggenheim doesn't have a shortage of art. They don't pay you to hang paintings for a show, in fact *you* have to pay for the insurance. Why? Because the Guggenheim is doing a service to the person who's in the museum and the artist who's being displayed."

As Godin sees it, power is shifting from content *makers* to content *curators*: "If we live in a world where information drives what we do, the information we get becomes the most important thing. The person who chooses that information has power."

This change is leaving folks who used to control distribution with less power to dictate terms. One of those folks is Mark Cuban. Cuban is a content creator. Or, more accurately, he owns assets that create branded content. He owns the Dallas Mavericks. He owns Magnolia Pictures. He owns HDnet. And he's got a stake in a whole bunch of other stuff. Cuban isn't shy. In fact, he's perhaps the most outspoken critic of content aggregation and curation.

"The content aggregators are *vampires!*" says the colorful Cuban. "Don't let them suck your blood." Cuban points to sites like Google News and the Huffington Post as the most aggressive content criminals. He tends to see no value in folks who gather, organize, summarize, or republish. He only finds value in content creation: "Vampires take but don't give anything back."

Not surprisingly, Godin wrinkles his nose at Cuban's vampire metaphor. In fact, he says it's all wrong. "When a vampire sucks your blood, you make new blood," Godin says. "That's different than when a human being eats bacon. The pig's over, it's done. The thing about information is that information is more valuable when people know it. There's an exception for business information and super-timely information, but in all other cases, ideas that spread win. I'm not talking about plagiarism; I'm talking about the difference between obscurity and piracy. If the taking is so whole that the original is worth nothing—like eating bacon—that's a problem."

And tech blogger Robert Scoble, known as Scobleizer.com, also disagrees with Cuban's horror-movie metaphor. "That's ridiculous. Cuban is fun to argue with, but it's ridiculous. I mean come on, the *New York Times* is an aggregator of a thousand people's work. More than that if you include letters to the editor, opinions, and guest posts and contracted posts and contracted articles. The *New York Times* has been doing aggregation for a hundred years. To say that's a vampire is just totally ridiculous."

Vampires. Bacon. Aren't we taking this carnivore metaphor a bit too far? Godin says that media outlets that trade content for exposure are offering a clear deal, one with obvious benefits. "If Oprah calls you on the phone and says come be on my TV show and tell everyone what's in your book, do you then say: 'How much are you going to pay me?' Of course not, Oprah doesn't pay people to be on her show," he says. "The chance to tell your story to Oprah's viewership is priceless. In fact, you'd pay her. Is Oprah a vampire? I don't think so."

Cuban fired back a response on his blog, Blogmaverick.com: "I love Seth, but he is simultaneously wrong and hypocritical. He makes my point very well when he says 'The person who chooses that information has power.' What does he think newspapers do? Randomly publish stories? Randomly assign stories to writers and editors? Of course not. The value in their brand comes from choosing stories, some of which come from 3rd parties and some of which they originate. By allowing themselves to be part of the Google Index or Google News, they become one of thousands of content options. They transition the power of information selection from their newspaper brand to the aggregator brand. That's just stupid."

And Cuban doesn't buy Godin's Oprah metaphor either. He says Oprah invites you on her show, while Google News and other aggregators simply take your content without your permission. Cuban sees Google's massive and undifferentiated search as making publishers commodities. On Oprah you are featured; within Google, you are lumped in with a massive pile of other data.

THE BALANCE OF POWER

Passionate advocates of curation such as Scoble think the shift we're seeing is a change in the balance of power. "Curation changes the value proposition," he says, "Because it used to be the *New York Times* had the value. Now something like Flipboard comes along and Flipboard can join the *New York Times* with the economists and CNN with the Associated Press, with me, with you joined together in one media thing." Scoble is talking about the emergence of a new class of devices and software, tablets like the iPad and software that uses intelligent aggregation from your curated friends and sources. His reader software of choice is Flipboard.

But even fans of curation like Scoble admit that the changes don't help mainstream publishers. Flipboard takes value away from publishers, making them one of many data streams. Scoble agrees with Cuban, but only up to a point: "Cuban is right that the value proposition is shifting, but to say that they are vampires is wrong. Flipboard adds a huge amount of value to me. And when people add value to my life, I don't call them vampires."

It's a stark disagreement, with curation fans and foes taking sides. But the argument is kind of moot. Content is going to become commoditized, and sites and publishers that have audience trust will need to become curators to remain relevant and keep the traffic and audience engagement they need to survive. Cuban can opine as much as he wants, but it won't change what the world looks like in five years. But of course that doesn't stop him.

Cuban's advice to content creators: cut off the aggregators at the knees. Throw the switch. Don't let your content be crawled or curated.

How does one of the Web's most successful bloggers and link aggregators respond to Cuban's taunt? TechCrunch's Michael Arrington says that turning away link traffic would be ridiculous. "When someone visits your site, they are doing you a favor. Not the other way around," he declares. "And when an aggregator puts up a link to your site, they are doing you a favor by sending you traffic. Not the other way around." And Arrington's widely read blog proved the value of being highly linked to selling to AOL for $35 million in the fall of 2010.

And Godin's proaggregation response is equally forceful: "The default should be you opt in to sharing. If you need to keep your book out of the library, if you want to opt out of Google, it's easy— it's a button. But even Rupert Murdoch doesn't have the guts to do that, because it would mean ruin."

So there's no doubt that these two smart guys will continue to disagree about the value of aggregation: Cuban says it is theft; Godin says it is manna from heaven. They return to their corners.

But what about curation? The human-powered filter that explicitly chooses the right stuff, adds value in organization and distribution, and provides content creators with ways to extend their brand? Surely Cuban sees the distinction, the gray area be-tween Google's algorithmic approach to content and the emerg-ing human-powered content curators? "It's just another name for branded aggregation. If they didn't need the blood from the other sites, they wouldn't take it," he says. "Putting different shades of lipstick on the pig doesn't make it a princess." Ouch.

"Of course, that doesn't mean they can't make money. They do," Cuban says. "But if the origination sites had the balls to just say no, most of the curation sites would wither away."

So Mark Cuban will preach the gospel of creators slamming the hammer down on curators, linked economy be damned. But didn't he invest in Jason Calacanis's Weblogs Inc., the blog network that later sold to AOL for $25 million? Cuban explained this away by saying that "Weblogs was all original content. My blog and oth-ers were aggregated. At no point was anyone's work used without their permission when I was active with the site. I'm not sure what it evolved into, but when I invested, it was purely original stuff."

Interesting. Brian Alvey, one of the founders of Weblogs Inc., says it started as a site that mixed created and curated content, but maybe Cuban simply forgot. It was a long time ago. Then there's Calacanis's next start-up, after the $25 million win, Mahalo. That's a site that aggregates and curates links. Cuban invested in that too.

It seems as though Cuban is against aggregation and curation unless he's an investor, in which case he's fine with making a boat-load of money selling a company that created much of its value by aggregating and curating. Which is okay. After all, Cuban's first fortune was made on a company called Broadcast.com which was sold to Yahoo for $5.9 *billion* in 1999; it was an early Web busi-ness that streamed links he aggregated from across the Web. As of the writing of this book, Cuban is number 400 on the Forbes Billionaires list, with a net worth of $2.4 billion. So while Cuban *says* that curation is bad, he's made his fortune by building and selling companies that embrace and profit from curation. My advice is to follow what Cuban *does*—not the combative and controversial things he says—if you want to make money in the emerging curated economy.

A SHIFT IN THE BALANCE

Seth Godin says curation is all part of the shift from an industrial to an information-age society. We're going from making things to finding and organizing things. Whatever you do though, you'd better be extraordinary at it.

"The industrial revolution is over," Godin says. "Karl Marx and Adam Smith said there are two teams, owners and workers. I'm saying there's a third team now, people who own their own means of production. They own the factory and they're a worker. That could be a blogger or a designer." Godin thinks there's power in being the one irreplaceable thing: the "linchpin."

And increasingly, the linchpin in the content world will be aggregators, not creators. Blogger Arrington says that today each piece of news lives and dies by its own meritorical links; aggregators and the real-time Web provide the curatorial fabric to help important and useful content rise above the noise.

"Aggregators are popular because they help users find the news they're interested in," Arrington says. "They serve a very real purpose and add value to the system."

While we're not going to outgrow our need for information, the changing economics tend to favor the small and nimble, or the individual curator—not the old media companies with large buildings and costly overhead. It seems we need a middleman, a curator, to help us find what's important. So what's really changing here? Are creators getting lazy? Is it simply that the act of creating is so much harder than the act of gathering? Or is it something else entirely—that the proliferation of data makes curating an urgent, essential, critically necessary function in our new digital world?

What's changed, in large part, is motivation. Journalists and professionals curate for profit, to build audience. And the mission of their management is to monetize that audience. But as Clay Shirky explores in his book *Cognitive Surplus*, individual curators have a much more altruistic motivation: "When publication, the act of making something public—goes from being hard to being virtually effortless, people used to the old system often regard publishing by amateurs as frivolous, as if publishing was an inherently serious activity. It never was though. Publishing had to be taken seriously when its costs and efforts made people take it seriously—if you made too many mistakes, you were out of business." The act of publishing is no longer costly or risky, and therefore the value as Shirky sees it was merely accidental.

And if you dissect Shirky's title, what he's saying is we're moving into a world were we each have an excess of brainpower. This brainpower enables us to participate in things like Wikipedia or open source software or Mechanical Turk, or any number of crowd-centric hybrids that let people participate on their own terms in making, sharing, tagging, and amplifying content.

Life in the Curation Nation is about power shifting, and in significant ways crowds of volunteer curators are replacing paid professionals. In fact, curated crowd knowledge is forcing a whole sector of experts and self-proclaimed pundits to challenge the wisdom of the crowd. Within the community of film critics, there is a shift from the time-honored, studio-driven review system to the Twitter-fueled instant pulse. In fact, there are more and more movies where the public and the film cognoscenti's tastes disagree, creating a battle between the public and the increasingly embattled professional reviewer.

Here Andrew Keen strongly disagrees, even if he knows it's a lost cause. He lobbies for a paid professional class of creative people. And he sees what he calls "the cult of the amateur" as edging out the paid professional: "I don't have a problem with some people doing stuff because they love it. But still the majority of creative people need to be paid for their labor. Otherwise they have to wait tables during the day. And that's what troubles me about a lot of this debate."

Perhaps nowhere is this battle more hard fought than in the world of sharp knives and equally sharp rhetoric. I'm speaking of course of the world of foodies and the elite highbrow world of the food critic.

Clay Shirky says the crowd-sourced reviews from actual patrons often provide more value than the expert restaurant critics who've made their livings and reputations making and breaking restaurants. Says Shirky, "Other functions of the critic, such as interpreting its chef's intentions or relating it to the history of a particular cuisine, remain, but overall value of the reviewers work shrinks because the world has change around him."

Curation-empowered individual voices and crowd-collected data challenge the existing established professional experts and tastemakers. The shift is significant and ongoing, and one that Keen says will have terrible consequences. "If we do away with professional curators, if all we're left with is amateurs, then we're in a worse situation. So all I'm saying is, it's good to have both. I don't believe that the amateur replaces the professional, just as the professional doesn't replace the amateur."

Could curation actually make it harder to survive as a creative professional? Keen says that's where it's headed: "The reality is that the creative artists—musicians, writers, filmmakers, animators, cartoonists—they're all finding it harder and harder to make a living. So in that sense I'm a cultural conservative."

The Web creates a power shift. The food critic was powerful because he wrote for a big-city newspaper. His voice was amplified by a media megaphone, and the scarcity of bandwidth and amplification tools gave him power. Sure, he had talent, but the megaphone didn't hurt. Now voices are aggregate and curated: Yelp gathers opinions and sorts the most coherent ones to the top. There's still plenty of room for individuals to build brands and have power and earn a living. But having access to a publishing outlet won't be the deciding factor going forward. You're going to have to have a voice and followers and a curatorial point of view. Vampires? Hardly. Quality curation, as it turns out, is darn hard work.

16

FINANCE, CURATION, AND PRIVACY

 s with all things that are new, the law of unintended consequences can spin wildly out of control. Today there is, by some measures, an epidemic of promiscuous sharing. Curation is driven by larger and larger numbers of people sharing their likes, dislikes, and habits with the world. Based on fast-moving trends like location-based sharing of data on services like Foursquare and experimental teen trends like sexting (texting of graphic sexual messages and images), it appears that the younger generation is willing to break down all barriers and share even their most intimate personal information. And perhaps the most dramatic area of data sharing that raises eyebrows is finance.

Personal financial data isn't something you'd ordinarily share with strangers. The stocks you own, the products you purchase, and your overall success or failure in the stock market are the kinds of things usually kept private. Heck, even among family members—sometimes between couples—the details of how money is managed and spent is a sensitive subject. But soon, your purchasing habits may no longer be private. Curation is having a major impact on privacy, as more and more of the financial services that we use invite users to share what was previously private information. Can curation change finance? A number of entrepreneurs are betting on it.

THE FACEBOOK OF FINANCE

Howard Lindzon is the current king of curation finance. Canada-born Lindzon applied his entrepreneurial zeal to social media and created StockTwits, a Twitter-powered site that captures the buzz of the market. As with many entrepreneurs, Lindzon took a number of swings at bat before he landed on a success. "I have learned more from my mistakes than my wins," Lindzon says. "I ridiculously overpaid for Cars Direct, Rent.com was more luck than my investment talent, and Golfnow.com was the one deal I am most proud of, as I spotted it early, helped put together the big investment and helped get it sold to Comcast."

None of those deals sounds much like curation or community, or even innovation. But then Lindzon turned to his passion, finance, which was an area he felt was stale and ready for reinvention. Along came Twitter, and the rest was history. Lindzon started what he calls the Facebook of finance in just 2009, and today it has over 100,000 registered users and receives more than 8,000 tweets per trading day.

But StockTwits isn't just an automated service, Lindzon knows that he needs to curate the stream in order to make sure he's got a clean feed to share with the Twitterverse. "People use $ ticker symbol to tweet ideas about stocks and markets. We then filter and curate based on that flow of messages," he says.

StockTwits employs actual human beings to be on the lookout for scammers or pump-and-dump artists promoting five-cent stocks. "It keeps the stream clean, so to speak, so we have a community of good people," says Joe Donohue, a New Jersey hedge-fund manager who's a featured tweeter on StockTwits under the name "upsidetrader."

But isn't financial information the most *private* data in a person's life? Do people really want to share their financial strategies and moves? Lindzon says yes. "Financial data has always been deeply private and for the most part remains so. It is hard to gather and easy to sell, so it's protected. It's finally changing. People don't really care if you know what they are buying. CNBC has been front running ideas for a decade in many indirect ways so that is not really an issue. Facebook and Twitter have just changed the way financial message boards and communities will evolve, and Stock-Twits is just part of this big open trend."

StockTwits has found a way to aggregate knowledge and turn it into marketplace knowledge. Can curated market data make you money in the market? Lindzon says it can: "I think the vested interest in sharing financially is it makes you a way better trader. The other motivation is ego and fame. Every vertical but finance has its 'American Idol.' Yet in finance, the same people get headlines year after year because of access. StockTwits will help push the right changes along."

The StockTwits mission is to connect traders to results, making them accountable rather than simply well-known because they went to an Ivy League school or because they have a large amount of capital under management. Not surprisingly, Lindzon says that Wall Street doesn't need more financial regulation, just better enforcement. And for StockTwits, enforcement means curating who can participate. "We kick people out at StockTwits," he notes. "Curation is important. Participating is a privilege, not a right, especially since we are a private and semi-open community. If we were totally open, we would quickly move to a very low value because people just don't know how to use the tools of the new social Web properly . . . *yet*."

The StockTwits concept is red flag for content creators and aggregators who think sources should be professional. Kevin Wassong is the president of Minyanville Media, a community of investment professionals. He says Lindzon's amateurs don't replace financial pros. "I can make pasta, but spaghetti Bolognese from Mario Batali tastes even better," Wassong says. "People want trusted professionals who can sift through an over-saturated market of information and bring them the best of the best."

WOULD YOU WANT TO MAKE YOUR CREDIT CARD PUBLIC?

While Facebook and Twitter have prodded people to broadcast just about anything they are thinking, doing, or thinking of doing— from what they ate for lunch to what movie they're going to see— Blippy wants to reveal more, by asking people to share what they buy. Yes, you read that correctly.

Blippy asks people to share their spending habits. If you register a credit card with the site, every transaction purchased with the card is displayed to your friends. Philip Kaplan was the founder of F*cked Company, the Web site that chronicled the dot-com meltdown. Kaplan joined the start-up after he became convinced that sharing purchasing data would be the next big thing. It might sound like oversharing to a ridiculous degree, but Kaplan is serious. The site's founders think it offers a new way to learn about deals and new products. And knowing your spending habits are being transmitted to a flock of friends might make you think twice before spending $500 on a pair of designer shoes.

Kaplan assured the *Wall Street Journal* that the idea is not quite a creepy as it might sound at first. "You can choose on a vendor-by-vendor basis," he says. "Like automatically post all my iTunes or Zappos purchases. You can connect a credit card to Blippy. A lot of people connect just one card to Blippy and use a different one if they don't want it shared. You can also connect without any credit card. You can just connect it to your iTunes account to just show what you're buying on iTunes."

And if you think there's danger of sharing too much personal information, Kaplan says there's more danger in being perceived as lame: "A woman tweeted and said 'Everyone's going to know about the vibrator I bought last week!' Well, she's writing it on Twitter, so clearly she doesn't mind people knowing . . . People are loosening up. The biggest risk is that their purchases are totally mundane and they're really super boring."

And Alexa Scordato, the digital native who has lived her entire life online, sees the debate as somewhat moot. Says Alexa, "I'm sort of resigned to the fact that the Internet owns me in the same way somebody could steal my identity by stealing my purse or my laptop. Then, you know, it's sort of a package deal." Alexa's generation can hardly imagine how they could participate in society without being online. It's a concept that's simply foreign to them. The Web is simply part of who they are.

For Kaplan, sharing everything is the default. Anything less seems like avoiding inevitable disclosure. "The big question is what happens when you take all this data that's previously been private like purchases and make them public? What will the world look like when you do that? We've seen a lot of people buying products they discovered because others bought them on Blippy."

As an example, Kaplan explains that he purchased a WiFi scale at Amazon, and since then four of his friends who follow his purchases on Blippy have bought one as well. I didn't even know that they sold WiFi-enabled scales, so I kind of get his point. Purchasing is a data trail that can broadcast your habits, your interests, a kind of digital endorsement: "I purchased this, therefore I recommend you try it too."

Kaplan continues, "You also learn a lot more about friends. One of my friends, I didn't even know he was a guitar player until I saw him buy a guitar. For businesses like gyms, insurance, airline tickets, it'll be harder to charge people different prices for the same thing if you knew how much everyone's paying."

But what if Blippy users don't want everyone else to know some of their purchases? In the brave new world we are entering, there are going to be some risks and some dangers. The blog Ven tureBeat.com uncovered the first instance of "unintentional sharing" of Blippy data just months after the site's launch. It was reported that Blippy had accidently published some users' credit card data. In the end Blippy found 127 transactions that had been made discoverable on Google, with four credit card numbers, but Kaplan responded by pointing out that the expiration dates weren't published. The larger point, however, is that as we share more data, the accidental sharing of personal information is inevitable.

Why did Blippy allow Google to crawl its members' pages, the source code for which included data not meant to be published to anyone but the individual members? Why is Blippy still searchable at all, instead of, say, blocking the search engine with a robots .txt file? Kaplan says that Blippy is no different than Yelp or any other sharing site—and it wants to be visible in the Google index.

The power—and the risk—of the Web is the growth of cleverer, interconnected computers. Kaplan says that has an upside, but a downside as well.

THE DOWNSIDE OF SHARING

Don't think that all this data is going only to marketers. That's just the start. Credit card companies are increasingly using complex customer profiles and behavior tracking to monitor cardholders' shopping patterns. While marketers are looking for ways to target you, credit card companies have another motivation altogether. They're looking out for risk. Change your buying habits abruptly from high-end retail to the local dollar store and there's a flag that you maybe facing a crisis: job loss, divorce, or death in the family. You may find your credit limit reduced or revoked. And that's before the credit-card counseling session paid with plastic, for example. Ben Woolsey, director of marketing and consumer research at CreditCards.com says, "The safest thing you can assume is that if it's not outlawed, they will do it." The practice of using data mining began as the economic crisis of 2008 started to show up in the subprime mortgage market. The fear was that if you defaulted on your mortgage, you might walk away from your credit card balance as well.

DailyFinance.com reports that some risk-management research firms are even collecting consumer data on social media sites such as Twitter and Yelp. Data mining seems like a throwback to the old bank practice of redlining, and the practice of using purchasing patterns to discriminate against borrowers of certain races or specific neighborhoods is illegal.

Rapleaf, a San Francisco–based data-mining company, claims it can predict which individuals might be a credit risk by virtue of who they're friends with on Facebook. If a person's friends pay their bills on time, that individual is also likely to pay on time. Rapleaf is one of a number of companies to collect and analyze the vast amount of personal data consumers create online. Its computers analyze your words on public sites like Yelp and Amazon and file them away in your social graph.

This is the kind of data that privacy advocates like Lauren Gelman, the executive director of Stanford Law School's Center for Internet and Society, finds most disturbing. Gelman fears that we may be sentencing our children to a life of being unable to escape the youthful indiscretions and innocent mistakes that have historically been a hallmark of growing up. She explains it this way: "Everyone should have an opportunity to be young and make mistakes, and put them behind you and move on. The fact is we're now living with this new technology that captures all these ways we try out different personas throughout our lives. I see this transformation going on in society, where people are no longer able to try things out or reinvent themselves, and I think that has big implications."

Can it be we're crossing a line from private to public that forever leaves us vulnerable to scrutiny or persecution from anyone who has a Web browser? While the act of curation often means providing data to the public cloud, what are your rights to your data after you've shared it? Currently, you have none.

Here's an example of the public cloud principle at work. Let's say you go to a local restaurant and have a terrible meal. Afterward, you post a review on Yelp. A year later you go back to the restaurant, and now with a new chef, the menu and the experience is delightful. Can you take down your Yelp review? Can you find all the places that Yelp has syndicated your data? What about all the sites that have gone into Yelp and scraped your review and reposted it? Crowd data is yours until you post it, but in most cases once it's out of your hands, it's going to be out in the ether forever.

Let's use another example, one that's closer to home. There's a powerful and growing collection of Web communities around health and wellness. Often these sites are a mix of personal stories, advice, and experiences. PatientsLikeMe.com is one of the largest and fastest-growing of these sites. Its simple mission connects patients with a "life-changing condition" to others with the same issues and challenges.

There's clearly an important benefit in creating curated communities around health issues. But there are privacy issues here as well. And, more interestingly, the site's Openness Philosophy states, "We believe sharing your healthcare experiences and outcomes is good. Why? Because when patients share real-world data, collaboration on a global scale becomes possible. New treatments become possible. Most importantly, change becomes possible. At PatientsLikeMe, we are passionate about bringing people together for a greater purpose: speeding up the pace of research and fixing a broken healthcare system."

The privacy policy on the site explains, "PatientsLikeMe removes pieces of personally identifiable information that can reasonably be used to identify you (i.e., "de-identifies" your data) prior to sharing information with third parties. PatientsLikeMe shares such de-identified data that relates to you, in some cases as part of individual records and in other cases in aggregate form, with third parties. For example, we may look at scientific questions such as, 'Do certain treatments work better for some types of people versus others?'"

So who's behind PatientsLikeMe? Big pharmaceutical companies, self-serving media companies, or carefully cloaked medical marketers? As it turns out, none of these is correct. The site was founded by Jamie Heywood, a former medical researcher whose life changed when his brother was diagnosed with ALS. He's been described as a guerrilla scientist, driven to use the power of crowd-sourced patient experience to dramatically speed up the way medical research data is created and evaluated. With PatientsLikeMe,

Heywood can reach out to huge numbers of patients with the same condition and the same questions.

Heywood explains it this way: "Imagine a world where in real time, every patient knows what will happen to them . . . the drug companies will be competing not to prove to the FDA they have some drug that modifies a signal to get through the process, but to convince the patients that they generate enough value to make their lives better." There's no doubt that there's huge power in real-time data that can collect and share information about patients with patients, and with the medical community. But as Lauren Gelman warns us, the current state of privacy is "binary": either you share or you don't. There's no way to define the way that the information you put out in the world can be used or gathered or tabulated or cross-referenced. And so while PatientsLikeMe may not share information about your health or condition with advertisers or insurance companies or employment agencies, there's nothing saying that another site with less rigorous privacy policies couldn't drop a cookie on your computer and then track your behaviors as you engage in research, review your genomic data, or post on a health-related forum or discussion board. The concern isn't that any one piece of data is revealed; it's instead about how marketers or others could collect a trail of data and piece together a portrait that would make your most private health issues visible to parties you don't want to share with.

This isn't fiction—far from it.

BLURRY-EDGED PRIVACY

Gelman says privacy is very much at risk, and the number of companies that are looking to create a digital snapshot of your private information is daunting. If the Web is built on sharing, and curation requires us to share more—and filter more—then the privacy infrastructure is going to have to undergo a major upgrade to catch up to the entities that are curious about, even predatory toward, your innermost secrets.

Gelman's solution is what she calls blurry-edged privacy.

The rapid expansion of the Web has facilitated one-to-many communications. Gelman says the next puzzle will be balancing the demands of free speech and the risks to individual privacy. This tension is being amplified as networks emerge that blur the line between private and public information. So-called blurry-edged networks are places where people post information generally intended for small networks of friends and family, but those networks are open to the wider Web.

Gelman says, "The technology that enables these communities creates an illusion of privacy and control that the law fails to recognize."

Her idea is to create a new set of privacy permissions, a template of rules that are agreed to across the Web. If it sounds a bit like what's been happening in copyright, well, then you'd be pretty smart. "I've been thinking about this project for a long time—when Creative Commons was launched a few doors down from my office at Stanford Law School, I thought: 'Why can't we do this for privacy?'"

It's a fair question, and one that folks are starting to take seriously. One of them is Jules Polenetsky, the former commissioner for consumer affairs for New York City under Mayor Rudy Giuliani. Polenetsky was named chief privacy officer for the advertising giant DoubleClick after the Federal Trade Commission launched an investigation into that company's plan to track consumer behavior on the Web and target ads, back in the Internet dark ages of 2000. Polonetsky then moved to AOL where he held the CPO gig, and now is the cochair and director of the Future of Privacy Forum.

Polenetsky explained to me in personal terms why today's privacy systems are deeply broken: "I live in a Washington, D.C., suburb, and the other day we had a storm and we lost power. I posted on Facebook and Twitter to get information about the outage and to share some details about the outage in my neighborhood. I wanted to share beyond folks who were friends and family, people in my neighborhood or region, but I didn't want them to have access to my personal information. I wanted to be able to define my sharing. Today there's no way to do that."

Polenetsky is of course talking about blurry privacy and wanting to have fewer binary sharing rules and more flexibility—adjustable based on time or geography or shared interests, but in control of the ownership of the information and protected from unwanted marketing or data mining. If Polenetsky had posted the question "Does anyone know a good doctor at Sloan Kettering?" would he expect to be targeted with cancer-drug advertising? What if his post triggered a rate increase in his health insurance premium? Data-mining technology and risk management together can turn the information we put on the Web against us.

In a world of curation, data is shared freely, and protections don't yet exist to shield us from the impact of our actions.

This isn't a genie that we're going to put back in the bottle. We're all leaving a trail of data wherever we go. Google CEO Eric Schmidt explains, "If I look at enough of your messaging and your location, and use Artificial Intelligence, we can predict where you are going to go," leaving the question of who "we" represents hanging in the air at the 2010 Techonomy Conference in Lake Tahoe.

Schmidt continued, "Show us 14 photos of yourself and we can identify who you are. You think you don't have 14 photos of yourself on the Internet? You've got Facebook photos! People will find it's very useful to have devices that remember what you want to do, because you forgot . . . But society isn't ready for questions that will be raised as result of user-generated content."

So what if you don't want all of your data to be public? Schmidt's comments on that require a bit of head scratching. "If you have something that you don't want anyone to know, maybe you shouldn't be doing it in the first place," Schmidt told CNBC. "If you really need that kind of privacy, the reality is that search engines—including Google— do retain this information for some time and it's important, for example, that we are all subject in the United States to the Patriot Act and it is possible that all that information could be made available to the authorities."

Of course, Schmidt dodges the issue here. Yes, your e-mails can be subpoenaed and your phone tapped by the government. But that doesn't mean your employer or your ex-spouse or a nosey neighbor should be able to poke around in your private data. The argument that you shouldn't do anything you don't want public is disturbing and wrong-headed. We do many things that are private and neither illegal nor objectionable: exploring belief systems or sexual preferences or legal remedies or health concerns. Privacy is going to become a central issue in the next 5 to 10 years, and Google doesn't serve our interests or its own by brushing it aside.

Does financial curation shift the balance of power from big banks and credit card companies to consumers and groups who've banded together? Clearly there are two forces at work here. As consumers put more data out, their collective interests can band together and form a voting block. Bad banks, bad companies, bad stocks all get outed quickly. But institutions do tend to fight back and use data mining to find patterns in your information. They can then use that data to market to you, to increase your interest rate, or to deny you a loan. It's hardly black-and-white. But that doesn't mean things aren't changing in a fundamental way. Lindzon explains,

"Consumers have all the power they need. Consumers have all the investing tools they need to make money. We have *no* excuses, just ourselves to blame. The institutions get away with what we let them get away with."

The disintermediation of services companies has been well documented. People who used to control data had power. People who needed data had to go through them. But that power center is gone, now that stock market data and analytics are all on line. Brokers and traders who used to control access to information will just need to find another way to make money.

So is this good for consumers? Lindzon believes the long-term trend of empowering consumer voices will continue to benefit the small investor. But he cautions that there are risks as well: "Curation and discovery are huge areas of growth on the net. In five years there will be new social credit scores and many new evil ways you will be getting screwed by data. But, those with good real credit have less to fear. The sites that curate and help discover will be huge hits in the next wave of the Web."

With a grin, and a bit of real pride, the maven of StockTwits says simply, "Community and knowledge are a new power."

So, it seems, at least in broad terms, that the cultural, legal, and societal frameworks we have in place today simply aren't engineered to manage the changes that the ever-growing tsunami of data is gathering and indexing. DANGER: SHARP CURVE AHEAD, the road sign on our digital landscape should read.

CONCLUSION

So, first of all, if I were sitting across from you I'd give you a big high five. Why? Because you're an inherently curious person who decided to devote a chunk of the most valuable thing you have (your time, of course) to this book. You invested attention. If you're one of those people who jumped to the conclusion chapter of this book and skipped the two hundred or so pages that preceded this one, you missed the point. Life is about the journey. The conclusions, as interesting as they are, are only half the point.

I set out to write this book thinking I knew a lot about curation, content, brands, and consumer behavior. I also thought I knew what a lot of smart folks thought about the subject.

After almost a year of interviews, with more than 60 people from a spectrum of disciplines, one single truth emerged that illuminates where we're going and who the winners will be. The machines we've built can't filter the future. They need us.

Here's an analogy:

Up until today you had a kitchen sink. You had a showerhead. Maybe a garden hose. Water came into your house or garden when you wanted it, where you wanted it, and how you wanted it. Water was there to help you make a cup of tea, water the plants, and take a shower.

Then overnight while you slept, the water pipe to your house was replaced by a fire hose. One of those massive canvas hoses that are six inches in diameter. Behind it, there is tremendous pressure: a thundering unstoppable gusher that quickly overwhelms the faucets, valves, and spigots that allowed you to harness and manage water.

You are flooded. Every faucet in your home is full-on streaming water into your formerly dry living room. Water is no longer a useful convenience or helpful and life-giving elixir. It is now a plague. A disaster. An unstoppable force that makes the idea of a shower or a cup of tea impossible.

Water is overwhelming your life. But water hasn't changed; it is the same substance. What has changed is the sheer volume of it, which quickly swamped all the tried-and-true systems that you'd come to expect could manage it.

You need new plumbing—and fast.

This new plumbing is going to take on some shapes and sizes you haven't seen in the past. Some new tools, some new technology, and some new behaviors and business practices. It's not a one-size-fits-all solution, and there are going to be some twists and turns along the way.

LOOK AT THE BIG TRENDS

In order to plan ahead and build a curation strategy that fits both your personal skills and the emerging billion-dollar opportunities, let's set the trends in context.

What Is Mobile?

There may be no better analyst for Internet trends than Mary Meeker. She is currently a partner in the Silicon Valley venture capital firm of Kleiner Perkins Caulfield & Byers and formerly a managing director at Morgan Stanley, serving as head of the investment bank's global technology research team. While at Morgan Stanley, her annual report on Web trends was carefully read and well respected. So when Meeker does the math and says that mobile users will exceed desktop users within five years, that's worth serious consideration. In 2015, mobile users will exceed 1.6 billion worldwide, on their way to 2 billion as desktop use levels off at about 1.8 billion. In particular, Meeker points to five trends converging: "3G, social networking, video, VoIP, and Impressive Mobile Devices." She doesn't yet have the iPad on her list of impressive mobile devices, but the report was released before the iPad hit the stores.

Driving the growth in users and minutes are Facebook and YouTube, social media and video. Video in particular is driving the rapid growth in mobile Internet traffic, with mobile data rising 39 times by 2014. Wow. Meeker points to Apple as leading the mobile innovation ecosystem for now, but she cautions that user experience and price will determine the long-term winner.

The shift to mobile Internet is going to have a profound impact on advertising, on-demand content, and e-commerce. In particular, Meeker reports annualized ad revenue per Internet user growing from $28 in 2005 to $46 in 2010.

The combination of location-based services, devices, mobile Internet users, and more content and e-commerce companies offering on-demand services is driving a remarkable shift in dollars and behavior. But Meeker is quick to point out that the ability to access a trustworthy billing system for micropayments (in particular Apple's iTunes store) makes impulse buys for both content and apps an appealing behavior for consumers.

Here, Meeker makes a compelling argument for why consumers are treating commerce and content differently on the mobile Web from how they do on their desktops. She points to four factors that are driving new consumer behaviors in mobile: secure payment systems, smaller price tags, established storefronts, and personalization.

The growing wins in mobile serve only to point out the frustrations/failures on the desktop Internet experience that have slowed the payment for content and commerce, including a fragmented payment system, difficulty in purchasing legal content, the impact of piracy, and the lack of clear legal content discovery. Mobile is winning because the Web is intrinsically more valuable when you take it with you: all the core values of the Web are enhanced by mobility. Social connections are more meaningful if you know where your friends are and if they can find you. Advertising is more useful, and therefore less annoying, if ads can respond to timely and specific needs, including offers and discounts.

All these reasons have convinced media advisor Terrence Kawaja of LUMA partners that there's a shift on the way that will bring attention and budget from broadcast TV to the Web. He points to the relatively tiny percentage of the U.S. advertising spend of $300 billion that goes to the Web. Today it's just 12 percent. Kawaja explains, "Much of the media optimization techniques honed in online can be applied to TV audiences, and a shift in agency dynamic and marketer mindset is key."

Kawaja says, ""Forecasts show the interactive channel growing to $50+ billion in five years," Kawaja says. "This represents a linear, evolutionary approach. The challenge is to think revolution, not evolution. Think of the new definition for *interactive* to go beyond online, including digitally addressable video (aka TV, offline commerce enablement, and mobile)."

As Kawaja explains, "Historical impediments to the growth of digital media are going away, convergence of digital (online and mobile) with traditional TV will open up a much larger market opportunity for digital players, and it is important to focus on holistic, cross-channel solutions to capture the larger TV and offline market opportunities."

Meeker and Kawaja's analyses serve to illuminate a dramatic and critical shift in the very nature of the Web and the economics that are growing around it. Within five years, the Web will be essentially mobile, location- and user-aware, and driven by micropayments.

The changes will further accelerate the growth of a la carte content, hastening the demise of cable-bundled programming and creating real economics for both niche ad supported verticals and micropayments for on-demand content.

What Is Real Time?

The thing about the shift to the real-time Web is that it's a change that no one asked for, much like the advent of 24-hour cable news. As Clay Shirky explains it, news used to end with the 6 p.m. sign-off the air. No more news till tomorrow morning—sleep tight. And you didn't need to worry about something happening while you were asleep, since there wasn't any way for you to hear about it. If news falls in the forest, and there isn't a 24-hour news channel, did it make a sound? It used to be, no—not without coverage. But Twitter changed all that.

It wasn't as though we thought we wanted to have hundreds of thousands of people, brands, and institutions with the ability to broadcast their thoughts, feelings, news, and favorite breakfast cereal in an open mic. But the world is wired for Web, and once there was an open channel, it was almost inevitable that there would emerge a tool to fill it. That Twitter—and the act of tweeting—has grown so quickly is simply proof of the inevitability of real-time data.

But not everyone thinks that real time solves a problem; in fact, real time further turns up the noise level in the data fire hose. So filter or be flooded, as content strategist Jeffrey MacIntyre says. "I used to drink from the real-time fire hose, because on the social Web everything was about real time," says *Engage* author Brian Solis. "Then I realized over the years that it's actually more about *right* time than *real* time. In fact, when information comes through, it doesn't necessarily mean that that's the right time to engage, capture it, and share it. I'm more successful now creating a list of information, relevant information, and then repackaging, repurposing, and broadcasting that information at the right time."

Getting people to pay attention to you—by following, friend-ing, linking, or otherwise engaging—will have real economic value, says Chris Brogan: "Attention is a currency, just like many others. We understand time and money as two interchangeable things. But attention is just as much something that needs to be arbitraged and disconnected from a 1:1 value. Said another way, 'Attention costs me time and time is worth money, so attention by extension is worth money.'"

Data will be created with staggering speed, and systems will need to evolve to find, gather, and package data so that you can get what you need, when you need it, in coherent and useful bundles.

What about Location?

Right now, devices know who you are, where you are, and what you want to do. But software hasn't been released that is smart enough to put the pieces together. Robert Scoble, of Scobleizer.com, shares his personal experience and frustration: "It's clear that mobile is taking over our world. I'm using my desktop and laptop com-puters less and less. So I'm using my iPhone and my iPad more and more. What does that mean to the world of curation? Right now, if you arrive in some place, like tonight, I'm flying to DC. My Memorandum isn't going to change based on my location."

He's referring to a customizable RSS newspaper called http://www.memeorandum.com that currently doesn't change content based on the location of the reader. Scoble says that now that devices are location aware, software is poised to catch up. "I live in Half Moon Bay, and my iPad knows I'm in Half Moon Bay 70 percent of the time. So it should know that I'm interested in local news from around my house. So if the mayor is doing something dastardly, why doesn't it show me that?" he asks.

That's just the tip of the iceberg. Will Foursquare allow you to choose favorite locations to check in automatically? Once you've given permission for a location to be one of your favorites, will it be able to reach out to you? We've seen this in the film *Minority Report*, where the billboard knows your name and invites to you to sample a new product or service. But it's hardly science fiction. Expect Starbucks to be able to say, "Hi Steve, this is your fourth visit this week. Would you like to try our new hazelnut-and-mocha cappuccino?"

What about Commerce?

When commerce goes mobile, real time, and location-aware, the very nature of buying and selling will change. Think of it in simple terms. You are a customer. You have needs and aspirations. Until now, advertisers had to make big, expensive guesses as to where you were. Most often they were wrong. So you ended watching ads from the American Beef Counsel even though you're vegan, or you ended up being pitched a new car just days after you purchased one. Clearly, this system is flawed. You got spammed, and the advertiser paid good marketing dollars to reach you with a message that only annoyed you.

Now, you've essentially gotten a unique customer ID number. It's tied to your mobile device and your name. Of course, it's your cell phone number. It knows who you are, where you are, and soon it will know what you search for and what you buy. Sound a bit creepy? Well, let's face it, selling you stuff was never pretty. But maybe, just maybe, you'll end up with better ads and offers that can be tailored to you, as well as some new systems and controls to block messages that you find offensive or objectionable. It's possible we'll look back at the era of mass media, with its barrage of ads that assault your sensibilities with inappropriate messages as the dark ages of marketing. It's not hard to imagine future generations saying, "Advertisers spent money filling the airwaves with messages that reached people who were uninterested or incapable of using their products? That was a crazy way to waste money."

What Is broken?

Search is broken. It's over. Done. Gone.

Why?

Search was effective when the Web was a library, notes blogger Vasu Srinivasan. But a library was a curated collection. And as such, each book in it had a Dewey Decimal System number and a proper place. Today, it's as if the library doors have been flung open and the shelves are now filled with literature, movies, comic books, cooking recipes, taxi receipts, old worn socks, boxes of love letters, worn truck tires, gum wrappers, and song lyrics. There is no rhyme or reason to what's on the Web or how it's categorized, or tagged. It's a data free-for-all, and it's just beginning. Today, we can check in on Foursquare or Facebook at a location. But what if your phone allowed you to automatically check in at your favorite places or if—better yet—*any place* you stop at for more than 10 minutes, it would fire off a check in. Your social network would be flooded with check ins. Someone, quick, find me a filter.

Here's the proof that search is broken: a search of my name on Google Images:

Now there I am—first result. But that's not me in the second or fourth. And if you get down to the second line of thumbnails, there are two women, a bunch of guys with name badges, and another woman. If you scroll down, there's even a pomeranian in a dog salon. Now, a few of are these false positives, such as the family using the iPad—it's a photo I took and tagged. So Google can't sort out a tag that says "This is Steve Rosenbaum" from one that says "Taken by Steve Rosenbaum." Metadata is tricky stuff.

But that's not my point. If you were in a restaurant waiting to meet me, this wouldn't help you. If you were a law enforcement officer picking up a fugitive on an outstanding warrant, this wouldn't help you. If you were an employer looking for information on me, this wouldn't help you.

Data can't be "close" or "almost right." It needs to be an absolute: *this* is Steve Rosenbaum, the guy you want.

The way to find out is to use Facebook. Either search someone you know that I know (a mutual friend) or read data that you know relates to me: CEO of Magnify.net, former magician, went to Skidmore College . . . things like that. You need to be able to do the human part, make the data contextual, in order for it to be useful.

This is but one of many examples. Try to search for a patch for a piece of software and you end up with old forum posts from five years ago. Try to find a restaurant review and you're pointed to a location that is out of business. You're more likely to use Google Maps to find a local vendor or destination than to search. I'm not suggesting that Google as a company is broken, just that the volume of data on the Web is going to increasingly have us sifting our "finding" behavior from raw search to social curation as our trusted methodology. We trust our community. And our community helps us find what we are looking for.

Search is over. Curation has begun.

And while search is about heavy iron and big, fast computers, curation is built at human scale. It narrows the wide Web down to a far smaller circle of friends, neighborhoods, and trusted filters. We're hungry for that kind of reliability—desperate for it, in fact.

A CURATION NATION

A very important speaker delivered a stirring commencement speech at Hampton University recently. He told the students: "You're coming of age in a 24/7 media environment that bombards us with all kinds of content and exposes us to all kinds of arguments, some of which don't always rank all that high on the truth meter . . . Information becomes a distraction, a diversion, a form of entertainment, rather than a tool of empowerment."

The speaker is crying out for clarity, for truth, and for a new way to find signal in the noise. Here is his conclusion: "All of this is not only putting new pressures on you, it is putting new pressures on our country and on our democracy."

Of course, you may have figured it out by now: the speaker was President Barack Obama. His message was clear: the era of overwhelming data requires discipline and new solutions.

This is the birth of Curation Nation.

This new nation of data will emerge to create order and rules, and form around the data tsunami that we're all collectively creating. Kristina Halvorson, a leader in the content strategy space, calls it governance, and there's no doubt that a new nation needs that.

So as you begin to wrap your brain around this idea of a Curation Nation, the question is what role do *you* want to play? Here are some choices:

- Citizens
- Shopkeepers
- Civic leaders

As a *citizen* of Curation Nation, you'll be a casual curator. You'll use the tools that make it easy for you to add data to your network of friends and followers. You'll "like" certain pieces of journalism, you'll review on Yelp, you'll report your location with Facebook or Foursquare. You may even aggregate all your links, approvals, and comments in a microblogging platform like Tumblr, or it may be that Facebook will be enough for you to keep your participation at a level where you're being a productive member of society.

Think about that for a moment. That phrase *a productive member of society* used to mean you had a job, a car, and a family. But now, being a member of society means participating in the conversation, the commerce, and the curation of the data stream. That's really significant—and exciting.

Passive participants will be off the grid; their digital vote won't count. And they won't be helping to influence the tides and turns of our increasingly digital world.

Then, as you walk down the block in Curation Nation, you'll pass by an almost limitless number of digital *shopkeepers*. These shops will be the new front door through which you'll enter a topic, a genre, a hobby, or any of an almost endless number of content niches and product categories. The barbecue site, the example we built together in chapter 6, is alive and well. The Web will shift away from nameless, faceless aggregators like Google News and low-cost generic content creators like Demand Media, and instead will emerge trusted sources that have brand name recognition, reputations, and a vested interest in providing links, clips, and recommendations that they actually believe in. Because these shopkeepers will value you as a customer, they will be proponents of scarcity rather than abundance. As Etsy has created a marketplace for quality handmade goods while eBay has devolved into a series of scammy storefronts and gray-market-goods e-taillers, the new digital shopkeeper will be able to create customer loyalty by providing expert advice, carefully curated products and services, and a clearly defined and authentic point of view.

Although shopkeepers will be prolific, think about how many delis there are in New York City and then transpose that number to the Web. There will be an uncountable number of sites that will cater to the Web equivalent of a local cliental. But there will be larger voices, more prolific, that will rise above their niche to become *civic leaders*. Voices of authority who will take a position, argue points, and gather points of view from a wide array of individual voices or sites. Already you can see the early members of this group taking shape: Arianna Huffington, Robert Scoble, Esther Dyson— individuals who've chosen to lead in content, technology, and health technology issues.

THE WORLD AHEAD

If you think the past five years were a dazzling fireworks display of change, you ain't seen nothing yet. We're just arriving at the tipping point, where content creation is truly democratized. The tools of content creation are in our pockets; cell phones are the location-aware devices that will allow video, photos, audio, and text to be created in bursts that will flood the network.

We're entering a world where the central magic is curation.

Consumer curation. Trusted media curation. Curation by the crowd. The world of curation will touch all parts of media, advertising, ecommerce, and education.

Because it's a driving trend, you can begin to see which technologies, companies, and brands will win in a curated world.

Advice from Our Friends

What are the key traits that can make you successful in the new world that's emerging? Scott Kurnit, who founded About.com, says it's about curiosity. He says when he hires people he asks: "How do I figure out whether this person is curious or not? 'Cause if they're curious they'll look around the corners, and then the trick is to make sure that they . . . that they either don't look too far around that corner or that they don't stick their head out . . . I think about when I stick my head out on Lexington Avenue, where this car is gonna wiz by . . . so, you know I guess it's curiosity with careful, 'carefultude.'"

Careful curiosity—is that you?

Robert Scoble says the key driver is passion: "Pick some niche that you're passionate about that you can totally own. If somebody says something about that niche, you should be able to see it in real time and be able to explain it to other people. If you do that and do that well, then you're going to be able to build up for that."

Passion and niches, that's Scoble's mantra. "Find a niche that you're passionate about, own it completely. Hopefully, you pick a niche that people care about and that is growing in importance."

Jason Hirschhorn, who was the head of Internet at MTV and then the copresident of MySpace, is putting his chips on curation: "I actually believe there is a golden age coming up for those who curate, and I think it's wonderful."

Finally, Jeff Pulver, founder of the popular 140 Conference, who at nine years old saw the future as being able to broadcast widely and then communicate one-on-one using ham radio, says the first thing you need to do is curate yourself. Pulver says, "You have to put yourself in a position where you can be successful. Sometimes people have to effectively fire their bosses in order to have a voice. Not everybody wants to be a CEO or have a big title, but people need to become CEOs of their lives. They have to be the ones to take responsibility for what they are doing and how they do it, and the people who are more vertically aligned with their goals and their passions or something which they strive for every-day have a much better chance of being successful than those who are not. To say that you need to work to put food on the table is true, but no one said that forever you have to be sentenced to a job that you hate."

For almost everyone I spoke to in writing this book, the emer-gence of a Web of curated content and the importance of people over machines had the promise of a golden age when people and their passions begin to create incomes and even profit for focused, passionate, committed curators. Pulver says it's a kind of digital sorcery.

"One of the magical things that I have discovered about the Internet is that anything is really possible. If you take that approach, you can do almost anything. It is the good mistakes that we make that sometimes we learn from and open our minds to things which we've never even thought about. That's a serendipity," Pulver says. "So if you are sitting at a desk and you are trying to figure out what to do with this real-time Web and curation. Number one is curate yourself. Number two is passion. What are your passions? What do you like to do? If you could spend your time doing things that you are passionate about, what would they be and what businesses do you see yourself being involved in that let you be passionate everyday and every moment of that day?"

"I think that we are all curators of our lives," Pulver says.

I began this journey with a clear sense that something was changing. I had a thesis, and I had evidence. But talking to so many smart people from so many worlds, I'm now sure that the change is more deep-seated and profound than I could have ever imagined.

We are all curators. We all will be sharing into the ecosystem of our friends and families. For some, it will be accidental. For others, it will become part of who we are. And for a few of us, curation will become our livelihood. It's exciting for me to see that we're turning a corner. The network is built. The data centers are in place. The next step will involve the human piece of the equation—humans are more-valuable machines.

Says Boba Fett: "The better man wins, droid."

It's all kind of magical, if you think about it.

A NOTE ABOUT SOURCES

Just as the world of media, content, brands, and the Web is rapidly changing, so is the nature of the book itself. In preparing to research and report *Curation Nation*, I made a list of all the subjects who I thought would have useful perspectives. Happily, almost all of them agreed to be interviewed for this project. Many of those interviews were conducted in person, and rather than take notes, the conversations were recorded and then transcribed. The rest of the interviews were conducted via Skype, and those too were transcribed. In both cases the transcriptions were turned around almost magically by a team of online workers known as Turkers, who are members of an Amazon service called Mechanical Turk. I talk more about Mechanical Turk in chapter 6, so I won't repeat the details here. Suffice it to say that the ability to have a Skype interview at 5 p.m. and have a transcript in your in box at 9 a.m. the next morning is for this author an awe-inspiring experience. The world moves quickly now.

I didn't want to weight things down in the text with footnotes and endnotes and such; in many cases when I quote people, their words are coming directly from interviews I conducted with them. So if there is no source attributed, that's why. The balance of the quoted material comes from books, blog posts, newspaper articles, and other reference material. In those cases, you'll find the appropriate citations listed.

ENDNOTES

Chapter 1

Alex Williams: "On the Tip of Creative Tongues" nytimes.com, October 2, 2009. http://www.nytimes.com/2009/10/04/fashion/04curate.html

Fred Wilson: "Email Bankrupcy" avc.com, May 11, 2010. http://www.avc.com/a_vc/2010/05/email-bankruptcy.html

Joanne McNeil: "The Editor and the Curator (Or the Context Analyst and the Media Synesthete)" tomorrowmuseum.com, March 28, 2010. http://tomorrowmuseum.com/2010/03/28/the-editor-and-the-curator-or-the-context-analyst-and-the-media-synesthete/

MG Siegler: "Eric Schmidt: Every 2 Days We Create as Much Information as We Did Up to 2003" techcrunch.com, August 4, 2010. http://techcrunch.com/2010/08/04/schmidt-data/

Steven Rosenbaum: "Creating a Happiness Culture: Zappos CEO Shows the Way" huffingtonpost.com, June 10, 2010. http://www.huffingtonpost.com/steve-rosenbaum/creating-a-happiness-cult_b_607621.html

Steve Rosenbaum: "AOL's Big SXSW Bet on Seed and 'Bionic Journalism'" techcrunch.com, March 12, 2010. http://techcrunch.com/2010/03/12/aols-seed-sxsw-bionic-journalism/

Rohit Bhargava: "Manifesto for the Content Curator: The Next Big Social Media Job of the Future?" rohitbhargava.typepad.com, September 30,

2009. http://rohitbhargava.typepad.com/weblog/2009/09/manifesto
-for-the-content-curator-the-next-big-social-media-job-of-the-future
-.html

N. Elizabeth Schlatter: "A New Spin Are DJs, rappers and bloggers 'curators'?"
aam-us.org. http://www.aam-us.org/pubs/mn/newspin.cfm

Jon Caramanica: "Ludacris as Curator of His Own Hip-Hop Museum"
nytimes.com, November 27, 2008. http://www.nytimes.com/2008/11
/27/arts/music/27luda.html

Carole Allen: "Kemp's Ridley Nesting Watch and Map" seaturtles.org,
November 27, 2008. http://www.seaturtles.org/article.php?id=1358

Clinton Forry: "Content Curation versus Content Aggregation: A Velvet
Mr. T Painting" content-ment.com, November 10, 2009. http://www
.content-ment.com/2009/11/curation-versus-aggregation.html

Chapter 2

Billy Linker: "Channel Focus: StreamingGourmet" magnify.net, March
6, 2009. http://www.magnify.net/blog/item/49MR3L1YW0NV46RZ
/Channel-Focus-StreamingGourmet/?from=hp.featured

Additional material from Amy Wilson re: StreamingGourmet from an
interview with the author, July 2010

"Wallace, DeWitt—Overview, Personal Life, Career Details, Chronology:
DeWitt Wallace, Social and Economic Impact." http://encyclopedia
.jrank.org. http://encyclopedia.jrank.org/articles/pages/6384/Wallace
-DeWitt.html#ixzz175HPPn00

Michael Kinsley: "Advice for Newsweek from Henry Luce" theatlanticwire
.com, May 21, 2010. http://www.theatlanticwire.com/editor-at-large
/view/article/Advice-for-Newsweek-from-Henry-Luce-11

"Cable Television History" retrieved from inventors.about.com. http://
inventors.about.com/library/inventors/blcabletelevision.htm

Diane Makar Murphy: "The History of Cable TV" ehow.com. http://www
.ehow.com/about_5068693_history-cable-tv.html

"Wallace, DeWitt—Overview, Personal Life, Career Details, Chronology:
DeWitt Wallace, Social and Economic Impact" retrieved from

encyclopedia.jrank.org. http://encyclopedia.jrank.org/articles/ pages/6384/Wallace-DeWitt.html

Alan Brinkley: "What Would Henry Luce Make of the Digital Age?" time.com, April 8, 2010. http://www.time.com/time/magazine/article/0,9171, 1978794,00.html#ixzz0n9k5AEGK

"Reader's Digest" retrieved from wikipedia.org. http://en.wikipedia.org /wiki/Reader%27s_Digest

Steven Rosenbaum: "What Susan Boyle Taught Me About Advertising" mediabizblogger.com, May 4, 2009. http://www.jackmyers.com /commentary/media-business-bloggers/44299967.html

Andrew LaVallee: "The Susan Boyle Bubble" blogs.wsj.com, April 16, 2009. http://blogs.wsj.com/digits/2009/04/16/the-susan-boyle -bubble//?from=hp.featured

Steven Rosenbaum: "The Conundrum of Costs: Ava Seave on Moguls and Curation" huffingtonpost.com, February 18, 2010. http://www .huffingtonpost.com/steve-rosenbaum/the-conundrum-of-costs-av_b_467978.html

Janet Maslin: "A Magazine Master Builder" nytimes.com, April 19, 2010. http://www.nytimes.com/2010/04/20/books/20book.html?_r=1

Patrick R. Parsons: "Blue Skies: A History of Cable Television" Temple University Press (January 28, 2008)

Chapter 3

Mercedes Bunz: "Huffington hits out at Murdoch speech" guardian.co.uk, December 2, 2009. http://www.guardian.co.uk/media/2009/dec/01/ arianna-huffington-murdoch-ftc

Ryan Singel: "The Huffington Post Slammed for Content Theft" wired .com, December 19, 2008. http://www.wired.com/epicenter/2008/12 /huffpo-slammed/

Ryan Spoon: "Perez Hilton Hits 14,000,000 Pageviews Yesterday. Wow." February 4, 2009. http://ryanspoon.com/blog/2009/02/24/perez -hilton-hits-14000000-pageviews-yesterday-wow/

Steve Rosenbaum: "Media: The Day Everything Changed" huffington post.com, November 17, 2009. http://www.huffingtonpost.com/steve -rosenbaum/media-the-day-everything_b_360990.html

Jay Yarrow: "Huffington Post Traffic Blows Past LA Times, Washington Post" businessinsider.com, October 19, 2009. http://www.businessinsider .com/huffpo-traffic-blows-past-la-times-washington-post-2009-10

Belinda Luscombe: "Arianna Huffington: The Web's New Oracle" time .com, March 19, 2009. http://www.time.com/time/business/article /0,8599,1886214,00.html

Steven Rosenbaum: "Why Content Curation Is Here to Stay" mashable. com, May 3, 2010. http://mashable.com/2010/05/03/content-curation -creation/

Jack Shafer: "A Tiny Taste of Mediaite: The fledgling media Web site leaves an acrid aftertaste" slate.com, July 6, 2009. http://www.slate.com /id/2222338

Laura McGann: "Huffington talks convergence, and 'monetizeable free'" niemanlab.org, May 19, 2010. http://www.niemanlab.org/2010/05 /huffington-talks-convergence-and-monetizeable-free/

Daniel Lyons: "Arianna's Answer: The Huffington Post may have figured out the future of journalism. But it's going to be a very difficult future" newsweek.com, July 25, 2010. http://www.newsweek.com/2010/07 /25/arianna-s-answer.html

Megan Garber: " 'The 24/7 News Cycle': David Carr, Arianna Huffington, and Mark Russell debate the future at ASNE" niemanlab.org, April 13, 2010. http://www.niemanlab.org/2010/04/the-247-news-cycle-david -carr-arianna-huffington-and-mark-russell-debate-the-future-at-asne

Steven Rosenbaum: "Web Aggregation Needs to Get Smarter" business insider.com, February 2, 2010. http://www.businessinsider.com /gideon-gartner-on-the-future-of-content-curation-2010-2

Steve Rosenbaum: "How Mediaite.com Is Making It Big by Thinking Like 'A Multi-Media DJ'" businessinsider.com, Jul 26, 2010. http://www .businessinsider.com/how-mediatecom-is-making-it-big-by-thinking- like-a-multi-media-dj-2010-7#ixzz11ypg4qQM

Steven Rosenbaum: "A Wolff in Web Clothing" huffingtonpost.com,

March 31, 2010. http://www.huffingtonpost.com/steve-rosenbaum /a-wolff-in-web-clothing_b_519972.html

Chapter 4

Steve Rosenbaum: "Bob Garfield: Mad Prophet of Madison Avenue" businessinsider.com, March 22, 2010. http://www.businessinsider .com/bob-garfield-mad-prophet-of-madison-avenue-2010-3

Bob Garfield: "What Part of 'We Hate You' Don't You Understand?" com castmustdie.blogspot.com, October 19, 2007. http://comcastmustdie. blogspot.com/2007/10/what-part-of-we-hate-you-dont-you.html

Tadas Viskanta: "Content vs. Aggregation vs. Curation" classic.abnormal returns.com, February 12, 2010. http://classic.abnormalreturns.com /content-vs-aggregation-vs-curation/

Bob Garfield / Fields Day Productions: "The 5 Stages of Comcast" youtube.com, March 3, 2008. http://www.youtube.com/watch?v= vOPzNqXQMqk

Rebecca Reisner: "Comcast's Twitter Man" businessweek.com, January 13, 2009. http://www.businessweek.com/managing/content/jan2009/ ca20090113_373506.htm

Frank Eliason: frankeliason.com. http://www.frankeliason.com

Karlene Lukovitz: "Mountain Dew Lets Fans Plan Tour, Events" mediapost .com, June 28, 2010. www.mediapost.com/publications/?fa=Articles. showArticle&art_aid=130980

Barry Silverstein: "Mountain Dew Finds Art of Engagement" brand channel.com, July 1, 2010. http:/www.brandchannel.com/home/post /2010/07/01/Mountain-Dew-Green-Label-Skate.aspx

Toby Daniels: "Q&A with Pepsico's Chief Consumer Engagement Officer, Frank Cooper" socialmediaweek.org, January 30, 2010. http:// socialmediaweek.org/blog/2010/01/30/qa-with-pepsicos-chief -engagement-officer-frank-rose/

Barry Silverstein: "When It Comes to Social Media, Pepsi Gets It" revenews. com, June 1, 2010. http://www.revenews.com/barrysilverstein /when-it-comes-to-social-media-pepsi-gets-it

Bonin Bough: "Pepsi Refresh Project: An Insider's View—Guest Post by Bonin Bough" beth.typepad.com, February 1, 2010. http://beth.typepad.com/beths_blog/2010/02/pepsi-refresh-project-an-insiders-view-guest-post-by-bonin-bough.html

Michael Arrington: "Comcast, Twitter and the Chicken (trust me, I have a point)" techcrunch.com, April 6, 2008. http://techcrunch.com/2008/04/06/comcast-twitter-and-the-chicken-trust-me-i-have-a-point/

Chapter 5

Steven Rosenbaum: "Confessions of a Newspaper Thief" huffingtonpost.com, March 25, 2010. http://www.huffingtonpost.com/steve-rosenbaum/confessions-of-a-newspape_b_513062.html

Rohit Bhargava: "Manifesto for the Content Curator: The Next Big Social Media Job of the Future?" rohitbhargava.typepad.com, September 30, 2009 http://rohitbhargava.typepad.com/weblog/2009/09/manifesto-for-the-content-curator-the-next-big-social-media-job-of-the-future-.html

Chapter 6

http://www.bbq-sauces.com/

Shawn Collins, cofounder, Affiliate Summit. July 26, 2010. In e-mail exchange with the author

Chapter 7

Jonathan A. Knee, Bruce C. Greenwald, Ava Seave: *The Curse of the Mogul: What's Wrong with the World's Leading Media Companies*. Penguin Group 2009

Josh Halliday, "Forbes to launch 'major upgrade' of social media" guardian.co.uk, August 3, 2010. http://www.guardian.co.uk/media/pda/2010/aug/03/forbes-social-media

Jeff Bercovici: "Lewis Dvorkin on the Future of Forbes: More 'Entrepreneurial,' 'Scalable'" dailyfinance.com, July 1, 2010. http://

www.dailyfinance.com/story/media/lewis-dvorkin-on-the-future-of
-forbes-more-entrepreneurial-an/19537682/

Marshall Kirkpatrick: "Google CEO Schmidt: 'People Aren't Ready for the Technology Revolotion'" readwriteweb.com, August 4, 2010. http://www.readwriteweb.com/archives/google_ceo_schmidt_people_arent _ready_for_the_tech.php

Dan Tynan: "Prepare for Data Tsunami, Warns Google CEO" pcworld .com, August 6, 2010. http://www.pcworld.com/article/202817 /prepare_for_data_tsunami_warns_google_ceo.html?tk=hp_new

"Jeff Jarvis" retrieved from wikipedia.org. http://en.wikipedia.org/wiki /Jeff_Jarvis

David Chase: "Forbes Magazine, The History" ezinearticles.com. http://ezinearticles.com/?Forbes-Magazine,-The-History&id=88697

David Carr: "A Gamble on a Weekly That Paid Off" nyimes.com, August 8, 2010. http://www.nytimes.com/2010/08/09/business/09carr.html? _r=1&ref=david_carr

Steven Rosenbaum: "Fast Company Founder on future of Curation & Magazines" huffingtonpost.com, January 30, 2010. http://www .huffingtonpost.com/steve-rosenbaum/fast-company-founder-on -f_b_443152.html

Steven Rosenbaum: "Is 'Everyone' the Media now?" huffingtonpost.com, April 8, 2010. http://www.huffingtonpost.com/steve-rosenbaum/is -everyone-the-media-now_b_530303.html

Clay Shirky: *Here Comes Everybody: The Power of Organizing without Organizations*. Penguin Press 2008

Chapter 8

David Sarno: "Twitter creator Jack Dorsey illuminates the site's founding document. Part I" latimes.com, February 18, 2009. http://latimesblogs .latimes.com/technology/2009/02/twitter-creator.html

"Twitter" retreived from wikipedia.org. http://en.wikipedia.org/wiki /Twitter

Kevin O'Keefe: "Twitter's growth continues at super-linear rate: Powerful

professional and business development tool for lawyers" kevin.lexblog.
com, July 5, 2010. http://kevin.lexblog.com/2010/07/articles/twitter-1
/twitters-growth-continues-at-superlinear-rate-powerful-professional
-and-business-development-tool-for-lawyers/

"Esther Dyson" retrieved from wikipedia.org. http://en.wikipedia.org
/wiki/Esther_Dyson

James Turner: "Tim O'Reilly - Why Twitter Matters for News" radar.oreilly
.com, May 7, 2009. http://radar.oreilly.com/2009/05/tim-oreilly-why
-twitter-matt.html

Rachel Sklar "Fair Use: Okay, Let's Talk About It" mediaite.com, August
13, 2010. http://www.mediaite.com/online/fair-use-okay-lets-talk-
about-it/

Chapter 9

Dylan Stableford: "Jay Rosen on Content Farms: Demand Media Not Evil,
But Still Demonic" thewrap.com, July 7, 2010. http://www.thewrap
.com/media/column-post/jay-rosen-content-farms-demand-media
-not-evil-still-demonic-19027

"Web Site Interest: curation." http://www.google.com/insights/search
/#q=curation&cmpt=q

Kara Swisher: "Demand Media Is Mad as Hell and, Well, Pens a Manifesto
(And Here It Is!)" kar.allthingsd.com, January 11, 2010. http://kara
.allthingsd.com/20100111/demand-media-is-mad-as-hell-and-well
-pens-a-manifesto-and-here-it-is

Saul Hansell: "Video: My New Job as Master of the Borg" saulhansell.
blogspot.com, December 11, 2009. http://saulhansell.blogspot
.com/2009/12/video-my-new-job-as-master-of-borg.html

Steven Rosenbaum: "Jason Hirschhorn . . . will Curate the Future!"
huffingtonpost.com, August 25, 2010. http://www.huffingtonpost
.com/steve-rosenbaum/jason-hirschhornwill-cura_b_693166.html

Mary Huhn: "Entrepreneur Makes Mischief with MTVi" nypost.com,
March 12, 2000. http://www.nypost.com/p/item_08qDyRtk5mGq9
PbLOpoG4H

Chapter 10

Steven Rosenbaum: "Curation, Crowd Sourcing, and Sexy Aliens" huffing tonpost.com, November 15, 2009. http://www.huffingtonpost.com /steve-rosenbaum/curation-crowd-sourcing-a_b_358402.html

Steven Addis: "Curator Economy" talentzoo.com, January 19, 2005. http:// www.talentzoo.com/news.php/Curator-Economy/?articleID=561

Dave Carroll: "Story" davecarrollmusic.com. http://www.davecarrollmusic .com/ubg/story

Chris Ayres: "Revenge is best served cold—on YouTube" timesonline .co.uk, July 22, 2009. http://www.timesonline.co.uk/tol/comment /columnists/chris_ayres/article6722407.ece

United Airlines Online Public Response to Dave Carroll YouTube Video: 9 Tweets July 13, 2009 by Dan Greenfield. http://www.socialmediatoday .com/SMC/109126

Chapter 11

Beth Negus Viveiros: "Keep the Brand/Blogger Relationship Transparent" chiefmarketer.com, August 9, 2010. http://chiefmarketer.com/social -media/0809-brands-bloggers/

Francine Hardaway: "Women Outperform Men as Social Customers" fastcompany.com, August 10, 2010. http://www.fastcompany .com/1680171/women-outperform-men-as-social-customers

"Work From Home Jobs": pcmoneymarker.net, September 27, 2007. http://www.pcmoneymaker.net/category/paid-to-blog

blogherads.com. http://www.blogherads.com/

Lizette Chapman: "Glam: the Next Media Giant?" fastcompany.com, August 5, 2010. http://www.fastcompany.com/1678205/glam-media -gets-tech-and-leaves-google

Michael Arrington: "Is Glam a Sham?" techcrunch.com, August 12, 2007. http://techcrunch.com/2007/08/12/is-glam-a-sham

Matt Marshall: "Glam to sign $1 billion ad deal—and draws critics" venturebeat.com, August 12, 2007. http://venturebeat.com/2007/08/12 /glam-to-sign-1-billion-ad-deal-and-draws-critics

Retrieved from glammedia.com. http://www.glammedia.com/publishers
/glam_publisher_network/

Chapter 12

Richard Waters: "Lunch with the FT: Chad Hurley" ft.com, June 25, 2010.
http://www.ft.com/cms/s/2/91518bb0-7fdf-11df-91b4-00144feabdc0
.html

Glenn Chapman: "YouTube serving up two billion videos daily" google.
com, May 16, 2010. http://www.google.com/hostednews/afp/article
/ALeqM5jK4sI9GfUTCKAkVGhDzpJ1ACZm9Q

Chapter 13

Kristina Halvorson: *Content Strategy for the Web*. New Riders Press 2009

Erin Scime: "The Content Strategist as Digital Curator" alistapart.com,
December 8, 2009. http://www.alistapart.com/articles/content
-strategist-as-digital-curator

Chapter 14

Jamie Beckland: "Social Media Content Curators Are Not 'Just Filters'"
jamiebeckland.com, April 6, 2010. http://jamiebeckland.com/2010/04
/social-media-content-curators-are-not-just filters/#ixzz11p
2suPRKhttp://jamiebeckland.com/2010/04/social-media-content
-curators-are-not-just-filters/#axzz0xMET1v4V

Jay Baer: "Do You 'Like' How I Look in These Jeans?" convinceandconvert
.com, June 2, 2010. http://www.convinceandconvert.com/facebook
/do-you-like-how-i-look-in-these-jeans

Dan McCarthy: "Social Content Curation, Facebook and Click-throughs"
viralhousingfix.com, February 5, 2010. http://www.viralhousingfix
.com/2010/02/05/social-content-curation-facebook-and-click
-throughs/

"Harvard on foursquare" news.harvard.edu, Janauary 12, 2010. http://
news.harvard.edu/gazette/story/2010/01/harvard-and-foursquare/

Chapter 15

Steven Rosenbaum: "Is Oprah a Vampire?" huffingtonpost.com, February 11, 2010. http://www.huffingtonpost.com/steve-rosenbaum/is-oprah-a-vampire_b_458507.html

Michael Arrington: "Everybody Forgets the Readers When They Bash News Aggregators" techcrunch.com, February 2, 2010. http://techcrunch.com/2010/02/02/everybody-forgets-the-readers-when-they-bash-news-aggregators

Steve Rosenbaum: "Seth Godin: Mark Cuban Is Completely Wrong About Aggregators" bussinessinsider.com, February 10, 2010. http://www.businessinsider.com/aggregation-vampires-2010-2

Mark Cuban: "Seth Godin Should Read His Own Book" blogmaveric,com, February 10, 2010. http://blogmaverick.com/2010/02/10/seth-godin-should-read-his-own-book

"Mark Cuban" retrieved from wikipedia.org. http://en.wikipedia.org/wiki/Mark_Cuban

Clay Shirky: *Cognitive Surplus: Creativity and Generosity in a Connected Age.* Penguin Press 2010

Chapter 16

Lucas Conley: "How Rapleaf Is Data-Mining Your Friend Lists to Predict Your Credit Risk" fastcompany, November 16, 2009. http://www.fastcompany.com/blog/lucas-conley/advertising-branding-and-marketing/company-we-keep

Rachel Sterne: "Internet Elite Predict the Media in 2010" groundreport.com, January 6, 2010. http://www.groundreport.com/Media_and_Tech/Internet-Elite-Predict-the-Media/2915610

Paul Boutin: "Another credit-card number Googled on Blippy: Philip Kaplan explains" VentureBeat.com, April 24, 2010. http://venturebeat.com/2010/04/24/blippy-credit-cards/

Liz Gannes: "Blippy's Philip Kaplan on the Last Frontier of Private Info" gigaom.com, December 22, 2009. http://gigaom.com/2009/12/22/blippys-philip-kaplan-on-the-last-frontier-of-private-info

Betsy Schiffman: "Who Knows You Better: Your Credit Card Company or Your Spouse?" dailyfinance.com, April 13, 2010. http://www.daily finance.com/story/who-knows-you-better-your-credit-card-company -or-your-spouse/19436105

Conclusion

http://www.comscore.com

INDEX

ABOUT THE AUTHOR

Steven Rosenbaum is an entrepreneur, an author, and a curator. He is the founder and CEO of the Web's largest video curation platform, Magnify.net.

Rosenbaum is known as the father of user-generated video, having created MTV's groundbreaking UGC series *MTV UNfiltered*, a pre-Web television project that handed cameras to young storytellers. Since that time he has built a career finding, organizing, and curating first-person storytelling.

Rosenbaum's work as an Emmy Award–winning documentary filmmaker includes *7 Days In September*, his film chronicling 9/11. That film gathered more than 500 hours of video around 9/11—creating a curated journey through the eyes of 28 filmmakers and citizen storytellers. The result was the curation of the world's largest collection of 9/11 videos: *The CameraPlanet Archive*, which Rosenbaum and producing partner Pamela Yoder donated to the National 9/11 Memorial and Museum. His film work includes long-form documentary projects for National Geographic, HBO, CNN, MSNBC, Discovery, A&E, and The History Channel.

As a blogger, Rosenbaum contributes to posts on technology, Internet video, and emerging digital lifestyle trends to FastCompany, The Huffington Post, Silicon Alley Insider, Mashable, TechCrunch, and MediaBizBloggers.

Today, Rosenbaum calls curation the "new magic" of the connected world—fixing the signal-to-noise problem and making the world contextual and coherent again.

He lives in New York with his wife, filmmaker Pamela Yoder; his two sons; and Louie, the best treeing walker coonhound in the Big Apple.